DIVERSITY, DISCIPLINE, AND DEVOTION IN PSYCHOANALYTIC PSYCHOTHERAPY

DIVERSITY, DISCIPLINE, AND DEVOTION IN PSYCHOANALYTIC PSYCHOTHERAPY

Clinical and Training Perspectives

edited on behalf of the
United Kingdom Council for Psychotherapy by

Gertrud Mander

KARNAC

First published in 2007 by
Karnac Books Ltd
118 Finchley Road
London NW3 5HT

British Library Cataloguing in Publication Data

A C.I.P. for this book is available from the British Library

ISBN-13: 978 1 85575 473 7

Edited, designed and produced by The Studio Publishing Services Ltd
www.publishingservicesuk.co.uk
e-mail: studio@publishingservicesuk.co.uk

Printed in Great Britain

10 9 8 7 6 5 4 3 2 1

www.karnacbooks.com

CONTENTS

ABOUT THE AUTHOR

Gertrud Mander, PhD, is a psychoanalytic psychotherapist and supervisor who trained at the Westminster Pastoral Foundation in London, where she was a supervisor and trainer of supervisors for twenty years. Apart from practising general counselling and psychotherapy she has specialized in supervision, supervision training, and brief therapy. She is a Doctor of Philosophy and a fellow of the BACP. She has published several papers in the *British Journal of Psychotherapy* and in the journal *Psychodynamic Practice*, has contributed chapters to several books, and published *A Psychodynamic Approach to Brief Therapy* (Sage). She has also translated Georg Groddeck into English and John Bowlby into German. The present book is a collection of essays written over two decades and reflects her wide interests in the field.

ACKNOWLEDGEMENTS

Several papers in this book have been published before, and are acknowledged as follows.

Chapter One, "Beginnings, endings, and outcome", was previously published in *Psychodynamic Practice* (2000), *6*(3).

Chapter Two, "From free association to the dynamic focus", was previously published in *British Journal of Psychotherapy* (2002), *19*(2): 203–218.

Chapter Three, "In praise of once-weekly work: making a virtue of necessity or treatment of choice?", was previously published in *British Journal of Psychotherapy* (1993), *12*(1): 3–13.

Chapter Four, "Dilemmas in brief therapy", was previously published in *Psychodynamic Practice* (2003), *9*(4).

Chapter Five, "Suitability and context for brief therapy" was previously published in *Psychodynamic Practice* (2005), *11*(4): 417–428.

Chapter Seven, "The selection of candidates", was previously published in *Psychodynamic Practice* (2004), *10*(2): 161–172.

Chapter Eight, "The stifled cry, or Truby King, the forgotten prophet", was previously published in *British Journal of Psychotherapy* (1996), *13*(1): 3–13.

Chapter Nine, "Some thoughts on sibling rivalry and competitive-ness", was previously published in *British Journal of Psychotherapy* (1991), *4*(9).

Chapter Ten, "The absent father and his return: echoes of war", was previously published in *British Journal of Psychotherapy* (1999), *16*(1): 3–15.

Chapter Eleven, "Fatherhood today: variations on a theme", was previously published in *Psychodynamic Practice* (2001), *7*(2): 141–150.

Chapter Fourteen, "Defiant resistance in the service of the impover-ished self. Herman Melville's 'Bartleby': an illustration of clinical casework" was previously published in *British Journal of Psychotherapy* (2004), *22*(2): 217–228.

The necessary permissions to reproduce these papers have been sought and granted. In respect of *Psychodynamic Practice* I have been asked to include a reference to the journal's website, which I am pleased to do (www.tandf.co.uk/journals).

I am grateful to the patients and trainees with whom I worked, from whom I learnt, and who inspired me to write these papers. I am also indebted to the Westminster Pastoral Foundation, where I trained as a therapist and supervisor and was given the chance to teach supervision and to train and work as a brief therapist. Particular thanks are due to Derek Blows, Paul Keeble, Mary Anne Coates, Edward Martin, Ann Scott, and to the many colleagues with whom I worked over two decades on the staff of the WPF.

INTRODUCTION

This book is a selection of papers written over twenty-five years of practising psychoanalytic psychotherapy, of training and supervising psychotherapists, psychodynamic counsellors, and supervisors. It reflects a preoccupation with the growth and diversification of counselling and psychotherapy, with the imperatives of training, supervision, and regulation, and with the significant changes in the profession due to the invention of brief, time-limited, intermittent and recurrent psychotherapy.

An overall theme is the conviction that what patients and therapists share is vulnerability, and that the therapist is a "wounded healer", whose reparative tendency informs his professional choice, his therapeutic empathy, and his capacity to bear the rigours of therapeutic work. Thus, an unconscious connection between the helper and the helped is the driving force of every therapeutic relationship, for better and for worse. Its responsible management requires thorough training, ongoing supervision, and a firm frame in order to contain the powerful forces operating when two strangers meet for the purpose of therapy.

The essays are located at the interface between the inner and the outer worlds, where the patient and the helper come together in a joint creative enterprise of talking, listening, and trying to understand each other. They offer the wealth of discoveries I made while working with patients, trainees, and supervisees and aim to contribute to the ongoing debate on the uses of psychotherapy in general, of long-term, time-limited, life-span or serial intermittent contracts. In recommending a model of recurrent psychotherapy, I have consistently focused on recent developments in the field of psychotherapy and counselling.

The range of subjects reflects two decades of professional experience and embraces many distinctive themes, some of which have since been taken further by other writers, such as sibling rivalry, frequency of meetings, the methodology of brief therapy, problems of fatherhood, methods of child rearing, identity, and abuse. The selection of topics represents my thinking as a dedicated clinician who persistently assessed and reassessed in her daily work the techniques and theoretical assumptions of her clinical and training practice.

I came into the field in the late 1970s as the result of a lengthy analysis and of translating (into English) a collection of papers by the German analyst Georg Groddeck, entitled *The Meaning of Illness*, followed by the translation (into German) of the first volume of John Bowlby's *Attachment and Loss*. This led to a desire to start training as a counsellor and psychotherapist, and initially I combined the training with my former profession of journalism. I started up in private practice, and in 1983 I became a trainer, supervisor and course organizer at the Westminster Pastoral Foundation in London. While continuing to translate psychoanalytic texts, I began to write clinical papers myself, some of which were presented at conferences before being published in various professional journals such as *The British Journal of Psychotherapy*, *Psychodynamic Practice*, and the BACP journal *Counselling*, which is now called *Therapy*.

Apart from practising general counselling and psychotherapy I have specialised in supervision, supervision training and brief therapy, have contributed chapters to several books and published the book A *Psychodynamic Approach to Brief Therapy* (2000). My 'mixed practice' has consisted mostly of once-weekly psychotherapy and supervision, with brief and time-limited therapy added a decade later, when I was asked to supervise a project for Counselling in Companies (started up by the Westminster Pastoral

Foundation, my training organisation, as an employee assistance programme), which offered free brief therapy to clients from various banks and corporate firms as a service provider.

I have always had the urge to write and all these essays were written spontaneously and sporadically. They do not pursue one particular theme nor do they add up to a system, as they were written whenever the spirit took me, or when interesting discussions with colleagues and trainees prompted me to think further about particular topics. Hence the title of this book, which emphasizes discipline and devotion as the essential ingredients when working with people suffering from traumatic life experiences or difficult childhoods.

*   *   *

The book starts off with a section on "Methods and models" and with a chapter on "Beginnings, endings and outcome: comparison of methods and goals", which emphasizes the demand for rigorous research into effectiveness, outcome, and evidence-based practice. There is now a confusing diversity of approaches and practices for today's patients to choose from. How do these compare and contrast in their goals and delivery? I call myself pluralistic and believe that we have to make a virtue of necessity, considering the enormity of needs in the community and the paucity of reliable information the public receives. When I recommend a model of recurrent psychotherapy (Chapter Two, "From free association to the dynamic focus: towards a model of recurrent psychotherapy") I base this on my experience of how many patients avail themselves of repeated therapeutic input of different length and style in the course of their lifetime rather than being content with one sustained period of analysis or counselling. Following Daniel Stern (1985), I see this serial format as the "continuation of a single therapy over the life-span", having realized that it is becoming more frequent as more therapeutic services and treatment approaches are available to people in need.

In the past decades there has been a successful introduction into the profession of brief therapy, time-limited, and short-term work, based on modest aims, which seems to indicate that many people are content when they get something that makes a significant difference and solves an immediate problem rather than embarking on the prolonged personality restructuring of orthodox analytic treatment, while those who can afford or choose full psychoanalysis will continue to get the in-depth treatment. The most frequent dilemma in brief work is whether there should or could be successive re-contracting or referral-on after the treatment has come to its agreed end in cases where the patient still seems to require more time to resolve his or her problem (Chapter Three, "Dilemmas in brief therapy"). There is no agreement in the profession and the jury is still out. Yet the situation continues to divide the traditional long-term clinician from the passionate short-term therapist, and this encouraged me to develop the notion of "recurrent psychotherapy", which is confirmed by Jung's concept of "individuation" and by the frequent use of the term "therapeutic journey".

My paper in praise of once-weekly work (Chapter Four, 'In praise of once-weekly work: making a virtue of necessity or treatment of choice') has been a bold challenge to the received notion that more always means better, and was based on the consideration of a vertical, alongside the horizontal, notion of time, with the weekly session being a moment of *kairos*, of fullness of time, of time with a difference, related to the timelessness of the unconscious. I am not claiming that everything is possible with reduced session frequency done with skill and conviction, but I am questioning the entrenched hierarchy in the profession based on quantity and plead for quality as well as a consideration of flexibility and realism concerning patient expectations. Frequency is a still a controversial issue in the profession (Stone and Duckworth, *Frequency of Sessions and the Analytic Frame*, 2003) and has often been used for special pleading. However, since I wrote the paper, the market has changed significantly and many psychotherapists now find it more difficult to fill their practices with patients requiring intensive psychotherapy at high frequencies. Some psychoanalysts do once-weekly work to keep their practices going and so do psychotherapists who work in the NHS. This does not mean, however, that once-weekly work has replaced the need for higher frequencies altogether, but rather that it has become the most popular method of the "psychotherapy for the people" which was recommended by Freud (1919) after the First World War as a feasible by-product of his five-times-a-week psychoanalysis , whose "pure gold would be alloyed with the copper of suggestion" in order to fashion what we now call psychotherapy or counselling.

A number of papers follow, which are the result of years of training and supervising scores of psychodynamic counsellors and psychotherapists. Chapter Five discusses "Suitability and context for brief therapy", Chapter Six is about "Bereavement counselling", and Chapter Seven, "The selection of candidates for training in psychotherapy and counselling", is a paper in which I examine the commonality I have identified between patients and training candidates when they present for their first interviews . I maintain that the shared vulnerability promotes the setting-up of the therapeutic alliance as well as enabling the counsellor's empathy and understanding, while the main difference is that the helper needs to have acquired the ability of self-reflection, which the patient seeking help has to develop in order to benefit from psychodynamic therapy.

The second section of the book is headed "Clinical and other matters", bringing together a mixture of papers exploring clinical case material or applying psychoanalytic theory to autobiographical and literary subjects. The first paper was prompted by a patient calling himself a "Truby King baby" and is a disquisition on the New Zealand psychiatrist Truby King, whose rigorous methods of child-rearing were ubiquitous in the Anglo-Saxon world during part of the twentieth century. His not always beneficial influence can still be traced in the psychic malfunctioning of certain patients. (Chapter Eight, "The stifled cry: or Truby King, the forgotten prophet".) The paper is an inquiry into the life of Truby King and his regime of four-hourly feeding that generations of mothers imposed on their babies against their primary maternal instincts, often to the detriment of their children's emotional development. I attempt to describe how reformers like D.W. Winnicott overturned these force-feeding methods, substituting child-centred procedures and liberating mothers, suggesting mirroring, holding, and attunement, and creating the benevolent notion of the good enough mother.

Another idea that was prompted by my clinical work led me to reflect on "Sibling rivalry and competitiveness" (Chapter Nine) in relation to many patients and to the difficult colleagueship of analysts and psychotherapists. I had become aware of an aspect of envy that is a universal experience owing to the presence of siblings in the infant's early life and in primary relationships rather than the innate envy that Melanie Klein located in the mother–infant relationship. I speculated on the origins of destructiveness in peer relationships, and on such traumatic emotional experiences as displacement and exclusion, tracing the theme in biblical stories, fairytales, and myths as an integral part of human existence that can be for good or for ill, depending on its management and strength. The role of the parents in the sibling scenario is explored, and so is its acting out in the transference and countertransference, unless the rivalry is turned into mutuality and the competitiveness into creative emulation, into comparing and sharing. Since then this theme has been taken further by Prophecy Coles in her book *Sibling Relationships*, and by Juliet Mitchell in two books *Mad Men and Medusas* and *Sibling Rivalry*.

The next paper is based on the clinical material of several patients that had alerted me to the important theme of "The absent father and his return: echoes of war" (Chapter Ten), which I discuss in terms of the trauma suffered by a whole generation during the Second World War, maintaining that it could be identified as a pathological agent in the psychological development of war children. The widely discussed concept of unconscious transgenerational transmission, coined to trace the effect of trauma on the following generation (Herman, 1992, *Trauma and Recovery*), enabled me to understand my patients' emotional difficulties in relating to others as a consequence of their dysfunctional fathering. Since then the theme of transgenerational transmission has been widely and creatively applied to the treatment of second-generation Holocaust survivors and to more recent genocides and ethnic cleansings. A number of conferences held by the Multilingual Psychotherapy Centre (Imago) have been dedicated to the exploration of this concept in relation to the persecution of European Romanies, the Armenian genocide, the ethnic cleansing in Bosnia, Kosovo, Rwanda, and to the plight of refugees and asylum seekers in general, who have become uprooted and are trying to find new homes and identities in Europe and elsewhere (J. Szekacs-Weisz, 2005, *Lost Childhood and the Language of Exile*).

I follow up the theme of fatherhood in another paper (Chapter Eleven, "Fatherhood today: variations on a theme") where I trace the rapid changes in fathering from the traditional patriarchal father to the absent or marginalized contemporary father in the nuclear family, to divorced fathers, step-fathers, and sperm-donor fathers of IVF babies. Reflecting on the implications of these changes for the children, for the decline of the modern family and for the important shifts in gender roles, all of which I have encountered in my clinical practice, also raised questions for me about the ethics of designer babies and of single motherhood with the help of modern technology. Since then there has been a book on *The Importance of Fathers* (edited by Judith Trowell and Alicia Etchegoyen), which recommends a rethinking of Freud's oedipal theories and the radical updating of psychoanalytic theory .

Chapter Fourteen is a paper called "The burden of being German", which deals with one of my ongoing personal preoccupations and arose in the context of a group relations conference based on the issue of origins and identity. Everybody's identity is a combination of fate as well as of choice, of the parents one cannot choose and of the person one becomes through learning from experience and in the course of the personal and professional choices one makes. I have traced my own formation and individuation through my exile by marriage from Germany to England, my acquisition of a second language and becoming bilingual, my embracing of another culture and of making a series of interlocking professional choices that combined journalism, translating, and becoming a psychotherapist. Parallel to the personal history, I describe the difficulty of having been born in a country that has played a traumatic role in contemporary history and is still attempting to come to terms with its responsibility for starting a devastating war and killing millions of people. In conclusion, belonging to an uneasy fatherland is a burden and a challenge with which I have been wrestling all my life.

Chapter Seventeen is a paper on the "Fear of death", which is personal in that it is not based on clinical material, and is about my developing thinking on mortality which began long ago when I was writing a doctoral dissertation on the seventeenth century English poet John Donne, for whom the fear of death was a central theme. Starting with Shakespeare's invocation of "the undiscovered country from whose bourn no traveller returns" (Hamlet, 3.1) and John Donne's "it is the going out, more than the coming in, that concerns us" ("Devotions upon emergent occasions, XVIII, Meditation"), as well as his "for whom the bell tolls; it tolls for thee" ("For whom the bell tolls"), I realized that the theme develops into an increasing preoccupation as one gets older and approaches death. Looking at the dignified death of the believer Jung, at the courageous assisted death of the atheist Freud, and at the variations of religious attempts to tame the fear of death (including the Baroque *ars moriendi*, which produced so much exquisite sacred music) I came to the conclusion, as have many people before me, that "no one wants to die alone". It is, of course, the process of dying rather than death itself that is most feared. But equally important is the need to be allowed to die with dignity, not to be put into a medical ward attached to drips and oxygen equipment and be abandoned to die in hospital alone as so many patients nowadays are (Philip Aries, 1975, "Essai sur l'histoire de la mort en Occident"). Erikson considered old age the life stage of "integrity versus despair", and believed that "growing old is an interesting adventure", an idea he complemented with the statement that "integrity equals the gathering of life into a meaningful pattern". The paper ends with an anguished poem by Philip Larkin, a menacing description of the grave by Andrew Marvell, and with Dylan Thomas's defiant "Do not go gentle into that dark night", and with the comforting sentence from Ecclesiastes that "to everything there is a season, and a time to every purpose under the heaven".

Finally, Chapter Thirteen is a paper called "Defiant resistance in the service of the impoverished self", which uses Herman Melville's short story "Bartleby the Scrivener" to illuminate some clinical work of mine with particularly difficult patients, reaffirming the importance of Freud's concept of resistance as a cornerstone of psychoanalytic theory together with the mechanisms of defence, with respect for the patient, and with absolute devotion to therapeutic work.

PART I
MODELS AND METHODS

CHAPTER ONE

Beginnings, endings, and outcome: a comparison of methods and goals

"In my beginning is my end", said the poet T. S. Eliot, enigmatically coining a phrase that would become meaningful beyond its immediate context in the *Four Quartets*—for instance, for therapists discussing the difference between long-term, open-ended analytic therapy and brief, time-limited therapeutic interventions. In the field of therapy, beginnings determine endings in most significant ways, and the two are inextricably connected. This has now taken on a particular significance, as in many therapeutic contexts these days we are faced from the beginning of treatment with a choice between offering long-term open-ended or short-term, time-limited contracts to our patients.

Freud compared analysis to the "noble game of chess" where anyone who hopes to learn it from books

> will soon discover that only the openings and end games admit of an exhaustive systematic presentation and that the infinite variety of moves which develop after the opening defy any such description. This gap in instruction can only be filled by a diligent reading of games fought out by masters. The rules which can be laid down for the practitioners of psycho-analytic treatment are subject to similar limitations. [Freud, 1913c, p. 123]

By this he may have wanted to indicate that the way a therapist started determines how he ends, though this cannot be predicted, only retrospectively understood, and is, therefore, difficult to get right.

"A patient will come into therapy successfully if the 'time is right' and the same principle applies equally to endings", states Jeremy Holmes in the "opening game" of a paper called "Too early, too late: endings in psychotherapy: an attachment perspective" (1997, p. 157), thereby flagging up one of the main difficulties for modern-day therapists who find themselves faced with the dilemma of how much therapy will be enough for individual patients, of how to begin wisely in order to end appropriately, and how to ensure a satisfactory and lasting outcome for both participants in the therapeutic enterprise.

In the beginning

For the therapist faced with a stranger who expects a cure for all the ills he/she is troubled by and hopes to be relieved of, there are no hard and fast rules, only experiences, opinions, hypotheses and inspired guesses as to who needs or will benefit from what and how to determine the relative length, intensity, and effectiveness of the contract that is offered at the beginning of treatment. Accurate and thorough assessing for suitability, ego strength, and self-reflection (Klein, 1999) is essential in order to make a prognosis and to define a realistic goal, since no one case resembles another and the curative uncertainties are arguably infinite. The "therapeutics" chosen depend on many factors, including the assessment context. If this favours brief therapy, then the beginning will include the ending in terms of the time-limited contract that is made and will include a set of selection criteria, a dynamic focus, and a negotiation of modest achievable aims. What usually happens is that the therapist's choice is made on the basis of clinical evidence, of personal experience of what has worked before, of availability, and ultimately of faith in a process that, though perhaps not yet fully understood, has nevertheless often been closely observed and proved to be beneficial. Other determining factors are the individual context in which the therapy takes place, the financial and practical resources on offer, the rapport and the level of motivation which exist at the beginning and which are the necessary fuel of the joint enterprise, and whether the therapy is allowed freely to take its time or is given a planned ending and circumscribed goal on first meeting.

The one thing that is safe to say is that time-limited practitioners will not have to experience the protracted indecisiveness of their long-term colleagues in relation to setting an ending. Their belief in the usefulness of working with the ending from the beginning is well grounded in experience and good results. They usually have a preferred number of sessions, perhaps determined by the contextual practicalities (e.g., in the GP practice) or set quite arbitrarily, like James Mann's twelve sessions, whose ability to be divided into threes and fours offers a handsome symmetry that can be honed for different therapeutic tasks and objectives.

There is a precedent in Freud's classic essay "Analysis terminable and interminable", where he describes a case when he "resorted to the heroic measure of fixing a time-limit for the analysis", "a black-mailing device about the value of which there can be only one verdict—it is effective, provided that one hits the right time for it" (1937c, p. 218). He adds "once the therapist has fixed the time-limit, he cannot extend it, otherwise the patient would lose all faith in him", which makes him the first truly time-limited therapist and further confirms his reputation of having invented practically everything single-handedly. In this same paper, he marshals all the arguments that have been levelled against analysis by its detractors. For instance, he asks the question whether there is such a thing as a natural ending to analysis. He also bemoans the inability of analysis to prevent a recurrence of symptoms or to act prophylactically, admits its practical uselessness in crises, and observes the ultimate irresolvability of the very transference phenomena that prolong the treatment. In effect, in the pessimistic mood of his old age, he demonstrates a general scepticism as to the absolute curative effects of analysis (thus giving his latter-day enemies plenty of ammunition with which to attack him), while joking sarcastically that Otto Rank's attempt at developing a method of brief therapy which focused on the primal birth trauma seemed to him "as if the fire brigade, called out to deal with a house that had been set on fire by an overturned oil lamp, contented itself with removing the lamp from the room in which the fire had started" (*ibid.*, pp. 26–27).

How to end well

In the early days, most therapy and analysis was, in fact, relatively short. Based on the assumption that it would take as long as was needed to remove symptoms, relieve depressive or persecutory anxieties, establish insight into baffling phobias, resolve relationship problems, or work through a period of mourning, it was confidently assumed that therapy ended when both partners agreed to do so and when patients had re-established a psychic equilibrium that enabled them, as Freud put it succinctly and simply, "to love and work". Gradually, however, it became apparent that most therapies lengthened, that strong dependencies and severe separation anxieties connected with the development of powerful transferences, together with the vain attempt at making the ending perfect, bearable, and clearly indicative of the task completed, made it more and more difficult to end. Indeed, these processes made ending a fairly fraught undertaking—one which, unfortunately, was often botched or mishandled and thus not truly "finished".

There are many definitions of the task of ending, depending on theoretical orientations. Most of them agree on the necessity of establishing strong ego functions, of dismantling no longer workable defences, and of reaching what Winnicott called the "stage of concern" and Melanie Klein the "depressive position". All of this amounts to an ability to face realities and, in Freud's classic phrase, to a "transformation of neurotic miseries into common unhappiness" (1895d)—a most admirable and desirable task indeed.

Like Freud, the Jungian analyst Michael Fordham found it difficult to find definite answers to questions of how to end analysis and stated wryly (1985) that, in his experience, ending had a way of taking place without the therapist's aim being achieved, something most of us probably know from our own therapeutic experience. Fordham did, however, draw up some very valid axioms that describe the process towards ending as "a gradual diminishment of the asymmetry in the therapeutic relationship though it never disappears". He than states, rather summarily, that "the patient achieves greater insight and control over his affects", which, once again unfortunately, cannot be taken as an universal truth. More accurate and to the point seems the remark that at last a time comes when the material begins to thin out, the associations have little in them, dreams diminish in number and become superficial in character, fantasies lose their compelling power, everyday personal and social difficulties become manageable and there are no transference crises. [*Ibid.*, p. 46]

So it is not surprising if therapist and patient begin to think that their work is coming to a close. In fact, they may become quite impatient to get on with other things. But do they really have to wait so long—until they are exhausted, so to speak, drying up and bored with the whole thing? The answer lies in another, more serious, point made by Fordham: "how to end so as not to reproduce unresolvable traumatic situations from the past" (*ibid.*, p. 47). It is clearly a premature ending that often prevents more timely and decisive decision-making, and it accounts for many of the complaints nowadays brought against therapists, and for some of the bad press we are getting in the media.

Managing endings without acting out and spotting the moment when it is possible for both participants to let go and say goodbye is surely one of the most important therapeutic skills. Needing intuition and experience as well as discipline, it is extremely rare. In my experience there is usually a moment when one or the other participant begins to think of ending without fear, and once the seeds of ending have thus been sown, there is no going back—and the less hesitation the better. The more the thoughts increase the more necessary it is to be decisive and to suggest first a tentative and then a definite ending date that allows the gradual unwinding and letting go to take its course. This is different from the chess endgame, where one or the other partner wins, whereas in therapy they both agree to let go and go their different ways.

Much therapy is ended abruptly or too soon. It stops due to initially unforeseeable events in the patient's life, to financial constraints, to sudden deaths and illnesses, to therapeutic impasse and to patients suddenly changing their minds. But, equally, therapy can also be ended too late, becoming "un-terminable" and unending, because separation has become unthinkable. Nina Coltart talked about the oddity of ending a therapeutic relationship of which

it is said, quite justifiably, that it is one of the most important relationships of one's life as . . . all levels of object-relating, closeness, intimacy etc. are at the very heart of analytic therapy. And it is not an exaggeration to say that although they, the patients, know that this will happen, some patients experience the agreement to end as a death sentence. [Coltart, 1996, p. 150]

The analyst Nina Coltart and the time-limited psychotherapist James Mann agree wholeheartedly that, against all resistance, protest, anxiety, and acting out, it is vital to make an ending total once it is set. While they both believe in the process, they disagree in respect of other vital points, in particular, the issue of dependence. For Mann (1973) and many other brief therapists, patient dependence is something to avoid at all cost because it prolongs the therapy unnecessarily. For Coltart and the long-term psychodynamic therapist, this is the moment when the patient begins to regress, when the transference unfolds, and when the transference neurosis has a chance to develop. In turn, this leads to all the complicated repeating, remembering, and working through that is considered necessary to arrive at a resolution of the twisted object relations and unworkable defences that the patient has been suffering from:

The patient ceases to suffer in his ways of relating and the acute but passing pains of insight take over from the personality problems presented at the beginning. Defences, of course, may have been taking years to build up and are only slowly dismantled, if necessary to be supplemented by ego itself and by defences that are more resilient and healthy. [Coltart, 1996, p. 149]

Holmes sums up this defence-dismantling and ego-strengthening goal of ending when he says "only when patients feel safe enough to give up their defences—accept the helplessness and dependence on the therapist—can they begin to progress towards an ending". Echoing John Bowlby (1988), he states categorically, "A good ending is possible once a secure base has been established, therefore the process can be relatively brief, when the patient's attachment pattern is basically satisfactory, as is the therapist's" (1997, p. 163).

Ending time-limited psychotherapy

Through dependence to independence—clearly, this traditional view of how to bring about deep and lasting changes in the patient's psyche was radically questioned by Mann. His method was, like other models of brief therapy, developed in a hospital context in order to cut patient waiting-lists and it turned out to have surprisingly good results just because he discouraged dependence and repression and built on the patient's knowledge of planned endings from the beginning.

The knowledge that the treatment will be finite and limited has a profound effect on the therapy: patients know that there is little time to waste and this encourages them to work hard in the therapy. Also, they know that the treatment will end in a fairly short time, and this allays fears of becoming dependent on the treatment and on the therapist, keeping them motivated to work hard. It is the general experience of therapists doing brief therapy that it is a richer and more affect-laden experience for the patients and the therapists.

Mann's rationale for making the ending a planned event was that in his experience the longer therapist and patient stayed together the less productive their work became, owing to complicated dependency and transference issues that produce a situation of inextricable enmeshment in which there is a strong wish to stay together and a wish for a perfect ending. In this situation, he believed, endings happen too soon or too late and out of necessity rather than choice. This leaves the sense of something unfinishable, of profound loss, and deep sadness. The efficacy of Mann's dogma of setting a firm time frame at the beginning maximizes therapeutic results and leads to dramatic changes, confirmed by research findings. Big questions, however, remain, such as how lasting these results will be and whether there might be more likelihood of erosion and relapse.

My own experience is that while it is always essential to keep to a deadline once it is set, and to work through whatever comes up as a result of this, there are a few people who return, after a some time, for a further stint of therapy—usually short, focused, but necessary—as they may have discovered that there are still issues that require attention. Like the teenager who has left home and returns for brief top-ups of home life, the returning patient indicates that their separation is as yet incomplete and needs to be repeated in order to become truly possible. Their attachment lessens gradually. There is nothing deplorable in this and, like Freud in "Analysis terminable and interminable", I believe that it should be permitted.

Mann's method provides a workable hypothesis of psychic functioning based on the realization that separation anxieties are
at the heart of much mental malfunctioning and unsuccessful object-
relating, and that only by setting a fixed time limit can
the ambiguity about ending treatment be eliminated. This ambiguity can be used as a defence by both partners to avoid confronting the
inevitability of separation. He maintains that, as a result of the
unconscious resistance, the majority of long-term psychotherapies
do not end with a planned and mutually agreed termination. The
experience of separation becomes the central feature of the time-
limited method and its aim is, according to Mann, for the patient to
"internalise the therapist as a replacement or substitute for the
earlier ambivalent object, thereby making separation a genuine
maturational event" (1973, p. 36). In effect, unconscious conflicts
and anxieties are made conscious and the experience of separation,
so far considered unbearable and unthinkable, now turns out to be
bearable and completable. This brave following through of a feared
emotional experience enables the patient to mourn the loss, first in
the presence of the object and then on his own.

The strategy of planned endings and time limits has a logic and
beauty of its own and ensures a predictability that is lacking from
much long-term work. It is rooted in the ancient wisdom of *carpe
diem*, of plucking the fruit while it is ripe, or of striking the iron
while it is hot. The outcome is a rapid change. There may, however,
be a fallacy in this argument, since it skips over the simple fact that
it is easier to separate from someone after twelve meetings, no
matter how rich, than after a relationship that has lasted for years.
Not everybody is capable of grasping the symbolism of Mann's
method, especially when there is the knowledge that the brief
involvement will end soon after it has begun. A defensive reaction of
"I might as well not bother to get involved" can be expected with
people who fear intimacy and are slow to engage or unwilling to
commit themselves.

Should the difficulty of a task be expressed in the length of a
contract, or is there, as Mann assumes, an optimal length of contract
tailored to each therapeutic case? Opinions differ, but the experience
of a time-limited contract will certainly shape the expected
outcome, the intensity of the therapeutic experience, and the
defences a patient will use to deal with it.

As a general principle, the outcome of time-limited therapy is likely to be best if there is some reaching of the depressive position and the recognition of ambivalence in relation to both the therapy and the ending of it. Mann speaks of the time-limited patients' inevitable disappointment with their therapists, of the necessary progression of the therapeutic couple from happy symbiosis to a measure of ambivalence experienced by the patients that starts in the second therapeutic phase when their habitual relationship problems emerge and the working through of these becomes necessary. Melanie Klein considered ending therapy in the context of maturation as an achievement of successful weaning which, for the baby, means coping with the rage at mother's capacity to come and go as she pleases. It marks the achievement of "unit status", of which Winnicott spoke in relation to the baby who has learnt to be alone in the presence of another (Winnicott, 1958). And, in the words of Bion (1967), "the absent breast is the beginning and the stimulus of thought: if the capacity for toleration of frustration is sufficient, the no-breast inside becomes a thought and an apparatus for thinking it develops" (p. 111).

Ending therapy presupposes a capacity to tolerate separation and loss that characterizes the resolution of the Oedipus complex. This capacity is hard-won and can get lost again and again, whenever regressive longings and unbearable anxieties become overwhelming. Equally, the gains of analysis, whether long-term analysis or time-limited brief work, might get eroded when the ego loses strength and the inner resources are depleted. Yet, once experienced, at least there is the knowledge of its possibility, and repeated experiences of facing and surviving separation should eventually lead to mature letting go in place of defensive denial or avoidance. The patient who walks out before the ending, or misses the last session, has not reached the maturity of being able to say goodbye forever and has not reached the stoicism of which Seneca speaks when he says, "as it is with a play so it is with life. What matters is not how long it lasts, but how good it is. Make sure you round it off with a good ending".

Of course, it takes two to make a good ending in therapy, and the therapist's capacity to tolerate separation and loss is as necessary and important as the patient's willingness to separate. The challenge for the brief therapist is that he or she needs to make the best use of the short time in which all sorts of tasks have to be accomplished while acknowledging the strong feelings due to attachment and separation and looking back over what has been done (or not done) and forward into the future. As I stated in a previous publication (Mander, 2000),

> it is inevitable that during the ending period previous experiences of ending and loss are remembered and emotionally reactivated, which is a chance to compare and contrast situations in terms of unfinished business, painful memories, regret, remorse and relief, and then to establish what can still be done to make amends, to work through emotions so far avoided. Often there is a realisation that ending is not as difficult as feared and that it can be experienced as energizing, and clearing the way to new beginnings rather than amounting to a frightening abandonment. [p. 105]

Aim and outcome

The analyst Alexander, one of the pioneers of brief therapy, coined the phrase "corrective emotional experience" (Alexander & French, 1946) to define the aim and necessary outcome of a successful therapeutic experience, no matter how short or long its duration. He maintained that such a corrective experience results

> from the difference between the original parental response and the response of the analyst during analysis which provides the patient with an opportunity to correct his distortions. The emotional experience in the transference lends conviction to, and is the necessary underpinning of, insight. Having thus reached some stability, this insight elicits new, more up-to-date and reality-oriented solutions to old conflicts. [Alexander, cited in Balint, 1972, p. 9]

New solutions to old conflicts could be said to sum up the aim of brief therapy succinctly, together with the modest claim of "making a difference" or, in the words of Gregory Bateson, of "making the difference that makes the difference" (1978). The important word for Alexander and his followers was "emotional". Rational insight is not enough; as everybody knows it needs to be backed up with, and underpinned by, a transformative therapeutic experience. The trouble with the application of the concept is that it can be falsely taken to mean concretely gratifying the patient's needs and understood as an advocacy of making up a parental deficit or a lack of caregiving rather than symbolically reworking an early developmental failure in the transference. In Winnicott's words

> In the end the patient uses the analyst's failures, often quite small ones, and often manoeuvred by the patient, and we have to put up with being in a limited context misunderstood. The operative factor is that the patient now hates the analyst for the failure that originally came as an environmental factor, outside the infant's area of omnipotent control, but that is now staged in the transference. So in the end we succeed by failing—failing the patient's way. This is a long way from the simple theory of cure by corrective experience. In this way regression can be in the service of the ego if it is met by the analyst. [Winnicott, 1965, p. 258]

The therapist has to fail, but this way round, supported by the therapist, the patient survives a re-enactment of the original failure, is more able to work through it, and is strengthened.

As with hindsight, the corrective emotional experience, coupled with a lived experience of the habitual and compulsive problem of finding a new and different solution, is the goal of all therapeutic endeavour that aims to involve the patient's understanding. It presupposes in the patient a willingness and an ability to change, to bear anxiety, and to endure uncertainty in the service of decisively restructuring his life with the support of a trustworthy therapeutic relationship that is experienced briefly, or over time, as a "secure base".

With this we have come to our third concept, "outcome". Perhaps we should tackle this in terms of expectations and goals at the beginning, and of results and consequences at the end, with some consideration of the lasting therapeutic effects following on from therapy.

In the climate of demands for evidence-based psychotherapy research, cost effectiveness, and professional accountability, outcome studies are essential, and much professional and academic research has been going on in the field. There has been a massive outcome research project undertaken for the National Health Service (NHS) by the CORE Systems Group (CORE stands for

Clinical Outcome in Routine Evaluation) based at the University of Leeds that is conclusively influencing the thinking about models, contracts, length, and endings, pointing to the evidence-based future of counselling and psychotherapy.

Outcome research in the field of primary care aims is establishing the effectiveness of GP counselling services, and, in particular, who can be helped, who might be harmed, and what kind of treatment "by whom for whom" is advisable (Roth & Fonagy, 1996). Quantitative studies based on research methods using clinical trials have been gathering conclusive evidence that there is a universal consumer demand for primary care counselling and that this is proving effective in treating depressive states and achieving symptom reduction (Corney, 1993; Hemmings, 1997, 1999). The measuring of psychic change, of improvements and longer-lasting effect, is more difficult to quantify and can equally be tackled by qualitative research such as the traditional single-case study—that is, an "account of the person in a situation which is descriptive of the process, the interaction and the therapeutic relationship, including a causal analysis that attempts to explain the observations found. Such research can be carried out in routine clinical practice and used for service evaluation" (Corney, 1999) both with brief time-limited and with open-ended long-term therapy.

I remember how, in the olden days in the agency where I worked, counsellors were asked to fill in a closure form on termination of their cases that involved ticking various categories: much improved, slightly improved, the same as at assessment, worse than at assessment, etc. This was primarily arbitrary, and depended on the counsellor's honesty, definition of improvement, and understanding of psychic change. Was it a measure of improvement in the clients' inner world or of changes in their external world? Was it an acknowledgement of success or failure, a statement about the therapist's competence, or an admission of the impossibility of generalizing therapeutic outcomes that allowed the counsellor a subjective discharge of feeling on the point of closing a case? The form's use for statistical purposes was, of course, negligible, yet it satisfied a need for classifying and wrapping up work done before closing a file, and therefore had its uses.

There is, and will of course always be, a difference of outcome for the two participants themselves: what the client might consider satisfactory may be far from the therapist's expectations, and to establish who is right is well nigh impossible. To use initial expectations as a yardstick and the solution of clients' presenting problems as an aim could be another approach. Yet, it might well be doomed to failure, as often the therapy covers areas that emerge well into the work, additional to the goals set at the beginning. Indeed, evaluation of outcome at the point of ending the work can be different from what is seen to have been achieved, or not achieved, a few weeks, months, or years later.

Follow-up

The technique of arranging follow-ups after termination—initiated by the Tavistock Brief Therapy team led by David Malan and Michael Balint in the 1960s—follows well-established medical practice. At regular intervals of three, six, or twelve months after ending therapy, patients are seen for a check-up to establish the lasting or proliferating effect of change achieved during therapy and to enable the patients to monitor themselves in the presence of their erstwhile therapists who, on these occasions, function as observers. Follow-ups look for evidence of continuing working-through on the part of the patient, of absence of symptoms, and of lasting ego strength, while recurrence of, or relapse into, previous complaints indicates a partial failure of the treatment and requires an adjustment of outcome indicators as well as measures to top up or resume therapy, if considered necessary.

The measuring of outcome is therefore contingent upon the moment when it is done as much as on the method and the criteria used. Where there are diagnostic profiles at assessment and terminal profiles at termination—a method first used at the Anna Freud Clinic (Fonagy & Target, 1996)—a definition of outcome can be based on a comparison of these two profiles. Where a General Health Questionnaire is used before and after a period of brief therapy, the comparing of the two forms can give ample and relatively reliable information about the therapeutic outcome at the point of the patient's departure. Changes have to be "clinically significant" in terms of "overall adaptation", according to the definition used for the Hampstead Clinic Adaptation Measure (HCAM).

The difficulty is the measuring of lasting results, unless there are systematic follow-ups over years that monitor the ongoing process of sustained self-therapy. But then, the goal of therapy is not necessarily the achievement of major changes, and brief therapy, anyway, does not talk about cure, but about making a difference, finding a solution, starting up a process of change. It can mean ego support to weather a crisis, finding the courage to leave a bad marriage, making a decision about a career change, or tackling a chronic situation in a constructive way. The outcome is not always positive, though a small change may set in motion other changes. Indeed, it may merely be the fact that someone has come for help that may lead to a belief in the possibility of change and to a different way of thinking about oneself that may persist and make a difference in one's behaviour towards others, too. When the outcome is the experience that therapy has helped, there is a changed perception of the value of taking one's troubles to another person and of entering into a self-exploratory dialogue with someone experienced in problem-solving, in understanding emotional conundrums, and in suggesting ways forward in chaotic life situations. The outcome may even be a referral to someone else, more specialized or suitable to deal with the matter in hand, and this may be a good experience of parental guidance and concern.

What has increasingly dogged our work is the expectation that we should help a patient make major characterological changes and mend substantial psychic damage and disturbances in mental functioning. This ambition can lead into deep waters, particularly when the initial assessment is over-optimistic and misleading as to the likely consequences of opening up hidden depths. One is entering a journey into uncharted waters, and diagnostic hypotheses need endlessly to be adjusted in the light of new evidence of pathology. This is as fascinating as it can be frustrating, but hardly ever are initial expectations fulfilled and the characterological changes usually remain imperceptible or fall far short of hopes and promises rashly made at the beginning.

Freud said "Psycho-analysis is always a matter of long periods of time" (1913c, p. 129) and he used to warn his patients that something that took a long time to develop would take a long time to unravel. He always allowed for a sizable period of ongoing assessment. Contrary to the views of his present-day detractors, he was no false prophet possessed by utopian visions, and his late essay "Analysis terminable and interminable" (1937c) speaks eloquently of this. Set against the difficulties of analysis, the modest aims of the brief therapist are pragmatic, avoiding embroilment in the depths of the psyche by steering clear of mainly interpreting the transference, though always monitoring it and encouraging the patient to do the work herself or himself: to find the solution, to solve the problem, and to attempt small behavourial, relational, and emotional changes.

It is, therefore, easier in brief therapy to describe improvement and outcome in concrete terms and, in some respects, also more satisfying to end, as the modesty of aims forbids expectations of major change and helps to focus on small achievements. The finality of coming to the end of an agreed contract also helps in that whatever has happened has to be accepted as the definitive outcome of joint work. The patient knows that they can do something like this again if need be and, when they are dissatisfied or disappointed, not much is lost except a belief in the effectiveness of therapy; i.e., they may not try again. This could be seen as a negative outcome, but it is not necessarily for ever and with another therapist it might be different.

Set against this is the rich tapestry of long-term intensive therapy, which is insight-orientated and, in Anna Freud's words, can be rehabilitative and give developmental help over time. It aims for a gradual integration of unacknowledged feelings, for stabilization, and for lasting adaptive changes, thereby producing an outcome that is difficult to put into definitive terms at the point of saying goodbye. It reveals its full significance only over time, sometimes over a long time in which, gradually, the full extent of its benefits become truly known to the ex-patient. Therefore, it has an outcome that could be called dynamic. Therapists will not know about this, and have to be content with the knowledge of what emerges in the last session in terms of outcome and results. They have to live with the fact that they will never know how the patient fares beyond the therapy—except, that is, when they accidentally hear about them or when a patient writes, sends Christmas cards, or gives occasional updates. One long-standing patient of mine, an actress who had started out as severely bulimic, surprised me recently by appearing in a lead role in a Hollywood film, something she had been adamantly refusing to do when she worked with me. My own therapy ended on a dream the night before the last session, in which I was convinced that I had two more sessions. My therapist interpreted this as a wish to return some day, and I now see it as an attempt not to give up the transference, and understand my unconscious wish for more time as probably an expression of gratitude.

CHAPTER TWO

From free association to the dynamic focus: towards a model of recurrent psychotherapy

I n his book *The Mystery of Things*, Christopher Bollas (1999) entitled a chapter "The goals of psychoanalysis?" After dismissing claims to alleviating suffering, to correcting destructive processes, to healing symptoms or changing the course of psychological development, he came to the conclusion that the goal was "free association" (p. 64). By this he meant Freud's fundamental rule, which states that:

> The treatment is begun by the patient being required to put himself in the position of an attentive and dispassionate self-observer, merely to read off all the time the surface of his consciousness and on the one hand to make a duty of the most complete honesty while on the other not to hold back any idea of communication, even if 1) he feels that it is too disagreeable or if 2) he judges that it is nonsensical or 3) too unimportant or 4) irrelevant to what is being looked for. It is uniformly found that precisely those ideas which provoke these last-mentioned reactions are of particular value in discovering the forgotten material. [Freud, 1923a, p. 238]

Bollas reaffirms Freud's statement that psychoanalysis does not provide a cure, and maintains that

as a moment in Western culture it founded a new and radically liberating state of mind . . . instead of being highly focused, directed and
aim[ing] at a special day of deliverance . . . it asks Western man to
find truth by abandoning the effort to find it . . . [1999, p. 63]

With this goal established for the patient, Freud defined the therapist's task as the adoption of an

attitude of surrendering himself to his own mental activity, in a
state of evenly suspended attention, to avoid as far as possible
reflection and the construction of conscious expectations, not to try
to fix anything that he heard particularly in his memory and by
these means to catch the drift of the patient's unconscious with his
own unconscious. [Freud, 1924f, p. 239]

Most psychotherapy trainings teach this important rule and the
practice of evenly suspended attention to tune into the patient's
unconscious. But the task is also to respond to and interpret the
patient's communications in a meaningful and, if possible, "mutative" way. This depends on the therapist's ability to free associate,
too, and to catch the ideas that are suddenly dropping into the mind
out of the blue, and that, according to Freud, "enter consciousness,
often with no apparent connection to previously spoken ideas.
Perhaps the mentality created by '*freie Assoziation*' potentializes
the arrival of the sudden idea" (Bollas, 1999, p. 66).

Shortening the treatment

In the decades since Freud formulated this revolutionary method
much has happened to his pure and simple goal. Bollas (1999,
p. 69ff) goes on to deplore what he calls "the diminution of free association which begins in Freud's work as well as in his followers' and
reflects important shifts in his model of conflict". It also reflects a
gradual move away from mainly interpreting the patient's resistance
and interpreting the transference. In the past fifty years modified
forms of psychoanalytic psychotherapy have been developed in
response to new populations of clients, in particular attempts to
develop shorter and more focused treatment methods than analysis.
In these the fundamental rule can still be observed, but it is no longer

paramount and thus "the pure gold of psychoanalysis is compounded by suggestion", as Freud had recommended when he advised his colleagues to practise a "psychotherapy for the people" (Freud, 1919a).

The analytic requirement for five-times-a-week attendance has now become limited to a minority of patients, many of whom are subsidized training patients, while more general access to analytic treatment has been modified widely to once- or twice-weekly psychotherapy and time-limited brief therapy. As Daniel Stern says in *The Motherhood Constellation* (1995):

> The history of psychotherapy is in large part the story of encounters between existent therapeutic approaches and new clinical populations for whom the existing concepts and techniques were not designed. Theories arise with specific clinical phenomena in mind ... At each major encounter with an unexplored illness or never-treated population, new treatment approaches emerge and these invariably have implications for the existing approaches. [p. 1]

As Freud had predicted, the demand for therapeutic services has increased vastly and there are now many new contexts in which these are offered to a multitude of clients who expect free therapy, as he had envisaged after the First World War. This has meant making a virtue of necessity by cutting frequency and length. Thus, everywhere these days charitable organizations, primary care trusts, educational institutions, and corporate employers are offering single or successive brief contracts of once-weekly therapy to people in need. This big increase in brief therapeutic services has led to a situation where most people in the western world have access to therapy, though not necessarily always the therapy of their choice or of appropriate length, because of money and time constraints. It has also meant that "free associating" is no longer the only basis of therapeutic discourse and that "focusing" has become an important word in the therapeutic vocabulary, indicating that the free flow of the patients' narratives and the clinical material can be subordinated to the therapist's cognitive selection and curtailment, the very thing Freud had intended to curb by encouraging free association.

In fact, many of his early analyses would nowadays be considered brief, though Freud had always seen his patients five times a week, had advised against a shortening of treatment, and was firmly against the therapist's imposing an ending to analysis in order to accelerate and move on the process. He had been critical of those of his colleagues (like Ferenczi, Rank, and Adler) who were experimenting with active methods of short-term work that he considered a dangerous adulteration of his technique. But, in his late paper "Analysis terminable and interminable" (1937c), he described a case where he himself had

> resorted to the heroic measure of fixing a time-limit for the analysis
> . . . a blackmailing device about the value of which there can be only
> one verdict—it is effective provided that one hits the right time for
> it. Once the therapist has fixed the time-limit he cannot extend it,
> otherwise the patient would lose all faith in him.

One could say that this statement makes him the first time-limited therapist, as it puts into a nutshell the most important principle of the time-limited model—consistency.

Freud also stated in the paper that analysis cannot always give patients permanent relief from their neurotic symptoms, and that it was not possible to "fully analyse" patients, as he had initially hoped. Experience had by then taught him that patients can experience a recurrence of old symptoms after the ending of analysis or that there could be an appearance of new material which might require more treatment, as there was no effective method to prevent as yet unknown neurotic conflict from coming to the fore in a crisis, however thorough and apparently successful the analysis might have been.

This was a frank response to the accusation of "interminability", which detractors of analysis, including adherents of time-limited therapy, have frequently used against Freud because of the slowness of the analytic approach and the complex entanglements that can be a consequence of analysing the resistance and the transference relationship. Bollas (1999) argues that the analytic approach is still the best method we have. However, having undergone substantial modification and enrichment, it has become a variable and flexible tool that allows therapists to practise in many different ways with long- and short-term contracts adapted to the needs of patients, to the therapists' personalities, and to the resources of the service providers. The question of how and when to end an analysis has remained as difficult as ever and there is much literature on how much or how little is needed by whom (Fonagy & Roth, 1996; Murdin, 2000).

Mann's time-limited therapy

Twenty years ago, in order to cut the controversy short, some people came up with a simple way out of the dilemma by deciding to set an ending in the beginning and devising a method of time-limited therapy that primarily addresses issues of separation, ambivalence, and loss. The first and most systematic practitioner–theoretician of this method, the American James Mann, believed that

> the problem of time with its meaning of separation, loss and death is as vital in the emotional life of the therapist as it is in that of the patient, [thus] only by setting a fixed time limit could the ambiguity about ending treatment be eliminated. In short: a fixed time limit forces both therapist and patient to confront the issue of termination with a minimum of evasion. [Mann, 1973, p. 36]

In this kind of time-limited therapy, the mastery of separation anxiety becomes the model for the mastery of other neurotic anxieties. The logic was simple and convincing and led to a statement of universal conflicts:

1.   independence versus dependency;
2.   activity versus passivity;
3.   adequate self-esteem versus diminished self-esteem;
4.   unresolved or delayed grief.

The nuclear focus

Mann's twelve-session therapy model has proved itself as effective. It is easy to learn and widely practised. It makes use of an important methodological breakthrough to deal with the interminability of analysis, which occurred in the 1940s, when the analysts Alexander and French developed the concept of "focal conflict" or "nuclear focus", by which they meant the pre- or semi-conscious symptoms which the patient presents when coming for treatment (Alexander & French, 1946). These presenting problems are assumed to "point the way to what needs to be analysed [in the transference] in order to free the patient from their unresolved nuclear conflict which has been an unconscious developmental obstruction in his or her psyche" (p. 67). All subsequent forms of dynamic brief therapy have used this formulation of the nuclear conflict as the theoretical basis for their therapeutic activity, whether they call it the dynamic focus (Balint, 1972; Malan, 1963), the central issue (Mann, 1973), the oedipal problem (Sifneos, 1975) or the core conflictual relationship (Luborsky & Crits-Christoph, 1990). The focus is seen to have a psychodynamic dimension, reaching into the past and connecting past feelings and attitudes with the present. As Alexander formulated it in the 1940s:

> Focal conflicts are derivatives of deeper and earlier nuclear conflicts ... which presumably originate during crucial developmental periods in early life. These remain mostly dormant or repressed, with one or the other of them becoming activated (or having remained active) and continuously appearing to underlie behaviour in the form of focal conflicts which can be identified as variations of the same theme. [p. 95]

This statement echoes the ideas developed by Freud in his paper "Remembering, repeating and working through" (1914g) in which he formulated a method of analysing and interpreting the neurotic pattern that emerges in the therapeutic process, a method that he described as "working through", i.e., a repeated working over of material which presents itself in various configurations due to the "power of the compulsion to repeat—the attraction exerted by the unconscious prototypes upon the repressed instinctual process" (Freud, 1926d). And, in a footnote to the case history of the Rat Man, Freud was the first to mention "the nuclear complex of the neuroses, which comprises the child's earliest impulses, alike tender or hostile, towards its parents and brothers and sisters" (Freud, 1909d).

With the identification of "unconscious prototypes" and of "nuclear conflicts", a way had been found to cut down on the mass of material produced by the patient's free associations and to focus on what were seen as essentials. This focusing can be said to be one of the primary tasks of the therapist on first meeting the patient and it becomes an ongoing discipline of the ensuing brief therapy. It has, in short, become the hallmark of all brief and time-limited therapies.

Balint's focal therapy

The homing in on the most important diagnostic clues in the patient's material was developed by the Hungarian analyst Michael Balint at the Tavistock Institute in the 1950s. As a medical doctor he had learnt to structure his consultations with patients as if they were "ten minute psychotherapy", for which he used what he termed a "flash technique". This was a move away from the traditional aim of "pinpointing the seat of trouble" to an alternative aim of

> providing the patient with the opportunity to communicate what-ever it is he/she wants in a brief, intense and close contact, and then following up on what has been communicated at subsequent meet-ings. The moment of the flash is that moment when communication is successful and the doctor has been able to hear, to sense and to think about what is being communicated in such a way that a shared moment of understanding occurs that allows what follows to have an emotionally substantial quality. [Pietroni & Vaspe, 2000, p. 142]

Here is Balint's description of how a focus was found, as a task

> which demanded a very high intensity of interaction between patient and doctor. This atmosphere helped the doctor to tune in with his patient's actual mistrust, confusions and clarity. If he succeeded in this task it amounted to a "flash" of understanding which united patient and doctor and was felt by both. Another way of expressing this experience is to describe it more poetically as a "meeting of two minds" or as the "moment of truth", the closing of a Gestalt or the "Aha" experience . . . It is sufficient that the event is felt and recog-nised by both partners and that this recognition is kept alive in subsequent meetings. [Balint, 1972, pp. 151–152]

The present moment

In his recent book *The Present Moment in Psychotherapy and Everyday Life*, Daniel Stern (2004) micro-analyses this "now moment" as the locus of psychotherapeutic change, as a moment in time that is not chronos but *kairos*, "when a 'real' experience emerges which is encoded in memory and rewrites the past" (*ibid.*, p. 22). Awareness or consciousness is a necessary condition of the felt experience, not the verbal account of an experience, and it will endure in the mind as a "moment of being", to use the words of Virginia Woolf (1977). Balint's "flash" can be translated into Stern's "intersubjective matrix", when two people make a special kind of contact which involves the 'mutual interpenetration of minds . . . a reading of the other's mind, when two people see and feel roughly the same mental landscape for a moment at least" (Stern, 2004, p. 75). These meetings, in Stern's opinion, are "what psychotherapy is largely about". His belief is that in psychotherapy the "intersubjective matrix" is the basis of the therapeutic relationship (which Balint had called the "harmonious mix"). It promotes the work of developmental repair in which the therapist's affective attunement and implicit knowledge of the patient's mind may bring about the desired change in psychic functioning. The past is brought into the present, the experience is relived, and this leads to a "journey of meaning-making" (*ibid.*, p. 195).

By using his "flash" technique, Balint had become the first analyst to conceive of a method called "focal therapy", which applied the notion of focal conflict to the patient's presenting problem and was structured around the concept of the a nuclear focus. He believed that

> in focal therapy the flash experience must be expressed by the thera-
> pist for his own use in fairly exact ideas, a process that is more or
> less identical with translating the flash experience into concise
> words. Without this precise formulation no focal plan can be
> devised, which means that the therapist will find it difficult to
> decide when and how to use *selective attention and selective neglect*.
> [Balint, 1972, p. 152–153]

The latter two strategies became crucial technical terms of the brief therapy that Balint, Malan, and a group of their colleagues at the Tavistock Clinic in London were experimenting with and developing systematically in an attempt to adapt psychoanalysis to a feasible form of brief therapy. They could be described as the inventors of the brief therapy that has since revolutionized the availability of therapy. By translating French's idea of the "nuclear conflict" and Freud's idea of the "unconscious prototype" into plain clinical language and developing a personal technique of focusing by using the therapeutic relationship, intuition, and the unconscious communication between therapist and patient, they formulated another example of the sequence: free associating, closely observing the patient, and imaginatively processing the material communicated, while waiting for an idea to conceptualize the finding. Following this powerful experience of a "brief therapeutic encounter" for the patient at assessment, the next important step was the therapist's putting it into concise words, making what is called a psychodynamic formulation, which then becomes the basis of the focal treatment plan that constitutes the necessarily brief "working through", lasting for 25–30 sessions.

Balint had a medical and an analytic training. He had brought along from the medical world an experience of disciplined time schedules and limited resources to inform this new method of focal psychotherapy. It was a truly inspired moment when the Tavistock team began to try out their innovative therapeutic model that was time-limited and focused rather than open-ended and free-ranging, while still remaining firmly rooted in analytic theory and psychodynamic thinking.

The dynamic focus

The dynamic focus is usually based on the patient's presenting problem and becomes the main theme of the work that proliferates into variations by free association, depending on the length of the contract. It can be an habitual inability to make decisions, a constant need to please and be compliant, an avoidance of conflict, or a problem with assertiveness, all of which will show up in patterns of work, in relationships with others, and in attitudes to oneself. It will need to be tackled (and linked to the transference) in order to establish self-esteem, a sensible management of aggression, and the ability to love and work—in short, to gain some freedom from neurosis of which Freud had spoken as the ultimate aim of therapy, in order to face the reality of the past and the present (1895d). The therapist's task is to home in on areas in the patient's life and psyche where he or she is likely to achieve such changes, however minute, that might make a meaningful difference, perhaps achieve a significant increase in risk-taking behaviour, in confronting painful issues, or in being honest about feelings towards others.

In an important paper on assessment, the analyst Hinshelwood (1991) used the American psychiatrist Menninger's tripartite structure of the psychodynamic formulation to forge an assessment tool by which he was able to establish the patient's "point of maximum pain". He maintained that in general the patient's core object relationship

> points directly to a core of pain which the patient is attempting to deal with. What follows from that are certain other kinds of relationships which are used to avoid the pain (the defences). We then have a way of ordering the various objects and the various relationships into a coherent narrative. [Hinshelwood, 1992, p. 172]

In other words, "the core object relationships pinpoint the focus of maximum pain and then make sense of the way in which other relationships are used in the attempt to evade the pain". The "point of maximum pain" could be equated with the dynamic focus as it is connected with the patient's core object relationship and with "other kinds of relationships which are used to avoid the pain".

When Luborsky and Crits-Christoph coined the phrase "the core conflictual relationship" (1990) as the seat of a patient's problem, they echoed Hinshelwood, Menninger, and Malan, all of whom are adherents of object relations theory. There are others who talk of core complexes, such as Jung and Glasser, or who home in with Freud on infantile traumata such as abandonment, separation, and other repressed infantile experiences managed by defences of the ego (Freud, A., 1936) or of the self (Klein, Kohut et al.): splitting, projection, avoidance, or denial. In every assessment the most important task is constructing a psychodynamic formulation and finding the dynamic focus, whether it is for analysis, psychoanalytic psychotherapy, time-limited or brief therapy.

Daniel Stern's description of identifying the important life experience that provides the key therapeutic metaphor for understanding and changing the patient's life is somewhat different from the classical theory of making psychodynamic formulations, and, as a brief therapist, I find it very useful. Stern claims that "this experience can be called the narrative point of origin of the pathology, regardless of when it occurred in actual developmental time" (Stern, 1985, p. 257). He thus sees development

> not as a succession of events left behind in history, but as a continuing process, constantly updated. The narrative point of origin can correspond with the actual point of origin, or not and the genesis of psychological problems may, but does not have to have a developmental history that reaches back to infancy. [*ibid.*]

Once the therapeutic metaphor is defined, the therapy proceeds forward and backward in time from that point of origin. According to Stern, most therapists would agree that one works with whatever reconstructive metaphor offers the most force and explanatory power about the patient's life, even though one can never get at the "original edition of the metaphor".

Stern's therapeutic metaphor is another name for the poignant image of narcissistic wounding that suggests that healing takes the form of permanent scarring, that old wounds can reopen and may remain lifelong potential danger areas, likely to produce crises when triggered off by some current traumatic event, or, as the saying goes, "when the past catches up with the present". Whatever we may call it—the core complex, the nuclear conflict, the narcissistic wound, the point of maximum pain, the organizing therapeutic metaphor—there is not always the possibility of permanent healing, of a resolution of internal fractures, of a cure for chronic mental illness or for a borderline condition. The ethologist Konrad Lorenz established that early imprinting is irreversible in animals, and when this term is translated into Balint's (1972) "Basic Fault" or into Bowlby's (1988) categories of "anxious, avoidant or insecure attachment", it is apparent that the human infant is as vulnerable as are goslings and ducklings, that therapeutic endeavours can be insufficient, that the "corrective emotional experience" and the "secure base" that patients hope to establish with the help of therapy may not last for a whole lifetime.

Recurrent therapy

Mindful of this, Freud and his follower, Erik Erikson (1950), recommended recurrent therapeutic input: the former when he spoke of relapse and the appearance of new symptomatology after ending analysis, the latter when he expressed the belief that each stage of the life-cycle presents the individual with developmental challenges that might lead to new crises, because of the reactivation of "nuclear conflicts" and of unresolved developmental problems requiring more therapeutic input. Jung's concept of "individuation" and the poignant image of therapy as a lifelong journey echo this statement, and recent infant observation studies have modified the classical psychoanalytic theory of psycho-sexual zones in infantile development into a theory of more pluralistic and lifelong processes.

Stern puts these points forcefully:

> It frequently happens that adult former patients who have completed successful treatments run into previously unexpected life crises, such as divorce or the death of a parent. Either they find themselves forced to deal with feelings and motivations that they never had to deal with before—in quantity or quality—or they find that previously effective ways of coping are proving unsuccessful in this new context. In either case they return for a second treatment to reapply in a sense the gains of the initial therapy to the new situation and enlarge the treatment effect. A large part of the motive to return to treatment is the clear feeling that the first one worked well. [1995, p. 191]

Sixty-five years ago Freud had recommended that analysts should periodically, every five years or so, go back into analysis and not feel ashamed about this as their continual contact with the patients' repressed material was always likely to reactivate their own repressed instinctual conflicts and they should be prepared to confront these regularly. Apart from such regular returns for more therapy, therapists nowadays also have ongoing supervision to face and explore the emotional problems surfacing in the course of their clinical work, and they constantly examine their countertransference to understand the unconscious projections and projective identification processes in the therapeutic relationship.

Nowadays, all this is well understood, and Freud's recommendations have become part of our professional ethics and practice. Successive therapeutic contracts are offered to the public at large over time, and the door is always left open to patients to return for more input if necessary. Thus, many patients receive some form of recurrent therapy in the course of their lives, coming back for more whenever they encounter a fresh disabling crisis. It is not unusual to have some treatment in adolescence for learning difficulties followed by some short-term counselling as an undergraduate and then engaging in analysis or long-term psychotherapy in later life, when relationships, work, or parenthood are temporarily unmanageable. More and more people have their first taste of therapy in some form of short-term or brief therapy, as this is now widely offered free in many contexts. It is, thus, very important that their first therapeutic encounter is a good experience for them, which they will be able to repeat later if necessary, and which will prime them for therapy by helping them to acquire self-awareness, or what Nina Coltart (1987, p. 25) has called "psychological-mindedness".

Serial life-span therapy

Serial therapy was first developed in the USA and called itself "Brief intermittent psychotherapy throughout the life cycle" (Cummings & Samaya, 1995). This echoes Freud's findings in his late paper ("Analysis terminable and interminable" 1937c) and Erikson's concept of life-stage developmental crises. When Stern talks of "serial life-span therapy", he raises the issue of

> a basic view of development during the entire lifespan, from the clinical point of view. If the major work of development is accomplished in early adulthood and can be more or less stabilized for a lifetime by giving the patient in therapy the self-righting processes to deal with all further developments, then one does not need the notion of longitudinal working through. But if one sees life-span development as a never-ending series of transformations that cannot be anticipated or sufficiently prepared for even by getting the coping machinery in good order, then the only difference between infancy—or adolescence for that matter—and any other period or phase of the lifespan is one of degree, that is rate of internal change and rate of encountering drastically new contexts. The need for a working-through process over time is then seen as normative and the timing of therapy may need to adjust to it in the form of some variation of the serial-treatment format. Such reapplications of treatment, in

this light, are neither retreatments nor second treatments. They are
simply the continuation of a single treatment across discontinuities
in a life-span. [1995, p. 192]

We pay visits to the doctor all through our lives, as we are liable
at different ages to develop different illnesses and age-specific
complaints that cannot be treated prophylactically or once and for
all. We take this for granted, more so since we now know more about
genes and their functioning in our physiological make-up. There
should be all the more reason to assume that our psychological
make-up is similarly vulnerable, and to be on the look-out
for the appearance of new symptoms of psychic dysfunctioning as
we grow older and find life more complex and stressful. Perhaps we
need to reformulate our understanding of the transference and be
more willing to shorten treatments in the knowledge that we could
always have more later, since we cannot foresee what life experiences are still to come.

Another aspect of the "therapeutic journey" is the fact that many
patients make use of alternative therapies or complementary medicine alongside psychotherapy to deal with the discomforts and
tensions in their lives. These "extras" are important indications that
the "talking cure" does not satisfy all patients and that it often
needs to be supplemented by other forms of healing that also happen
in relationship with another (Budd & Sharma, 1994). It is difficult,
in most instances, to establish how much they influence, support, or
hinder the ongoing psychotherapy and whether they could be called
a resistance to, or an affirmation of, therapeutic needs. What it
amounts to in the end, however, is the patients' admission that they
are not entirely self-managing or self-sufficient and that this is why
they turn intermittently (or promiscuously) to others for help.
In this connection I also want to mention the fact that another
powerful therapeutic model has been gaining ground over the last
few years that is favoured by many doctors, and by the government,
as seemingly more effective than the psychodynamic approach—
cognitive–behavioural therapy (CBT). This offers a structured treatment that is also available in self-help format. Many patients
believe that it is less painful and more cost-effective than the
psychodynamic approach. CBT is a serious rival, but it may well be

more suitable for some people and, although very different, must not be discounted. As there are many religions, so there are many therapeutic approaches. What really matters is what works for whom!

The focal therapy team Balint and Malan devised a method of following up their cases over a period of years after termination that was based on the traditional medical follow-up of a patient after discharge. These follow-ups were intended to establish whether the changes achieved during therapy were lasting and to enable the patients to monitor themselves in the presence of their erstwhile therapists, who functioned as observers on these occasions and arranged for referrals if required. Follow-ups look for evidence of continued working through on the part of the patient, or for renewed psychic turbulence and reactivation of endemic focal conflicts. Apart from the follow-ups' value as research material, they could be used to help people get help earlier and more willingly than they usually do, and to remain conscious of their psychic functioning as vulnerable and as a source of ongoing psychic conflict and struggle.

David Malan's recent book (2003) followed up three of his analytic cases, all of which had a "happy outcome", over long periods of time (in one case over fifty years!) and found that what determined their successful outcome was "the use of life experience" and "management and not just understanding". Consequently, he recommended the use of psychodynamic psychotherapy as a treatment combined with psychiatry and medication, a flexible interdisciplinary approach offering psychiatric, medical, and analytic techniques with the overall aim of "the transformation of self-destructiveness into constructive use of experience, developing the capacity for self-analysis, and bringing about a change from compulsion to free choice, from ought to want" (p. 90). Not surprisingly, this resumé is close to Freud's famous statement that psychoanalysis aims to "transform neurotic misery into the ordinary unhappiness of life" (1895).

CHAPTER THREE

In praise of once-weekly work: making a virtue of necessity, or treatment of choice?

Introduction

When I first began to think of this subject, I intended to evaluate the once-weekly work I do in my private practice and supervise at the Westminster Pastoral Foundation (and privately) to examine some of its results and satisfactions and, perhaps, to start a general debate on the virtues of the once-weekly psychotherapy model which is practised widely in agencies or in the NHS and is also offered widely in private practice. I soon realized that I had opened a can of worms, particularly in relation to the discussions on frequency of sessions that have been exercising the profession as a result of the psychotherapy regulation process. I decided to avoid the difficulties around labelling by choosing the neutral word "work", rather than the perhaps more specific "psychotherapy" or "counselling", although I confess that I personally prefer psychotherapy to counselling, because it connotes "healing" rather than suggesting "advice-giving", and because the term counselling is much misused and abused in the press. However, that is not the subject of this present work.

As I need to value what I do in order to do it reasonably well, I persisted with the task and discovered first that there is a general confusion on the subject of frequency and of who needs when and who can practise what, with an underlying assumption being that everybody should do only what they have been trained for. I also discovered that the assumption may go back a long way, to a famous statement made by Freud at an international psychoanalytic congress in Budapest (September 1919), when he said that "It is very probable that the large-scale application of our therapy will compel us to alloy the pure gold of psychoanalysis with the copper of suggestion", implying that other methods not exclusively based "on the line of investigation which recognizes the two facts of transference and resistance" might be necessary. He concluded by insisting that

> Whatever form this psychotherapy of the people may take, whatever the elements out of which it is compounded, its most effective and most important ingredients will assuredly remain those borrowed from strict and untendentious psychoanalysis. [Freud, 1919, pp. 167–168]

Freud thus acknowledged reality, while emphasizing fundamental principles. Yet, in a way, he inaugurated the hierarchy that we are now inscribing in tablets of stone, gold being the most precious metal—though no longer the basis for most currencies. Other metals have other useful functions and some are alloyed with gold or gold-plated!

By using this potent metaphor Freud inaugurated a system of value and status that has persisted to the present day and is difficult to ignore. There were inherent issues of elitism, class, wealth, and ideology here—something for the rich and something for the poor—and Freud was well aware of these when he chose the expression "psychotherapy for the people" and suggested a system of philanthropic or state subsidizing for this. He envisaged that hypnosis might play its part in this, yet made no mention of any other technical differences; for example, with regard to how often or how long patients should be seen for this treatment. When he mentions frequency of attendance in "Further recommendations on the technique of psycho-analysis: on beginning treatment", he describes his analytic method laconically thus:

> I work with patients every day except on Sundays or public holidays. That is, as a rule, six days a week. For light cases or the contin-

uation of a treatment which is already well advanced, three days a week will be enough. [Freud 1913c, p. 127]

This is a statement of fact and the reasons given for it are based on his experience. It is also well known that he could be flexible, if necessary, and that most of his analyses were short by today's standards:

Any restrictions of time beyond this bring no advantage either to the doctor or the patient and at the beginning of an analysis they are quite out of the question. Even short interruptions have a slightly obscuring effect on the work. We used to speak jokingly of the "Monday crust" when we began work again after the rest on Sunday. When the hours of work are less frequent, there is a risk of not being able to keep pace with the patient's real life and of the treatment losing contact with the present and being forced into by-paths. [Freud 1913c, pp. 127–128]

With his daily sessions, Freud set a precedent for "classical analysis" that became an orthodoxy and, for some, a status symbol. Strangely, there has been little research done to back it up until a 2002 LCP Symposium "Exploring once-a-week work", and the book by Stone and Duckworth (2003), *Frequency of Sessions and the Analytic Frame.*

Once-weekly work—a psychotherapy for the people?

My training institute (The Westminster Pastoral Foundation) decided at its inception to offer its clients and teach its trainees a "psychotherapy for the people", based on the "pure gold of psycho-analysis", and it adapted for this purpose the canon of psychoana-lytic theory (which has retained its dominance since Freud through many modifications). It was alloyed with the copper of counselling, more specifically pastoral counselling, which made it a compound combining tradition and evolution in a constant state of trans-formation yet also linked historically to a much older, religious tradition of psychic healing.

This once-a-week model still reflects its original connection with the weekly rhythm of church life, worship, and confession, but it also owes its persistence to other customary weekly rhythms and, last but not least, to sheer necessity. As Freud had realized after the First World War, when there was a dramatic increase in people whose neurotic conditions needed the kind of help he could offer to only a few, who had the money, the time, and the urgent interest—the WPF realized that, if it wanted to help the many, it had to spread its resources—not thinly, but prudently. As the results were encouraging (judging by the growth in client numbers), its particular brand of once-weekly client work has remained the bedrock of its training and counselling service for the past three decades.

When I did my training twenty-eight years ago, the frequency was never questioned, and I am still convinced that the model works, or rather, is good enough for a huge proportion of clients who knock at the WPF's doors. As supervision is also practised once a week, I have come to feel comfortable with the weekly rhythm, though in my private practice I also see people twice a week. I believe that the WPF made a virtue of necessity and that one can be effective and satisfied doing once-weekly work, pitching expectations realistically and curbing one's competitive and envious feelings in relation to analysts and psychotherapists who practise at higher frequencies. After all, group and family/marital services, and the whole field of brief and time-limited therapy, are also offering once-weekly work, which means in blanket terms giving people a regular space in their working week when they can attend to urgent personal matters in the presence of another.

The need for status and the experience of personal therapy at higher frequencies seem, for some people, to cast doubt on the value of once-weekly work. This is understandable and yet it is also deplorable, particularly as the people who are in need of this work seem to be on the increase in our economic climate, and the necessity for good clinicians is obvious. I believe, and have been confirmed in this belief by others, that once-weekly work is in some respects more, rather than less, difficult than twice- or three-times a week work, because of the need to make the hour memorable and meaningful for the clients to encourage them to persist, and because of the pressure of numbers on the therapist, who has to hold in mind many people's stories and process more diverse clinical material.

Whether the long gap between sessions is necessarily experienced as more frustrating may be questioned once a habit is established, as also may be the assertion that deeper analytic work cannot be done consistently in one session a week.

My first client became regressed after a few months of working together, and our transference relationship went through all the classical phases, requiring rigorous interpretation in order to keep pace with the psychic changes, which were considerable over six years. With the help of close supervision I learnt how to hold her through periods of primitive rage, to contain her high anxiety levels, to survive her prolonged attacks on me in the transference, and to work through a host of issues relating to sexual and physical abuse in her childhood. It was this first relatively successful experience of what can be done in prolonged once-weekly work, this "baptism of fire", that convinced me of its usefulness, and it has been confirmed again and again by other cases of my own and those of other people, trainees and colleagues. I wonder whether a full analysis could have achieved more and quicker change and maturation in this client. One thing is clear—it is often the beginners—without much experience, unjaded and unprejudiced and boldly prepared to go with their clients wherever they take them—who have good results; but supervision is an essential of the process as is their personal therapy.

Making a virtue of necessity

When I speak of necessity I mean it in the reality sense of circumstantial constraint relating to time and money: unavoidable and reality-based, and, hence, always needed to be worked on at two levels. When clients say they want help or someone to talk to, they usually think that it is normal to come once a week, and they also do not have a clear and realistic idea of how long it might take unless they know something about therapy or have been in it before. At this point, the therapist decides (or the agency norms or resources dictate). Once a week is an "imperative need" and "indispensable", to use two of the five meanings of "necessity" in the *OED*, but I have also worked with people at lower frequencies over quite long periods of time. This only works when the motivation is high and the process is sufficiently established to allow for some ongoing working through in the interim. What I mean by motivation is a combination of *Leidensdruck* (high levels of suffering), sufficient ego strength to bear lengthy separations, and the internalization of the therapist as a good object. Paradoxically (or understandably), I usually find less resistance in these situations and, when I compare outcomes, not necessarily less satisfactory results, which appear to be due to ongoing processing by the client with the therapist in mind. Personally, as far as I know, I am without desire to increase or reduce the frequency of sessions for my own benefit, as I believe in abstinence and try to fall in with the necessity when I am as certain as can be that I have to.

My experience as a supervisor is that supervisees who talk about clients in terms of "needing twice a week" are often those who are most anxious about not being able to contain them or about not being good enough, or those who are angry about having to work with people they consider too disturbed (in which notion they can be supported by anxious supervisors). I think we do not really know how to correlate disturbance levels with frequencies, and often rely on intuition or prejudice for recommendations. On the one hand, we know that it requires considerable ego strength to undergo the intensity of analysis; on the other hand, high disturbance levels need the firm containment that is implied when we speak of the therapist's auxiliary ego and superego function that is the basis of all supportive work.

There are other, non-quantifiable elements of our work, such as hope, belief, experience, and personality match. And, as we are working with human beings, the craft elements of skill and method are never enough. So much of what happens is, and remains, unconscious and unknowable. We cannot really be certain of what the client needs until we have tried and seen what works. Nor can we make objective comparisons. I find the difference between once- and twice-weekly work very noticeable in individual cases, particularly the transition points, when there is a radical change of perception and intimacy, a qualitative difference in the transference, but to compare cases with each other objectively with regard to results is as difficult as comparing individuals to each other.

Issues of choice, goal and method

I would like at this point to refer to some articles that have relevance to these issues: first, the papers read at a conference on Psychoanalysis and Psychoanalytic Psychotherapy, published in

1988 in *British Journal of Psychotherapy*, 5(2). The contributions made by Joseph Sandler and Heinz Wolff, in particular, are interesting in that they throw into question the "more means better" assumptions and emphasize the difference rather than establishing norms of better and worse, calling for more research into what works when and what therapists actually do. Four years later, an article by Ruth Barnett ('Two or three sessions?' (1992) raised the issue systematically; the author put the question to herself when she was raising the frequency of sessions with patients: "was I agreeing in the best interest of the patients, or might there be an ulterior motive in myself?" The editorial to that issue (*British Journal of Psychotherapy*, 8(4)) spelt out this question:

> Frequency is important but what importance and how important? These questions affect psychotherapists. A good deal of status for the therapist may often attach to how near to the psycho-analytic five-times-a-week he works. Nevertheless, as Ruth Barnett says, the frequency of sessions significantly affects patients—though perhaps in different ways. There is often a need to tailor the frequency to the patient. More equals more intense equals better, does not necessarily apply.

Clearly, more thinking and research work needs to be done on this issue. As for transference work, this surely is possible and necessary across the whole range, depending on the individual patient and the style of the clinician, though time constraints make its explicit use more limited in once-a-week work and there are, of course, vast differences of methodology between pure analysis and psychotherapy. Here is a definition I find plausible:

> The most marked difference between psychotherapy and psycho-analysis lies in the handling of their transference. In Psychoanalysis, the goal is to bring about the resolution of the transference neurosis so that the patient comes to regard, understand, and relate to the analyst as a real person, and thus freed from their transference projections, distortions, and idealizations. In the psychoanalytically orientated psychotherapies the centrality of the transference is the underlying dynamic of the therapeutic relationship and techniques of clarification, confrontation, and interpretation are utilized. In psychotherapy it is frequently more therapeutic (or

possibly just customary) to leave untouched a selection of the patient's projections and idealizations of the therapist, since they can help to maintain the person's stability, even though some magical thinking may be involved. [Schwartz 1990, p. 85]

The main difference, it seems, lies in the method, not in the goals, though:

> these operate at different levels and at a different pace [and] frequently psychotherapy begins when the patient is in a critical situation and is only anticipating a focused resolution. The focus in psychotherapy is much more towards reality, reinforcement of ego strengths and reconstructions. An uncovering process is not sought to the same degree and regression is dosaged . . . the therapist should know what should or should not be done or approached, based on an understanding of the underlying dynamics and a clear assessment of what the patient is capable of handling. [*Ibid.*, p. 91]

Encouraged by this, let me now play the devil's advocate and state a bold hypothesis: it may not be the quantity, but the quality that counts, the quality of the relationship with the therapist and the quality of the experience that happens within it and through it. We have long since been disabused of the hope and belief that anyone can become fully analysed, i.e,. fully conscious, mature, or normal. We have pitched our goals more realistically: with Freud, to enable the client to love and work (*lieben und arbeiten*); with Jung, to "individuate", confront and integrate the shadow; with Klein, "to reach the depressive position"; with Winnicott, "to feel real, become able to play and to be creative". In other words, therapy has worked when it has made a significant difference in somebody's life that can be sustained and, by way of subtle ripple effects, will generate further difference and change in the internal world and/or in the external world—a difference in a person's experience of self and others.

Therapy has also been conceptualized as the healing of psychic wounds, or the strengthening of ego functions, as the letting go of no longer functional defences, as the integrating of splits and parts, as the growing from immaturity to maturity, and all these are models, metaphors, and preferred ways of description, depending on the therapist's theoretical or cultural orientation. There are no certain predictions at the outset as to which of these things are going to happen, if any, nor can we say with certainty at the end what has happened intrapsychically in the course of the painstaking process of making conscious previously unconscious conflicts and complexes. If the outcome, to quote Freud again, is "an elimination of neurotic misery, and a better ability to bear the ordinary unhappiness of life" (1895d), we have achieved what was implied in the original request for help. This is a somewhat pessimistic view of saying that somebody has achieved a reasonable degree of stability, psychic equilibrium, and personal identity, a better quality of life, and the capacity to carry on the process of continuous self-exploration and self-analysis. "Know yourself", exhorted the Delphic oracle.

As for descriptions of the intricate processes and of the progress in individual cases, these are necessarily partial, whether they be the therapist's or the client's accounts of what happened in sessions or in the whole course of a therapy situation. We always have to fall back on approximations, assuring ourselves that we can trust the process, and observing our own and the client's minute feelings and reactions, while we try to decode the complex details of communications we receive during the therapeutic discourse. Freud (1914g) described the work as "remembering, repeating and working through". This is a generalized approximation of how we work with the client's clinical material in the transference, the general method of which there are myriad variations and permutations. In supervision one gets an idea of how different everybody's work is, depending on the personality and the personal history of the therapist, and on the mix and match of every individual therapeutic relationship in every individual session, which creates a developing therapeutic process *sui generis* in every case.

Quality in once-weekly work means continuity, reliability, safety, and support. It is always difficult not to get drawn into a client's need for gratification, let alone one's own needs for it, and this underlies the useful but much misunderstood concept of therapy as "corrective emotional experience". It does not, of course, mean becoming the good parent, but facilitating the client's working through the painful disappointment and destructive rage of not having had the kind of parenting environment that would have promoted a reasonably balanced affective functioning. The demand for, and granting of, more sessions could, for instance, be a satisfying of the need for gratification, while not fulfilling it can be experienced as a cruel withholding; yet talking about, interpreting, and working through it with reference to the transference might be more genuinely therapeutic when it leads to insight into patterns of need and transference issues. It presupposes, however, an ability in the client to use and understand symbolic language in the therapeutic discourse. As this is often not there, particularly in the beginning, it also presupposes an ability in the therapist to teach this language sensitively by fostering the making of links in the client's life story, and the understanding of how their expectations of parents and other significant figures relate to their expectations of the therapist in the here and now of the sessions.

John Klauber's (1986) statement that "each patient repeats in each session something of his whole life history" may have a special relevance to once-weekly work, where, I believe, one has to think of pieces of work rather than sequences as in four- or five-times-a-week analysis. The structure and content of every individual session may have to be taken as complete in itself, and when a door opens in the course of it, it may have to be shut again in order to allow the client to leave the session and to function reasonably for the rest of the week. The secret is to do this and yet somehow to hold the process over until the next session, which will be the next piece of work and yet will connect with what has gone before, like a link in a chain. The client's frequent question, "what were we talking about last time?", acknowledges this situation and appeals to the therapist to remember her and to hold the therapy together for her. Hence, the basic need for continuity links with the basic need for reliability, for being held firmly in the therapist's mind over the gap of a week. The question, of course, may also be a reproach ("we started something that was not completed") or a checking out ("am I important enough for you to remember?") And it is also always a way of indicating that the process has been painfully interrupted and that restarting it is difficult, almost a new beginning every week, and if there were a longer break it may not be possible to do this any more.

Time and frame: kairos/chronos

All this relates to the different sense of time and space that is experienced on entering and leaving the therapeutic container. One bit of important theory taught to me during my training came from theology. It links up well with the analytic concept of setting, frame, and boundaries, and has stayed with me as a precious and useful bit of knowledge on which I base my once-weekly work. It is the concept of *kairos*, one of two Greek words for time, the other being *chronos,* clock time. *Kairos* describes time when it is special, significant, and meaningful. Applied to the regular therapeutic hour it implies that this hour of the week is set aside from ordinary existence, and is qualitatively different from all the other hours in the week, a slice of vertical time, so to speak, as opposed to the horizontal flow of time. Time with a difference, related to the timelessness of the unconscious and of eternity, to existential, subjective time, when the prosaic rules of clock-time are suspended. Past, present, and future can come together, form links and meanings, and produce intense experiences for the two participants in the time-bubble. These may initiate qualitative psychic changes and make a significant difference in their internal life. *Kairos* is a moment in and out of time, the special moment that is meant in Wordsworth's verse:

> There are in our existence spots of time
> That with distinct pre-eminence retain
> A renovating virtue, whence our minds
> Are nourished and invisibly repaired. [1850, II: 208–210]

The Greeks used the work *kairos* to describe the fullness of a sacred moment—of truth or revelation—and in this sense of time and space it captures the powerful impact of the hour when the therapist meets the patient, signifying the distinctive otherness of this meeting that breaks like a shaft of light into the mechanical flow and the routine of clock-time, bringing two people together in an encounter qualitatively different from other relationships and in a dialogue that is not like ordinary conversation. In this heightened atmosphere people go into trance-like states, go temporarily mad, have visions and delusions. They also learn to speak a new language, and they remember, imagine, and communicate in ways they never knew they were capable of. This, we know, is the peculiar magic of this particular hour, potentially creative or destructive, depending on the handling of the opportunity and the timing of responses.

When we talk of the importance of time boundaries in therapy, giving particular attention to the beginning and ending of each session, we acknowledge the power of *kairos*, the significance of meeting for it and of separating at the end of it. It is especially important because of the felt gap between sessions that can mean release, abandonment, or a time for working through, depending on what happens emotionally and relationally and what the patients take with them or leave behind. One of my patients, who terminated after four years of work, called it the cornerstone of his week, a space which he had reserved, religiously, for the exploration of his nightmarish dreams and his violent phantasies, and where he tried to work through them to a new sense of being real and able to manage them rather then acting them out. When I saw him for a period twice a week, at his request, he went into a dissociated state and seemed on the brink of a breakdown. This made me seek a psychiatric consultation and return to once-weekly sessions, which calmed him down and proved in the long run more useful.

Kairos can happen once a week or five times a week, as a time dimension that breaks into clock-time with a difference. In a more secular vein, it equates to the "constant analytic frame", a term coined by Bleger, that modifies Winnicott's concept of the analytic setting by applying to it the totality of all the phenomena included in the therapeutic relationship—those that make up the process and those within the process (Bleger, 1967). This constant structure of the analytic frame has the same function for the patient that the maternal holding has for the child's developing ego. Flegenheimer compared it metaphorically to the "darkness in the cinema, the silence in a concert" (Momigliano, 1992, p. 35).

Bleger's "frame" became the basis of the methodology of communicative psychotherapy, developed by the maverick American psychoanalyst Robert Langs (1994). He emphasized that once the ground rules of the therapeutic frame have been stated and agreed between the therapist and patient, they have to be strictly adhered to, as deviations or modifications can have traumatic effects on the patient, reviving anxieties around earlier trauma and parental failure. Langs was not saying anything new, but he was saying it more loudly and exclusively, with the conviction of someone who knows how easy and tempting it is to break the frame and become abusive. Pointing at deviancy in the profession, from the earliest days of Freud analysing his friends and his daughter, Langs exhorted the therapist to read the patients' communications consistently as encoded narratives relating to validation or deviancy from the frame, and in this emphasis on listening between and behind the lines of what the patient says he joined hands with Patrick Casement's urgent message in *On Learning from the Patient* (1985).

The security of the frame, the safety and sanctity of the therapeutic container, is a fundamental therapeutic prerequisite of any therapeutic model, whatever the frequency or orientation. It emphasizes the absolute necessity of reliability and of vigilant narrative processing in this unique object relationship, where conscious and unconscious communications are always totally intertwined. When there is no ongoing security there can be no basic trust for the patient, the frame can be experienced as entrapping or leaky, and this will lead to resistance and ambivalence. Accurate decoding, which is Langs-speak for interpreting, is necessary to prevent stuckness or acting-out of basic assumption behaviour such as fight or flight. Langs' strict demand is for vigilant adherence by the therapist to ground rules and frame, and it follows that supervisory error and frame-breaking can also be transmitted to the therapeutic dyad. He implies that unconsciously and instinctively we are all potential frame-breakers, and we always need to listen to the patients' material with this awesome basic knowledge in mind.

The message that the frame is sacrosanct allows itself to be translated into the notion of *kairos* and into Winnicott's clinical image of holding and providing, like the mother, a facilitating environment, an intermediary, interactional space. With Langs there is a dark note, of power and abuse, of the shadow aspect of the profession, something archaic as of sacrilege and of violence, reminiscent of Freud's warning that if we can do good it follows logically that we can also do harm, and that this needs bearing in mind all the time while we are handling the powerful forces of the unconscious. This is reminiscent of the story of the sorcerer's apprentice.

Transference in once-weekly work

The concepts of *kairos*, frame, and holding imply a use of the symbolic function, and they connect with the essential as-if quality of the work embodied in the transference, This is active in once-weekly work in the sense that it is a powerful holding and binding agent, an ingredient in what looks like a habit, when it is more like a spell and the illusion of a life-line. Its existence enables and compels the patients to come regularly for their hour, to leave when their time is up, and to exist in the interim, once it has established its hold on them. It is the therapist's responsibility to remain aware of the strength of this agency of dependence and ambivalence and its inseparable counterpart—countertransference. Equally, he or she is responsible for holding the frame when a negative therapeutic reaction makes the patient fearful or unwilling to enter it, makes it difficult to be in it together for long stretches of time, and sometimes even impossible to use it constructively.

Handling the negative transference in once-weekly work is as much an art as it is with higher frequencies. The therapist's task is to allow it and endure it, with all the hate, the fear, and the retaliatory urges experienced in the countertransference, while enabling the patient to enter and leave the therapeutic container in a frame of mind that makes it possible for him or her to function in the external world without disastrous acting-out, or to continue coming to therapy without too much disruptive acting-in.

Once again, it is important to retain one's hope, belief, and trust in the process, holding the frame and fostering the effectiveness of the therapeutic *kairo*s. And also, once again, the beginnings and endings of sessions are critical points to watch, as are cancelled sessions, threats of giving up or destroying the therapy, and the continued denigration of the work, which may be a defence against envy, against intimacy and dependence. In cases of borderline and narcissistic disturbance, this may go on for months, even years, and yet the patient keeps coming, week by week, hating it and yet needing it, and waiting/hoping for change. In retrospect, the necessity for it becomes apparent, proving the firmness and survival of the therapist as much as the tenacity of the patient's transference, and laying the basis for firmer selfhood and healthier functioning. When psychic change comes, it is inconspicuous, fragile, easily lost, and the weekly gap becomes for a while particularly difficult to bear, while breaks are experienced more sharply and may be catastrophic. Whether change is lasting and turns into metamorphosis depends on the many unknowns and mysteries of our profession.

In the subtitle I speak about necessity and about treatment of choice, a distinction that is difficult to make, since both may involve resistance to handing oneself over to the therapist and to focusing on the therapy while putting one's life on hold. I was taught, and believe, that one must go with the resistance, while interpreting it as it arises, and that in once-weekly work with a patient this is fruitful in the long run because it allows the patient to set the pace, using the gap between the sessions to digest what came up and recovering equilibrium before the next bout. Freud's objection to lesser frequencies was that the work might become "obscured"; I believe that this objection may not make enough allowance for the ongoing nature of unconscious therapeutic processes, once established—the intensity of which varies, of course, from individual to individual and from time to time. The therapist may not be able to "keep in step with the real events in the patient's life" and it may sometimes take the patient much of a session to open up or to fill the therapist in on the happenings of the week—and yet the telling will always be unconsciously selective and hence full of symbolic meanings. The therapist has to keep on the ball—to read attentively between the lines or, if necessary, stop the flow appropriately. The former and the latter require constant thinking on one's feet and making acutely sensitive interventions.

Suitability

As for the choice of people suitable for once-weekly work, this becomes as much a matter of one's experience as of the patients' voting with their feet. When the transference is weak or not interpreted, they may feel unheld, particularly during the initial phase of anxious ambivalence (which accounts for the fact that self-doubting trainees "lose" patients in the first few months more frequently than experienced therapists). I do not know how many five-times-a-week analyses are aborted, though, to judge from psychotherapy trainees' experience with their training cases, there seems to be no dearth of those. The distinction between supportive and expressive work that for some determines session frequency, and recommendations as to who needs what and when, are difficult to make, and how we distinguish between the two unless we consider the constant interpretation of the transference as expressive and reconstructive/empathic work as supportive, with Kleinians and Kohutians thus neatly split into two camps, though not necessarily on frequency. Supportive work seems, in my opinion, to be more often a function of the therapist's personality and/or benevolent attitude towards the patient than a genuine technical choice. As with mothers, therapists cannot be what they are not, except in the patients' projections. The support gained from once-weekly work can last a week or an hour—time is plastic—and one timely or correct transference interpretation may reverberate over weeks, while a verbal *faux pas* can be disastrous.

I believe that we are artists rather than scientists, but it is not enough to have creative talent; we also need a solid and strong crafts base. The craft of processing what is brought to the session once a week has two aspects: allowing space for the realness of events and for the patient's reactions to these, as well as reading them in the context of the ongoing transference. It is this sort of decision-making based on an understanding of the unconscious dynamics that characterizes once-weekly work: recognizing priorities for the patient, choosing an intervention out of a multiplicity of possibilities, and trusting one's instinct on what to respond to and which way to go. Ideally. this will then amount to a sequence of "remembering, repeating and working through", in which some aspects of the patient's life history are involved, and these sequences will accumulate constructively over time.

Of course, there is much misunderstanding, mismatch, and missing of opportunities, and far too many pieces of therapy cannot be seen through to a satisfactory conclusion for patient and therapist. I once conducted a survey of all the cases I had seen and was astonished by how many terminations had occurred for external reasons, such as the patient's moving away, having a baby, finishing or starting a course; not to mention the ones who do not engage or who decide to stop abruptly, leaving one with a sense of unfinished business and a question mark. But probably the most difficult part of the work is when it is with someone in whom the maturational processes are stifled to the point of extinction. These people with borderline or severely narcissistic psychopathology need help in order to survive, and may use us as a life-line, but they may not be able to change substantially, whether in once-weekly or in five-times-a-week work. They also seem to be getting more numerous—or rather, we are getting more able to understand, if not to improve their conditions, with the help of the theories on narcissistic and borderline conditions developed in past decades. Over the many years that I have practised a once-weekly model, I have realized that while quite high levels of disturbance can be handled in once-weekly work, when the patients feel held in a reliable ongoing situation, the changes may remain minimal.

I feel rewarded when the work continues on a steady level, ensuring the patient's reasonable functioning in their external and internal world. I find every session uniquely interesting, and the different way I am being used and perceived constantly fascinating. Over the years I have pegged down my expectations considerably, and have become more realistic about what I can do or not do.

Conclusion

In order to survive and to restore myself, I constantly need to turn to the "pure gold of psychoanalytic theory", and when I read the *International Journal of Psycho-analysis* and the *British Journal of Psychotherapy*, or new books on object relations, narcissism, and neuroscience, I am fascinated by theories which make me understand some of my patients better and I feel validated by others that I have "found" myself in the process of working with someone and that, to paraphrase Alexander Pope, "I have never been able to express so well"; but I also realize that I cannot work the pure gold of psychoanalysis, of pure transference and resistance analysis, as I have not been trained to do so, nor experienced it myself, and thus would not presume to do it except in the more commonplace "copper" form of once- or twice-weekly psychotherapy.

We need the lifeline of theory to feel contained in moments when we do not know what we are doing and what is happening, because, to quote Eisold (1994), "theory and stress go hand in hand . . . there are many ways that a therapist can be thrown off balance and every time that happens some aspect of theory will become important to him" (p. 789). Eisold goes on to say, "In the isolation of the consulting room, particular theories or beliefs provide lifelines, so to speak, back to the therapist's own analysts, supervisors and teachers, linking them to a community of like-minded practitioners" (*ibid.*, p. 791). Theories confirm identity, but as system or abstraction they may sometimes interfere with, rather than promote, unbiased responsiveness to the individual detail of material presented by patients. As clinicians we are not truly like scientists, who hypothesize, experiment, and validate data objectively; we are more like artists, who respond intuitively to experience and have creative ideas, use well-timed interpretations, the right word at the right time.

We also have to select and translate constantly what we find useful and digestible in psychoanalytic theory into a personal language we can speak and practise fluently, otherwise we will remain confused in our professional identity and, hence, confuse our patients and trainees. When I examine carefully what I believe in, I find it is a patchwork of not always consistent bits of theories, and I often find it helpful to read the same material in as many different theoretical ways as possible, pluralistically, so to speak. "A repertoire", says Adam Phillips, "might be more useful than a conviction" (Phillips, 1993). All theoretical approaches to the truth are partial, relative, and probably personality-related. But to Freud, who was the only begetter, the creator of a "whole climate of opinion", in the words of W. H. Auden, I return again and again and I feel privileged to be able to read and reread him in the elegant original.

CHAPTER FOUR

Dilemmas in brief therapy: referral-on, topping up, extended contracts

This chapter examines three central concerns for the short-term therapist at a time when therapy is widely available free of charge in the community, in a model that has been called "intermittent serial life-span therapy". Issues of referral-on, topping up, or extending contracts are experienced as dilemmas or as temptations, depending on what therapists believe their clients need and what their clients may demand of them. Short-term therapy has become accepted in many contexts, with therapy no longer used as a once-and-for-all solution to clinical problems but as a serial method over time that includes topping up and re-contracting. After an initial agreement of brevity, depending on the client's disturbance levels at assessment and on availability, there may be the need for referral-on after the end of a brief contract, when clients may be offered a different, long-term service, or they may be recommended to return later in life for more if and when this becomes necessary. Flexible contracts, rather than rigid rules about the termination of therapy, are being practised in many contexts, depending on "what works" and how methods can be adjusted to new evidence. There is danger of collusion or control, and this can lead to therapeutic dilemmas, which involve taking acceptable risks, or to therapeutic temptations that are due to the desire for narcissistic gratification, benefiting the therapist rather than the client in terms of power or eros. Being able to let go of clients and manage issues of loss, grief, and greed requires a measure of maturity in the therapist that aims for good-enough results rather than striving for perfect endings.

There is no longer any doubt that brief and time-limited therapy has come to stay. After much controversy, its usefulness for certain client populations has been established, and the profession at large has accepted its validity. Nowadays, most psychotherapists practice both long- and short-term work when it offers itself, and this has led to a situation where both/and, rather than one or the other, obtains, depending on personality type, opportunities, resources, and work contexts. However, there are a number of quite specific dilemmas for the brief therapist that are still controversial, and it may be worth spending some time on three of the most obvious.

To start with, there is the issue of referral, both referral in and referral out, which depends on the careful assessment of clients' suitability for time-limited work. Most brief therapy happens in institutional settings and thus involves a number of people apart from the therapist, which means that referrals both at the beginning and at the end of a piece of time-limited work require a thoughtfulness and expertise that is not always available. What a client is offered usually depends on what inclusion or exclusion criteria are used by clinicians, what they believe can be done, who assesses the prospective patient and how the therapy is set up, conducted, and terminated. Because of limited resources, the patients do not always have the choice of what they get, and this is dictated by availability and prognosis of potential outcome.

Contexts vary enormously. In some, as in educational settings, there is open and easy access, in others, appointment procedures and numbers of sessions may be strictly fixed. It is important to note whether referrals are made by the clients themselves, by doctors, tutors, relatives, or through service providers such as employment assistance schemes. Contracts can be negotiated by the therapeutic couple or by service managers who hold the purse strings and stipulate the number of sessions allowed. When counselling happens at the GP practice, at corporate and workplace settings, in schools or universities, clients are told that therapy is finite and funded, and do not expect open-ended or long-term work. They tend to come with self-defined problems and expect rapid symptom relief, though the psychodynamic assessor will usually insist on taking a brief personal and psychiatric history and will try to establish a limited dynamic focus to work with. Starting clients off will depend on whether they are ready to engage in an active working alliance and have sufficient trust to reveal at assessment the extent of the emotional crisis that has made them seek help. The dynamic focus will then be defined on the assumption that the emotional turbulence may be caused by a psychic conflict representing the return of repressed material from their past, which the skilful counsellor attempts to identify, to concentrate on during the brief joint work, and hopes to resolve within the contracted time.

There is usually an initial agreement of brevity, though, depending on the disturbance levels found, there may be an understanding that referral-on may be necessary straight away or possibly later on, involving a change of therapist and/or a change of venue, after negotiation with the client and the provider. This does not undermine the value of the brief work, but it will mean that the client has to be prepared for the kind of ongoing help that is needed supplementary to their thorough induction into clienthood and will involve a change of therapist, be it referral to a psychiatrist, into a group, to a more specialized agency, or a private practitioner if they can pay for it.

At this point it seems important to recall the medical and pastoral beginnings in which analysis, psychotherapy, and counselling originated, and the gradual ways in which, after a period of experiment, pragmatism, and much individual effort, a general practice of helping people with their psychological problems has developed. This has happened over the course of a century, during which psychoanalysts and social workers came to believe that disturbed minds need as much attention as diseased bodies, and that the traditional mind–body duality can no longer be upheld. The understanding of how psyche and soma are influencing each other in subtle and unconscious ways, and how social systems affect individuals, increased as helpers became aware of what happens in families where parenting is brutal and inadequate and affects the emotional development of children, and when they realized that this could no longer be tackled by the traditional methods of precept and admonition.

For centuries, the caring for troubled minds was the domain of the church, while the medical profession was looking after the physically sick. In our time, the physical and mental welfare of people has increasingly become the responsibility of the state, and with the growth of psychotherapy, the introduction of the NHS and the statutory social services, a situation has come about in which people can expect their personal problems to be taken care of and funded publicly, instead of having to pay for physical and psychological help, as in the past, when the vast majority had been left to fend for itself.

The development of brief and time-limited modes of counselling in the past few decades is a direct consequence of these momentous changes during the twentieth century, which our therapeutic ancestors had only dimly glimpsed after the end of the First World War, in which a whole generation had been traumatized, and was affected physically and emotionally by its consequences. It took a long time and another terrible, even more total and devastating war, before there was a significant increase in public awareness that people could be healed, not only medically but also therapeutically, from the wounds they inflicted on each other, be it in war, in the environment of the family, in the competition among nations, or in the inhuman living and working conditions many people have to endure.

In his book *The Faith of the Counsellors* (1965), the sociologist Paul Halmos described graphically and critically this "coming of the counsellors". As he was writing in the 1960s, the author was unable to foresee how dramatically new therapeutic methods like groupwork, family therapy, and time-limited counselling would change the scenario of health provision and lead to the present situation where everybody has access to free counselling, though not always of the length and intensity they might want or need. It used to be the churches who provided people with pastoral care from the cradle to the grave, then the hospitals and GP practices opened their doors to everybody in need of medical care, now there is the availability of brief counselling at every stage of a person's educational and working life, which fulfils a similar promise of life-long care and counselling.

In the USA, this new situation has been called "intermittent lifespan therapy" (Cummings & Samaya, 1995).

. . . If one sees life-span development as a never-ending series of transformations that cannot be anticipated or sufficiently prepared for then the only difference between periods or phases of the life-span is one of degree, that is, rate of internal change and rate of encountering drastically new contexts. The need for a working-through process over time is seen as normative, and the timing of therapy may need to adjust to it in the form of some variation of the serial treatment format. Such reapplications of treatment are neither retreatments nor second treatments. They are simply the continuation of a single treatment across discontinuities in a life-span. [Stern, 1995, p. 192]

In other words, long-term and time-limited therapy are not necessarily one-off therapeutic treatments, as the first generation of theoreticians believed, they can be used serially whenever appropriate and necessary during the long journey of life, depending on the individual and on the vicissitudes they encounter along the way. The short-term model is not a substitute for the long-term open-ended modality that used to prevail, but an alternative to this. Dependent on the context where it is offered, it is a time-limited, repeatable approach to the therapeutic needs of human beings, which are unforeseeable and unpredictable and cannot be prevented or treated prophylactically once-and-for-all, just as physical illnesses cannot be foreseen nor warded off by magical panaceas.

Returning to the notion of referral, this means that nowadays a client's therapeutic CV can run parallel to his or her medical CV and will involve alternative visits to medical and/or therapeutic practitioners, as the need arises. Depending on the stage of a client's developmental situation, there may be a first piece of therapy in childhood, followed by another piece of brief counselling at university, then by further therapeutic involvements, long-term or briefly, on starting work, getting married, starting a family, getting old and facing death; in short, whenever there is a short-circuit or a crisis in the developmental process that requires assistance or threatens a breakdown.

Therapy can thus be seen as a series of necessary repair jobs during the ups and downs of life, whenever coping becomes temporarily unmanageable, and it can lead from an initial brief therapeutic input to a referral to long-term psychotherapy, or to another service, be it medical, psychiatric, group or family therapy, as is considered necessary by different helpers in the life-long process, which thus becomes structured into an ongoing facilitating environment where clients will feel held and contained in various transferential scenarios that have to be managed carefully so that transitions do not become traumatic and changes of therapist are possible.

The hope is that there will be transformation and integration somewhere along the way, significant changes in an individual's psychic functioning and in their personal situation in the external world. The ultimate goal, of course, is to strengthen ego functions, to dismantle no longer workable defences and to reach what Winnicott called "the stage of concern" and Melanie Klein "the depressive position", an ability to face reality.

Of course, not everyone will need the serial treatment, as most people learn to manage the working-through processes by themselves. Everyone, however, is nowadays assured of its availability and can make use of reparative and supportive "re-applications" whenever there is an agreed need. This requires careful contracting, particularly if there is a transition from one practitioner to another as the client needs help to manage the shifting transference situation and to be matched carefully to a different therapeutic environment.

What follows is a clinical example of serial life-span therapy.

A client of mine, who is an artist and started therapy with me twelve years ago, has needed intermittent therapeutic input after she had finished an extended period of ongoing twice-weekly work. She was brought up in a family where nannies were the norm and had a strained relationship with her mother. Initially, I provided long-term open-ended work to help her overcome a severe eating disorder, which included regular use of laxatives and persistent somatizing. Gradually recovering and stabilizing a partnership with a man much older than herself, she decided to have a baby, which meant permitting the motherhood she had denied herself when she aborted a baby conceived with an abusive boyfriend. We terminated the therapy shortly before she gave birth to twins, but she soon returned for a brief piece of work in order to understand why she had problems with breastfeeding. A few years later she returned again, because she had had an affair with a married man and wanted to save her own marriage, which had been endangered both by this and by her partner's bankruptcy that had left the task of breadwinning to her. She understood that she had been angry with him for abdicating his responsibility and accepted that she once again needed to do some therapeutic repair work with me, with whom there remained a transference bond. I would not be surprised if she returned again at another time. The children are now at school; how will she manage their adolescence?

Working for a university counselling service, I have been able to observe another type of serial process repeatedly at close range. Students are at a vulnerable developmental stage, during which they may come temporarily "off the rails" as the new demands of independence and competition tax their weak ego strength, which may require a visit to the counselling service. This may end successfully after a few sessions, or they may drop out and show up again later during their time at university. As they are guaranteed open access during the entire length of their studies, it is not uncommon to resume the work started and left unfinished at a later date, to ask for a "topping up", or "returning" until they have done as much as they require this time. For the counsellor, this becomes a job closely resembling the parenting some of these young people demand in vain from their parents, from whom they have not quite managed to separate in order to start their adult individuating. It is a form of piecemeal brief therapy that can become a dilemma for the therapist until he/she identifies the stop and start of these encounters as an age-appropriate acting-out. It may be the only way the student client can manage the unfamiliar intimacy and intensity of the therapeutic situation. Possibly the full rigour of a strictly time-limited contract is equally uncongenial to their particular developmental stage, which would mean that enforcing it sternly according to orthodox rules would be counter-productive.

Allowing the student to return, to stop, and to continue at their own pace seems to be an age-appropriate way of getting help, but it requires great flexibility on the part of the therapist, who is trained to work in the analytic discipline of regular meetings. The end of term, or the advent of the summer vacations can act in a similarly dramatic way, as does the planned ending of a piece of orthodox brief therapy. The knowledge that there is no more time seems to speed up the maturational processes and to achieve a good-enough ending.

In employee assistance programmes (EAPs), early drop-out rates are fairly high as many clients develop an initial resistance. Some agencies allow their clients to return, usually after a year, for another piece of funded brief counselling, which is a chance for further topping up and firming up a positive transference with their counsellors, the agency, or their employers. In GP surgeries counsellors are known to use various methods of successive contracting, or of spacing out sessions over time, which can constitute a valid form of holding for those who cannot use the once-weekly or time-limited model constructively (Pietroni & Vaspe, 2000). All these procedures are adapted forms of serial intermittent therapy, which have the advantage of both brevity and limited time, and are tailored to the various developmental stages and pathological conditions that clients are presenting with in the practice, fitting into the complex practicalities of the context. It is important to note that the GP counsellor works within the medical appointment model and the EAP therapist within the short-term contract culture of corporatism, in both of which there can be shifting transferences to various people that may be split and need holding. In the educational context of schools and universities, the counsellor may be used *in loco parentis* or even team up with parents if need be, which means remaining cognizant of adolescent development and its particular psychic patterns and maturational processes.

Some time-limited therapists believe—mistakenly, I think—that their metholodogy is suitable for all pathological conditions, if carefully administered. Like their clients, they may occasionally mistake surprising improvements for lasting change and initial flight into health for progress. In practice, severe addiction or sexual perversion is rarely amenable to one brief therapeutic onslaught, nor is it possible to shift persistent personality and eating disorders in a few sessions of concentrated work, and as for more serious personality problems or psychopathic behaviour, there seems as yet no effective way of short-term help. With brief therapy an initial inroad can be made and an important psychological process can be set in motion, but it will need the repeated and determined working through in the transference that is only possible in long-term work to eradicate an entrenched habit of high infantile anxiety levels and to equip clients with healthy alternatives to primitive defences or to facilitate mature anger management and relationship skills.

When staggered over a period of time, however, serial brief therapy can offer a secure base to return to by agreement. It can begin to address entrenched psychological problems when it identifies original fears of being abandoned and repeatedly reinforces the experience of being helped, while allowing a well-prepared ending and the acceptance of loss that James Mann (1973) considered one of the key issues of time-limited therapy. Clients may feel listened to for the first time, make a firm therapeutic relationship, and may have a good therapeutic experience that makes them willing to return and attempt another necessary piece of work in their own time, which can be long-term, open-ended, or time-limited.

The third issue is the extending of contracts. I was taught in the 1980s that the time-limited therapist should never convert a contract for an agreed number of sessions into a long-term therapeutic engagement, because this meant collusion or inconsistency. As Freud insisted, "once the therapist has fixed the time-limit, he cannot extend it, otherwise the patient will lose all faith in him" (1937, p. 218). Nowadays, in supervision, I encounter counsellors who allow themselves to extend contracts when they believe that this would be neither sharp practice nor a pernicious transference situation undermining the beneficial therapeutic process. I have to give them the benefit of the doubt and observe how they slow down and transform their active brief working style into a more repetitive and considered working-through of dynamic material. The twin danger is collusion or control, when therapists are keen to fill their private practice or when they try to avoid their inevitable separation anxiety. The gain would be a systematic consolidation of insight and the creative use of a well-functioning working alliance, but it requires a conscientious examination of the passive client's regressive or dependency needs and of one's motives—are they altruistic or narcissistic? Is it the client's benefit or one's own that guides the decision and who pays?

An example is the case where an EAP clinical manager encouraged the counsellor to keep on working with a client who had asked to go into long-term ongoing work with her after five sessions funded by his employer. They had made a good working alliance and the client's great fear of breakdown needed to be contained quickly. It had seemed from the beginning that brief work would be counter-indicated, and the work so far had been an extended assessment of the severity of the client's condition and of his motivation to embark on, and pay for, an extended piece of therapeutic work. As he had lost both his parents in childhood, it might well have felt like abandonment if his counsellor had insisted on an ending with her at this point, so carrying on together was decided to be good enough.

Instead of insisting on "never", one should consider "what works" and adjust the method to new research evidence. Most psychotherapy research is based on brief therapies, and outcomes are almost always evaluated in terms of symptom reduction. There are, however, a number of very relevant findings, for instance in *What Works for Whom? The Critical Review of Psychotherapy Research* by Roth and Fonagy (1996). This is an important report commissioned by the National Health Service that systematically examines the different therapeutics of existing therapy options and offers guidelines for diagnosis-based treatment selection. It has been shown that psychodynamic brief therapy is superior to waiting-list control, and that, on average, the most significant amount of change occurs early on in therapy, with sixty-two per cent of clients maintaining that they have been helped within thirteen sessions (Garfield, 1994). Research has also found that there seems to be a "dose-reponse curve" (Howard, Kopta, Orlinsky, & Brown, 1986) which shows that the longer therapy continues, the more the returns diminish, and that by session twenty-six about three quarters of all total gain has been achieved. For brief therapists, one research finding is that despite good results in the short run, long-term follow-up shows that many patients tend to relapse. Research results may be influenced by researchers' allegiance, and there is no easy definition of what "being helped" means. Change has to be clinically significant, but since short-term therapy has the modest aim of problem-solving, of symptom relief, and of "making a significant difference" (Bateson, 1978) rather than wide-ranging character restructuring, this may mean no more than that a small change is likely to set in motion other changes, which may lead to a belief in the likelihood of further change, and to different ways of thinking about oneself that may make a difference in one's behaviour towards others. There may also be a changed perception of the value of taking one's troubles to another person and of entering into a self-exploratory dialogue with someone with extended experience of working with troubled people.

This experience in relationship with another has been seen as a "corrective emotional experience" (Alexander & French, 1946), i.e., a meeting facilitating an encounter qualitatively different from previous experiences with significant others, in reality and in the transference. It results from the difference between the original parental approach and the response of the therapist in the transference, and provides the clients with the opportunity to correct their distortions. It lends conviction to insight, which elicits new and more reality-orientated solutions to old conflicts. Rational insight alone is not enough, but needs to be backed up by a transformative therapeutic experience.

There is a difference between a dilemma and a temptation. The first is a position of doubt and perplexity, of being caught between the two horns of a practical or moral conundrum, which requires examining one's assumptions, thinking about positive consequences, taking risks, and perhaps getting it wrong. The second is a desire for something narcissistic or gratifying—eros, power, satisfaction. The point I have made about extending contracts can be seen as one or the other: if the first, then it is the choice of a necessary action based on professional integrity; if the second, then self-analysis, further therapy, or clinical supervision would be advisable for the therapist, because unconscious instinctual needs might be involved. One may want to keep a client, or do something for them that breaks rules and boundaries; there may be favouritism, an unacknowledged erotic transference, or anxiety about not giving them enough. Brief and time-limited therapy is always set against the pressure of time; as the poet Andrew Marvell put it, "but at my back I always hear / Time's wingèd chariot hurrying near". This pressure often enhances the work, but it may also lead to botched endings, when the client is not ready and would be traumatized. An example was a woman student who had paranoid fears about people staring at her face, which she considered masculine. When, in supervision, the question arose as to whether she might be heading for a breakdown, she surprised her therapist by rallying round in the final session, as if she had unconsciously derived ego-strength from her therapist's holding her in mind with concern and could use this experience of containment to give up her dismorphic anxieties and not to feel abandoned.

When supervising counsellors doing short-term work, one is often told "this client needs long-term work", and it is important to examine this statement in terms of the dynamics and the transference in each individual case. Referral-on can be a dilemma or a temptation. It can be necessary at the beginning of a contract if a client shows symptoms of long-standing personality disorder, it can come up at the end of a contract if the client requests it, or when the counsellor is anxious that disturbing symptoms have increased and that something else has become necessary, such as a psychiatric consultation, ongoing long-term psychotherapy, or an alternative therapeutic approach. It can be now or in the future: if the former, it might be an admission that the brief work has been inappropriate; if the latter, it could be a confirmation of the necessity for serial intermittent therapy and will be an assessment of the total situation in which the present piece of work is only one of more, possibly many, pieces.

Students can feel affirmed when they are told that they might need more long-term intensive therapy later on in life. When this is left to their own initiative, they understand, in the spirit of Freud (1937), that there is the likelihood of more crises in the future that might need more therapeutic input. Only if it devalues the brief therapy is this questionable, or if it is played out against a background of "second-best".

A recent case made me understand the fine line between a therapeutic dilemma and a temptation in short-term work. In supervision, a counsellor talked about a client who was troubled by bouts of blind murderous rage, phantasies of axeing strangers and going berserk. His partner had arranged brief counselling for him through her EAP, and in the initial assessment session he opened up a can of worms. He felt despair of ever managing his enormous anger with a mother whom he had experienced as bitter and twisted, setting him up against his father. Because of the severity of his disturbance, the counsellor first considered turning him down for brief therapy and referring him on to a psychiatrist, but then she changed her mind and offered him ongoing assessment in the remaining five sessions, since he had already opened up to her. The client asked whether she would take him on in her private practice, but she resisted this temptation, while agreeing to help him think of therapeutic alternatives after they finished. He was an out-of-work actor, and would not be able to pay for further therapy unless he got a temporary job. They discussed the possibility of his becoming a clinic patient with a psychotherapy organization, if he could not be found an NHS psychotherapy placement. The client agreed with the counsellor that the focus was for him to take responsibility for himself, and give up the rescue fantasy of finding an acting role that would get him the attention of an audience. The agreed goal of ongoing therapy would be for him to find a way of facing his unmanaged anger and turning it into creative action.

The brief therapist has to be realistic. We genuinely do not know what lies in the future for any of our clients, though we always hope that they can be helped to take full charge of their lives again and that we can leave it to them to deal with the inevitable working through of problems to come. That depends on how much reflective capacity and self-awareness they possess, or have acquired in the process, and how much of their core problems can be shifted. It also depends on whether the two principal temptations of the brief therapist have been resisted: the tendency to believe that only they can give their clients long-term psychotherapy, and the wish to hang on, particularly if one has become fond of a client or if a passive client cannot let go.

I often compare brief therapy to the short story, in contrast to the novel, which resembles a long-term therapy experience (Holmes, 1997). These two narrative forms serve different purposes and attract different writers and readers. The same can be said of the different therapeutic genres, and it underlines the complex issue of personality differences: an episode instead of a chronicle, a sharply focused limited time instead of the diversity of a whole world, a particular event instead of a multitude of freely associated happenings—these are different narrative methods applied to different goals. Emphasizing a part instead of embracing the whole can point to contrasting personal preferences and the use of different tools: a magnifying glass instead of the broad brush. Clearly these activities open up different talents in their practitioners, and not everybody is good at both. The two temptations I mentioned above may point to the prevalence of the latter in a counsellor, to a longing for lasting relationships and an unconscious deferment of completion, while their absence may characterize a counsellor who avoids intimacy, can live with quick changes, and deals with the ending of relationships pragmatically and stoically, rounding them off in the manner of the short story writer who finishes his story with a pithy punch-line and makes a significant point, taking the satisfied reader to a good enough ending.

Notions such as growth, the development of self-understanding, or working in depth, depend on an amplitude of time and space, while opening windows, enabling a transformative experience, and setting something in motion are possible in a flash. Both genres can deal with relationships, but client dependence is not encouraged in the brief encounter that involves an ending from the beginning. Some therapists can take on both styles and function equally well in either by using different parts of themselves, others may not be able or willing to switch gear, fall into the temptation of attempting both and fail, or mix the styles inappropriately. There are episodic novels that fail to add up to a whole and rich short-stories that squeeze a whole life into a significant chain of events.

The secret for the therapist is to know themselves and to closely monitor their weaknesses. For instance, being able to bear the repeated hellos and goodbyes of brief therapy may depend on how the therapist has managed the meetings and partings in their own life, and their ability to focus on significant psychodynamic details will be a function of how they analyse their own life experience in terms of linking past and present. Both are essential features of working briefly and of being able to let go of clients who have finished their contract in order to take on new clients without hankering after the previous ones. This requires a firm belief on the counsellor's part in the effectiveness of what he or she is doing, and a measure of maturity that allows for good-enough results rather than striving for perfection. For this to happen, the counsellor's expectations and the client's expectations need to be matched, so that they can get there together rather than being out of step when the ending comes. Realism is based on the knowledge that in many cases the client is new to counselling and that the therapeutic encounter will need to be good, otherwise they will never be able to ask for help again.

All this has to be set in the context of supervision, where dilemmas and temptations can be openly discussed and resolved without acting out by either party. The working through of grief and mourning, in particular, should be facilitated by the supervisor, who may help the counsellor to face their own difficulties with loss that may counteract a successful ending and to confront their feelings of guilt about not having done enough for the client. A warning about getting too involved is often useful, as is the assurance that endings always mean new beginnings. The joint experience of facing and surviving separation in brief therapy is one of its valuable learning points.

All the time both counsellor and supervisor will do well to closely observe their countertransference, because this is as important in brief therapy as it is in the long-term mode, a vital tool to pick up clues and to understand the clients' unconscious feeling states. As untimely transference interpretations could encourage dependence and regression in the client, the brief therapist has to be sparing and judicious when interpreting the transference, in order to discourage the development of negative transference, will constantly watch the therapeutic process, to trace and verbalize all transferences to the context, to the institution, the GP, or current relationships. It is useful at assessment to work with the two triangles described by Malan (1979)—the triangle of conflict and the triangle of person—that allow psychodynamic formulations, and to test the client's ability for forming a working alliance by attempting a "trial therapy" based on transference interpretations before embarking on psychodynamic work. Pearson (1995) recommends staying with the patient's metaphors and

> allowing a variety of ways of projecting the relationship problems, as research shows that patients can improve symptomatically with short-term work that does not include analysis of negative transferences and that high frequency of transference interpretations seem to be related to poor outcomes. [p. 47]

CHAPTER FIVE

Suitability and context for brief therapy

he argument of this chapter is that a client's suitability for brief or time-limited therapy is determined by various factors, including context. There is still agreement on the validity of Malan's selection criteria, which included "mild illness, recent onset, high motivation and response to trial interpretation", yet many additional issues have since emerged and need to be considered. For instance, the counsellor's suitability, training, and work experience, the counsellor's assessment skills and ability to establish a dynamic focus, the clients' capacity for self-reflection, their ego strength, and their response to a trial therapy in the first session. Then there is the importance of the various contexts in which, nowadays, much brief counselling is offered free to clients, whether in education, at the workplace, in primary health care settings, or by charitable organizations. This means that issues of money and markets have come to the fore, and an initial differential assessment needs to be carried out in order to decide which method or model of therapy is best for the client. Matching the counsellor's personality to the needs and the pathology of the client, and matching the treatment to the client's developmental stage or life stage crises, are other aspects of the work that determine the issue of suitability. In the end, as always, there is much that remains unknown about what works for whom and how the client's decision to take up help is made.

I begin with a case encountered in the context of an employment assistance programme. The client, a thirty-eight-year-old woman who worked in human resources for a city law firm, came because she wanted to explore why she was unable to settle down with a man. None of her relationships had been long term and she was worried about remaining single. There was something plastic about her, a professional persona that was impeccable. Her history revealed that her mother had developed multiple sclerosis (MS) when she was fourteen and had died some years ago, unable to speak in the last stages of her disease. The client had been a keen rower, and had aspired to participate in the Olympic Games, but was not chosen for 2004. In the first session she broke down and cried when she talked about her mother's death. This made her go back to the service provider to ask for more sessions, indicating that she had been deeply affected when she shared her story. Was she suitable for brief work? Two issues made the counsellor hesitate: the unfinished mourning for the mother, who had been ailing for so many years, and the fact that the client was working in human resources, advising clients at their workplace. Was she asking for more, i.e., long-term work? And, how could she get what she needed: serially, intermittently, or in an open-ended form?

The suitability of clients for brief therapy is no longer as hotly discussed as it was in the 1980s, when many forms of short-term, time-limited and brief therapy first came on the scene. These have become accepted, some of them are funded by the government, and they are available in a plurality and diversity of contexts to different client populations: in education, in primary health care, in workplace settings, and all kinds of specialized services for bereavement, alcohol, drugs, and sexual abuse.

Suitability criteria for brief therapy were first established by David Malan (1976) and were divided into "radical" and "conservative". He described the conservative view as "Only acute illnesses in basically well-adjusted personalities are suitable. Brief methods should be used only when long-term methods are not available", and the radical view as "good results can often be achieved in severe, long-standing illnesses and brief methods may in certain cases be more suitable than long-term methods. Quite far-reaching changes are often possible".

Malan listed his selection criteria as "mild illness, recent onset, and good motivation"; in other words, as Freud had said, "the patient should be ill enough to seek help, but not too ill to make use of it", i.e., patients who arrived at "propitious moments in their lives, had oedipal problems, some satisfactory relationships, and demonstrated good contact and response to trial interpretation". Moreover, it seemed important that "the patient's life problem can be clearly defined and offers a clear-cut theme or focus for therapy" (Malan, 1979, p. 243).

Malan's contemporary, Sifneos (1979), treated only patients with oedipal problems and excluded pre-oedipal conditions, contrasting anxiety-provoking treatment with anxiety-suppressive therapy, and tailoring contract lengths to the patients' presenting problems and psychopathology. Another of the early practitioners, Habib Davanloo (1980), maintained that "the patient's response to a period of trial therapy was the best indicator of their suitability for the treatment", which he considered an "unlocking of the unconscious". These pioneers based themselves on Edward Glover's (1955) classical list of decreasing treatability—hysteria, conversion symptoms, compulsive neurosis, character disturbance, perversions, addictions, lack of impulse control, psychosis—and they guided the first generations of brief therapists through the controversial discussions in the profession about brief and time-limited work until the wide public availability of different brief versions and the advent of employment assistance programmes shifted the focus dramatically to issues of money and markets, contract length, technique, and modest goals.

There are now many contexts that offer funded brief therapy to people from all age groups and walks of life. The main question is still how to separate clients who *are* suitable from those who are not. For instance: what should one offer the forty-year-old train-driver and father of four children by two marriages, who asked for counselling at a community counselling service called "Open Door" because of his intermittent depression, and began his assessment session by telling the counsellor that his mother had died when he was twelve and that he wanted to do a training in psychology? Should he be given twelve sessions to help him come off his medication and focus on his childhood loss and his mid-life crisis, or should he be invited to enter open-ended long-term work to explore everything that was troubling him? Or how much time should be offered to the seventy-seven-year-old woman who was busy running committees in her community and having extensive treatment for bowel cancer, who was complaining of her husband's lack of interest in sex with her and had lost touch with her three grown-up children years ago? Would one decide to give her open-ended counselling and listen to her tales of woe, or offer her a dozen sessions in which to help her reconnect with her children before her almost certainly imminent death?

These two cases from my supervision practice appealed to the brief therapist in me and I encouraged the counsellors to focus on loss and mourning in both cases and thus to enable the clients to deal with a life-stage crisis rather than address the full complexities of their life stories and emotional problems. I was reminded of the primary importance of context in brief work, of the variable client populations who need treatment, and of the diverse styles and therapeutic attitudes of available counsellors that determine a client's suitability for brief therapy. Many contexts offer very brief and time-limited contracts to specific clients—at the workplace, in schools and universities, at GP practices, or charitable services. Most of these clients are newcomers to counselling, their knowledge of counselling is scant, and they usually expect instant help in a crisis. Usually, the decision as to whether they are seen briefly is determined by the counsellor's judgement and experience, or by the availability of resources, while the client's motivation, ability to self-reflect, to tell their life story, and to establish a relationship may be of secondary consideration.

Many contexts are now specifically geared to offer short-term contracts, and what clients get depends on how skilfully they are assessed in their first session and on the work experience the counsellor has. I believe that almost everybody can be seen briefly, if only for a thorough assessment, but I also believe that brief therapy is best when it is a first therapeutic experience. When it works, and when the client feels helped significantly, it can lead to more and longer, or to a different kind of therapy at another time in their lives. If it does not work, if nothing helpful happens, and there is no "meeting of minds" (Stern, 2003), it may have been a waste of both the participants' time, but perhaps not much will be lost, except when the client has experienced the therapy as traumatic and felt abandoned when it ended. What is most important, therefore, is that the context is well set up, is containing for both the client and for the counsellor, and that the parting of the ways is handled appropriately. Then there may be no more than disappointment; the client has had a taster and did not take to it, the counsellor has had a try and failed. The lack of a good outcome may, however, seriously affect clients who have experienced previous failures in their lives and think of themselves as failures. Then the skilled therapist needs to contain the damage by suggesting and negotiating referral to a more appropriate service, attempting to get the client seen for a longer time, or suggest another alternative, in which the client can feel understood and held.

Of course, some clients may never try again. Failed attempts may give our work a bad name, but therapy is not a panacea. What matters in the long run is that there are enough practitioners who are trained to do their work well and responsibly and who are able to fit the method to the recipient. Many clients can be helped first time round by a stint of brief therapy, when they have understood something better, made some changes, and had a good experience of being listened to. It can encourage them to try again later on, when they need more, or a different kind of, help. Much depends on the match of personalities and especially on the quality of the assessment. This needs to be carefully done on the basis of personal experience of how much to open up in somebody, of what is on offer and, ultimately, of faith in the process. Then it can enable the client to acquire a more reflective attitude towards their problems and their life story, to use the following sessions creatively and to repair some deficit or to regain their balance.

Much depends on the counsellor's training. There is still a tendency to assume that doing brief therapy is easier than long-term work. A common mistake is to think that beginners start with short-term work and that with increasing experience they learn to keep their clients longer and to go deeper. In fact, they often lose their clients in the early stages, because they mistake flight into health for success, when they are unable to establish a working alliance that ensures the client's cooperation. Beginners often have their first counselling experience in placements that offer brief contracts, and they may find it difficult to help these clients focus on problems that can be worked with briefly and dynamically. They may launch anxiously into the work without assessing from the life story whether clients are capable of establishing trusting rapport, whether they can reflect on themselves, are articulate enough to communicate their difficulties, and can make meaningful links in their life story that pinpoint the problems with which they are presenting.

Beginners may also be anxious about getting it right, about giving clients enough, about understanding what troubles them or where they are developmentally, and they may be unable to practise the necessary "selective attention and selective neglect" that is needed to find a focus in the clinical material. They may also find it difficult to set modest goals and to contain the masses of information a client may flood them with. This means that they have to be thoroughly trained and selected *for their suitability* to do brief work, since they need to get hold of where the client is psychologically and developmentally, how well they respond to the active dialogue of the brief method, and how much self-scrutiny they are capable of. Moreover, they have to have had some experience of therapy themselves, both brief and long-term, both as practitioners and in their own personal therapy, so that they know what the client may be experiencing during the work.

Choosing clients suitable for brief therapy thus requires a shrewd eye for the clients' most troubling emotional problems, for their ability to establish and to use a relationship, and for the psychological-mindedness that facilitates a therapeutic dialogue. The Canadian analyst Habib Davanloo (1980), one of the grand old masters of intensive short-term psychotherapy, believed that clients' suitability was established by subjecting them to the "vital ingredients of the treatment that was to follow", that is, to a "trial therapy", in the first session. This would test their ego strength, their availability for using interpretation, their defensive structure, and their motivation for change. And all the indications or contraindications should be judged in context. There are also dimensions of personality style, of matching expectations, and of developmental profiles, which are significant, when suitability is decided. Davanloo's selection criteria, like Glover's treatability conditions, would seem to apply to any candidate for psychotherapy of whatever length, as is a sufficient level of articulacy, of intelligence, and of a capacity for involvement in a dialogue.

Settings

It is also rewarding to consider the treatment contexts and the candidates' age group when establishing their suitability. Much brief therapy, for instance, is offered to young adults in educational settings, where the clients' most frequent pressing issue is the age-specific separation from their parents and from their home, which tests their maturity, autonomy levels, and sense of identity. In other words, they inhabit a transitional space between a restrictive or contained environment and the risk-demanding open territory of young adulthood. The counsellor working in this setting with adolescents will have to focus on these issues in order to establish how far individual clients have succeeded in the developmental tasks of achieving independence, of starting to individuate and to form an identity, whether they have the strength and resources to cope with the necessary parting from their parents, and why they are faltering in making career choices and becoming functioning adults.

The same separation–individuation dynamics will probably be repeated in the brief therapy relationship, and much will depend on how the therapist handles the parallel processes between task achievement and therapy termination. Brief therapy may generally be the treatment of choice for young people because of the developmental position they have reached and need to reach, and a regressive open-ended treatment would run counter to their developmental task of achieving independence from family and parents.

Separation issues also operate in bereavement counselling, where the clients' suitability for brief counselling depends on their capacity to mourn, to let go of persistent ambivalent attachments, and to resolve unfinished business with the dead. This can be facilitated and strengthened by an emphasis on the time limit and by working with the count-down method towards an agreed ending that becomes an example for the stages and closure of the necessary mourning.

Primary care contexts

In the GP practice the counsellor will be dealing with a motley crowd of clients, with high rates of depressive, anxious, and somatizing clients whose capacity to face difficult emotions is often impaired and habitually channelled into bodily symptoms. A willingness to face defensive and deep-seated strategies of avoidance determines the patient's suitability for brief work, and once again the choice might depend on the patient's ego strength, their self awareness, and motivation for change, since "they are going to exchange their chronic suffering for the acute but passing pains of insight which take over from the personality problems presented with initially" (Coltart, 1996, p. 149). Another difficulty in this setting is the method of referral from doctor to counsellor, which requires the patient's active participation in a therapeutic dialogue rather than medication, and this depends on the doctor's knowledge of and belief in the efficacy of counselling. In this context, a good collaboration between the doctor and the counsellor is of vital importance, as the client's transference is to the practice, and is therefore split between doctor and counsellor, with the doctor assuming an ongoing paternal role and performing a gatekeeper function, which will always influence the counsellor's working alliance with the patient and their assessment. There are also issues of funding, as GP practices are accountable to their mental health trust, which is paying the counsellors, and the doctors have the first say on the selection of patients for therapeutic treatment.

Most surgeries nowadays employ practice counsellors who do brief work. Some of these practice CBT and offer patients structured time-limited treatments which many people consider less strenuous than psychodynamic counselling and more cost-effective. Patients go to their doctors with all kinds of practical, emotional, or somatic complaints, and it is important that they are engaged fruitfully in a tentative exploration of emotional conflict that could help them understand what they really need. They might be encouraged to have a series of short-term sessions spaced out over time with the approval of the doctor. This work could constitute the beginning of a change towards treatability in a psychodynamic manner, and then lead on to referral out to another service. Much of the diagnostic work is hypothetical, may be based on trial and error, and may be the assessment of chronic conditions that might take some time to improve or for which new solutions may not be found. There is always the need to beware of false optimism.

Suitability for successful short-term work in the primary care sector is an elusive subject, and most brief work in the medical context happens because it is an available rather than an optimal solution to patients' conditions. The heart-sick and worried-well patients who people GP surgeries may not be "cured" by the primary care counsellor, but research indicates that the patients' symptoms can change, that they can find emotional relief, and often appreciate this resource as an offer of help, as a good experience of support and of being listened to, and as an incentive to go on hoping. In the end, probably only a multi-disciplinary approach will shift many of these conditions over time.

Employee assistance programmes

Another context in which client suitability for time-limited work is a complex issue is the fast-expanding world of counselling at the work place and of employment assistance programmes, where many therapists nowadays earn part or most of their livelihood. The allocation of EAP clients is in the hands of the service provider, which refers clients to the counsellors who are on its books, usually on the basis of geographical proximity. In the initial assessment session the client's suitability to be treated is established on the basis of the presenting problem(s), and of the psychodynamic focus that can be formulated by the counsellor together with the client after taking a personal and medical history. All this depends on the rapport and understanding achieved between the two participants. On beginning treatment an agreement is necessary to contract for the number of sessions allowed by the service provider, which becomes the moment of choice and of skilful negotiation between client and therapist. Who decides what happens now? If the counsellor has misgivings about the client's suitability, will this alone decide the issue? Does the client have an independent say and can he or she demand they go ahead together? Will the counsellor need to go into more detail for a decision if they disagree? Can the counsellor use persuasion to achieve a decision or does the client's behaviour decide? Is the outcome always a compromise?

Clearly, clients play a decisive part in establishing the suitability of working together, depending on the strength of their motivation and on their initiative of making a choice for the therapist, for whom they may decide unconsciously in their vulnerable state. This complicates matters considerably, as their motives might be mixed. Are they taking a risk? Do they not care whom they get? Is there already an unconscious transference developing that reaches back to their primary relationships?

The client's part in the choice

The question of suitability never is a one-sided affair decided by the therapist. Even when an agreement is reached at the end of the first session to go ahead together, this does not always happen. Clients sometimes change their mind and decide not to return, perhaps because they are ambivalent, they may not have much hope that counselling is suitable for them, or they just vote anxiously with their feet. This is not an option the therapist has, but the client's decision prevails in this situation. Yet the therapist may have a change of mind on discovering that the client proves to be more disturbed or needy than at first appeared. This may then require a joint decision to find another option. When the client returns, the sessions have to go ahead and this means that the client has decided the issue of suitability. Then the therapist is duty bound to enter into a process that has started and must decide how he or she conducts the work to lead to a satisfactory outcome, which may well be a referral into long-term work if the client shows signs of regression or dissociation that needs more containing ongoing work.

Thus, the decision-making is never simple, and the client can be more active in having a say than is expected by the counsellor. Stern (2004) describes how in any kind of therapy there is a momentum of "moving along" that overrides clear-cut decisions of suitability. In this "intersubjective matrix" it is uncertain who is in control; the process simply takes over and needs to be trusted. In some respects, therefore, suitability can only really be known with hindsight, when the counselling has worked, when the focus has been well formulated, has provided insight into the client's problems, leads to a resolution, allows for mutative interpretations, creates a surprise or a new understanding: in other words, when a process has been set in motion in the client's mind that has therapeutic consequences. In the end this means that the choice of suitability is always hypothetical, even though it can turn out later to have been very accurate.

In the context of EAP work, it seems that the client who gets allocated through the service provider often does not know, at first, what they are getting themselves into, and they usually need guidance about whether they have come to the right place. As the counsellor is guaranteed to be paid, not by the client but by a third party who gets paid by the client's employer, the first interview is a sounding-out of what is on offer, what the client's expectations are, where the client is emotionally and developmentally, whether they can tell a plausible life story, engage in a dialogue, what their emotional baggage is, and what in particular has brought them in. This establishes the parameters, but it is not always a clear assessment for suitability.

The important fact is that EAP clients are usually self-referring, which means that they have a reason for asking to see a counsellor— something of very recent vintage that makes the question "Why now?" so important. Another fact is that the counselling is free for the client, and that the experience is a brief encounter, which is easier to embark on than the uncertainty of an open-ended commitment. The counsellor's first task is to make the encounter meaningful and to focus on a problem that can be tackled creatively rather than embarking on a lengthy exploration that might become uncontainable. What matters is that there is instant rapport that can lead to a moment of change, however small. Clients who are not sure what they want will often not take up the offer of more sessions, but they may have been affected by having been listened to in an unusually attentive way that may have made them curious about something they did not know about themselves. The briefness of the encounter matters less than the quality of it.

The EAP client often comes with issues relating directly to their workplace, to their colleagues and their bosses, which means that the counsellor has to be sensitive to the organizational dynamics and needs to connect these with deeper personal and relational dimensions that may not be immediately obvious. It is worth finding out why the client is working with a specific organization: one client who worked with Amnesty International came from a background of political instability and she found her trips to the

Congo very traumatic until she discovered parallels with her own background, which explained why this was so and the knowledge of this dynamic enabled her eventually to change her job.

There are often sensitivities about confidentiality issues; the client may have been sent by their organization because of persistent absenteeism, or it may turn out that he or she is a drug or alcohol abuser, which may require more time and a more specialized treatment than is on offer. The counsellor will have to negotiate with the service provider for more sessions, perhaps for a referral-on, or for a form of intermittent brief therapy that is spaced out over the length of time it would take to make a significant difference to the presenting problem. In many cases, counselling can turn into a whole package of treatments that involve other approaches on top of or instead of talking. Not everybody, whether client or counsellor, is suited for this complex task, or capable of negotiating with the organization and/or the service provider.

EAPs vary in their generosity and methodology—many of them nowadays allow the counsellor more than one period of brief work with their clients, or the clients are permitted to re-contract with their counsellors on a private basis for ongoing therapy. Private practice is less suitable for brief therapy because of scheduling difficulties, but experienced practitioners are able to establish flourishing consultancies for corporate referrers that rely on them for the management of their work force. This requires good financial and administrative skills.

In all the contexts I have mentioned it is essential on first meeting to establish the degree of pathology and the type of defences a client uses. Equally important is the client's motivation and willingness to engage. When this amounts to trust, there can be instant rapport; when there is resistance and rigid defensiveness, this will mean ambivalence or high levels of anxiety and the therapy will take a long time to get under way. The accuracy of initial assessment is the prerequisite for achieving a psychodynamic formulation, establishing a working alliance, and attempting a trial therapy in the first session.

As for the issue of "working through" after the brief therapy finishes, this is debatable, because it requires an ability of corrective self-scrutiny that not every client is capable of or will acquire in the course of the brief therapy. If they haven't, there could be an erosion of what was done during the therapy or a return to the status quo. Much depends on the outcome—whether the client has resolved an important issue, has reached the depressive position, has been able to internalize the therapist, and has learnt some lessons from the therapy experience.

Finding new solutions to old problems could be said to sum up the goal of brief therapy succinctly, together with the modest aim of "making a difference" or, in the words of Gregory Bateson "to make a difference that makes the difference". There should also have been some emotional re-enactment, since rational insight alone is not enough and needs to be backed up by a transformational experience. There may also be a difference of outcome for the two participants themselves: what the client might consider satisfactory may be far from the therapist's expectations, and to establish who is right is well nigh impossible. Indeed, evaluation of outcome on the point of ending therapy can be different from what is seen to have been achieved or not achieved a few weeks, months, or years later. In the end there is the possibility of more therapy at a later stage—for which the brief therapy may have been an introduction, a rehearsal, and a strengthening of motivation.

It is vital that the brief therapy, though a brief encounter, amounts to a therapeutic experience that becomes internalized and enables an ongoing process of "working through" after a good-enough ending. The memory of having been helped significantly will then become an incentive of seeking help again if necessary, with the same or with another therapist, perhaps even with some alternative form of therapy, not necessarily of the "talking" variety; for instance, with CBT or with one of the newer models, such as eye movement desensitization and reprocessing (EMDR) or "energy therapy", which are becoming very important in the market of brief therapy.

I often compare brief therapy with the short story, in contrast to the novel: it is an episode, instead of a chronicle, a sharply focused limited time, instead of the diversity of a whole world, or in the words of William Blake, the experience of "see[ing] a world in a grain of sand, . . . / And eternity in an hour". It opens windows, enables a transformative experience, sets something in motion that becomes healing and life-altering, and may usher in the depressive position, which means giving up the pleasure principle for the reality principle, enables reparation, mourning, and the internalization of the counsellor.

It might be interesting to finish with a case of trauma debriefing in brief therapy, with a client whose partner disappeared in the recent *tsunami*. The young couple had been living together for a while in a relationship that had not yet stabilized and the man had gone off to Thailand on his own to a town that they had once visited together. There was no contact after the *tsunami* had struck that particular part of Thailand, and the client was in despair about what to do.

The first reaction had been action, i.e., go to the town where the partner had gone, but then she heard from her partner's sister that he could not be traced there. Then she realized that she was angry with him and felt guilt (the typical mixture of grief emotions) and uncertainty about her own role in what had happened, which needed to be vented.

This was followed by a preoccupation with closure, which began to shift when she attended the family's memorial service, which became a cathartic ritual in place of burial and started the process of finally coming to terms by giving up wishful thinking.

She still needed some support with moving out of the flat they shared but which had belonged to him, and with the sorting out and letting go of his belongings, another very painful part of the bereavement process, which meant that she had accepted that he had definitely gone for good.

Moving into another flat, she encountered a good friend of her late partner and struck up a relationship with him, which was a comfort, but it also made her feel guilty and that forming another relationship was premature.

Somewhat further on, she tentatively began to think about a future without him, and it became slowly possible to make more realistic plans.

The counsellor accompanied flexibly the various phases of the process, which divided up the nine sessions allowed by the client's employer into the beginning, the middle, and the end of the process that at first had seemed endless.

There was a break for Easter before the last session, and when the client came back, she said she felt she had done enough counselling for the time being. It had been invaluable for her and she now knew where to go if she needed more, but she wanted to experience standing on her own feet again. In view of her age (twenty-nine), this seemed sensible, and emphasized the age-specific theme of "individuation", the resilience of the young and an avoidance of regressive dependence.

There had been no time or space to go into the client's life history, as the focus was the bereavement, though past losses were mentioned and taken into account, and when the two of them met for the last counselling session, this seemed sufficient for now. It was a mutually planned and well-prepared ending, and a moving experience for both.

As a piece of post-traumatic debriefing the work was exemplary, as the client had shown herself up to the task in hand and as suitable for the brief treatment, yet not yet ready for more.

CHAPTER SIX

Bereavement counselling

eath is not easy to talk about, nor is it easy to counsel the bereaved, as everybody experiences when it is a friend or family member, or knows from their own experiences of having been bereaved. And it is a universal truth that grief is the price we pay for commitment and that it is the consequence of investing emotion and affection in another. This means that it is a natural process that sets in automatically after a bereavement or a major loss. Commonly, the bereaved are helped by their support system of family and friends, but not everybody is able to allow the mourning process to take its natural course towards an acceptance of the fact that their loss has really happened. Mourning can be a very painful experience and people who find this more difficult to bear than others may remain stuck in it for a long time, become seriously depressed, or even mentally ill. In other words, grief can be complicated, it can even become chronic, and then the natural process does not move easily through the dynamic stages of searching, anger, guilt, and depression on the way to gaining a new identity and restarting life without the lost person.

The most famous case of protracted mourning is, of course, Queen Victoria, who became a widow at forty-two when Prince

Albert suddenly died of typhoid fever. She was so grief-stricken by her untimely bereavement that she withdrew for ten years from all her public duties, first to the Isle of Wight, and then to Scotland. She only reappeared when her son Edward caught typhoid, from which he recovered miraculously, and this event shocked her out of her retirement. For the rest of her life she lived surrounded by images of her dead husband and always wore black, never smiling on any of her numerous photographs. Grieving thus became a lifelong habit with her, and this is not at all unusual. People have gone to extraordinary lengths to honour their dead—another example is the Taj Mahal in India, one of the most beautiful buildings in the world, which was built by a grieving husband as a memorial to his wife, making sure that she would never be forgotten.

It is another universal truth that grief initially feels very much like a derangement or a mental illness, as it usually comes with symptoms of severe psychic pain, of sleeplessness, depression, and endless obsessional reminiscing, all of which is an integral part of the elaborate mourning work, of remembering, repeating, and working through. These symptoms are interfering with the ordinary life processes and may take months to subside before the bereaved individual can begin to relate normally to others again, and enjoy their family, their work, and their social life. Everybody's experience of bereavement is different, of course, depending on their age, the quality of their relationship to the dead, on their religious beliefs, and on their particular personality, and serious complications are certain to arise when there was a high degree of psychic ambivalence, of unresolved hostility, and of unfinished business in the relationship with the dead. This takes much longer to work through, particularly when it is rooted in psychic disturbance predating the loss, and it will exacerbate, stall, or derail the natural mourning process. Then it can become a major hazard to mental health.

Contributory factors are the specifics of death: whether it was sudden, timely or untimely, self-inflicted, accidental, or violent, whether and when there have been previous losses and also what the surrounding or precipitating events were; in short, whether there was a disabling trauma and no possibility of preparing for dying and death. These are important determinants of grief reactions, leading someone who has been bereaved to adopt strategies of denial that may continue well beyond the fatal event, may sabotage the necessary reality testing and block the recalling and working through of memories. Freud spoke of this eloquently in his paper "Mourning and melancholia" (1917e), in which he contrasted the lengthy reality testing of normal mourning with the self-accusatory ruminations of melancholia, and implied that the former might lead to the latter in certain circumstances of identification with a bad object, when anger against this may be turned against the self.

Reality testing is another word for the incessant searching in the early phase of grief, when there are symptoms of psychic withdrawal, of physical restlessness, and of manic hyperactivity that prevent the bereaved from participating in the external world. What is typical or atypical grief is thus difficult to define, as there are transitions from one to the other and as many different individual reactions to bereavement as there are bereaved persons.

But there are certainly distinct degrees of complication in the mourning process which will seriously incapacitate its sufferers and impair their psychic functioning. At this point, a bereavement counsellor could come in usefully with an offer of supportive listening, encouraging the bereaved to talk about what seems to be holding up their recovery, and exploring the background to their complications in order to restart the natural process and remove the difficulties in its way. It may emerge that there was denial or avoidance of the loss, because the bereaved was unable to acknowledge the separation and hanging on to wishful thinking that it had not actually happened. The death may also have been sudden or unprepared for, so that the bereaved defended against it by going into the basic assumption behaviour of flight or fight, which happens in groups or families. It may be traumatic and overwhelming, and it can also be truly catastrophic—like an earthquake or a *tsunami*.

I recently encountered a young woman who had not been able to face up to her mother's death after a lengthy terminal illness and believed for months that she was still alive somewhere, even though she had attended the funeral and all the indications were that the mother was dead. This state of affairs became unbearable when her searching reached fever pitch, when she lost all sense of reality and plunged into a state of agitated depression that made her incapable of reasoning and completely unreachable. She had somehow lost her self. Someone finally persuaded her to get in touch with a bereavement counsellor, whose sensitive listening and shrewd understanding helped her let go of the delusion and false hopes and gradually facilitated the grief and mourning processes she had so stubbornly avoided. This was a turning point and mitigated her distress. She learnt to understand that she had been suffering from intense separation anxieties and had defended against these by denying the facts that were staring her in the face. One could also say that she had been insecurely attached to her mother and that she became emotionally liberated when she at last managed to accept her mother's death, which meant that she could start a perfectly viable new life, carrying on with the counsellor into a more general exploration of her life story and slowly constructing another identity. Her mother had been internalized, and she gradually built up an active life and turned to running support groups for other people. She had made the change from dependence to independence, had in fact gone from breakdown to breakthrough with the help of competent bereavement counselling that enabled her to finally accept the reality of her mother's death.

This case demonstrates how a brief counselling relationship can break the deadlock of denial and prevent the outbreak of mental illness as a consequence of unbearable loss. The daughter had become open to change after facing the reality of her loss and, in consequence of this, her vital functions and the natural processes of mourning had been kick-started.

Freud paired and contrasted mourning and melancholia as progressive stages of pathological grief. Describing the former as a natural process leading to the reinstatement of normal functioning after a painful period of repeatedly working through fond memories of the person that is lost, he analysed it as a process, in which the loss of part of the self is transformed by reinstating the dead into a new self-identity. In melancholia, by contrast, a similarly depressed and inward state of mind turns into endless self-accusations and guilt feelings that resemble a conflicted and ambivalent identification with another. Melancholia cannot become mourning as long as there is a narcissistic wound that cannot heal. The self seems irreparably damaged.

The act of grieving, Freud told us

> involves grave departures from the normal attitude to life. It remains peculiar among derangements. It never occurs to us to

regard it as a pathological condition and to refer it to medical treatment. We rely instead on its being overcome after a certain lapse of time. We view any interference with it as useless and even harmful. [1917e, p. 237]

Melanie Klein made a similar assessment in her "Mourning and its relation to manic-depressive states":

The mourner is in fact ill, but because this state of mind is common and seems natural to us, we do not call mourning an illness. More precisely I should say that in mourning the subject goes through a modified and transitory manic-depressive state and overcomes it. [1940]

When the time-limited bereavement counsellor identifies a depressed situation like this, it can be necessary to refer the bereaved to the GP, a psychiatrist, or, better, into long-term counselling, because more time is needed to work through the deep depression. Often there may turn out to be more complications than the recent loss, maybe previous losses or a psychiatric disturbance. Also, love has often been seen as a form of madness, by Shakespeare, by Freud, and by other writers, because it can plunge the lover into states of dissociation and delusion.

Let me describe another case of mine, of a married woman who was preoccupied by trying to conceive by IVF when her husband died of a brain tumour after a protracted period of illness, during which neither of them ever dared to mention the possibility of his dying. Afterwards, she was distraught with grief, accusing herself of failing him, going into denial, and becoming convinced that he would come back one day and reassure her that he was all right. After months of waiting in vain, during which she wore herself out by compulsively telling her story to whoever she came across, in desperation she sought therapeutic help. When I first met her she was clearly on the brink of madness and I had to contain her terror, gently helping her give up the delusional fantasy of her husband's return. After this there were months and months of going over the details of his terrible illness and death, of suing the doctors for negligence, of accusing herself of not being awake at the actual moment when he died, of choosing a particular gravestone for her garden, of complaining about not being understood by her mother, her father, her siblings, and her friends, and demanding more patience from me than I ever knew I possessed.

This endlessly protracted mourning process eventually turned into a free-ranging personal therapy that lasted for years, gradually revealing a severely conflicted relationship with her father, who had never given her the recognition she craved. Her hysteria and the incomplete mourning for her husband morphed into bottomless self-pity, and into a severe case of melancholy. By telling this clinical story, I want to emphasize how difficult it is to stop the mourning process from developing into chronic melancholia in someone I would now definitely call a borderline patient.

Thank God for bereavement counselling and time-limited work. If this is done well at the right moment it can achieve miracles. Clients can become actively involved in their grieving to stop the work from spiralling out of control, and thus can be helped to understand that their painful feelings are normal and a necessary part of letting go of the dead person. They can learn to think of their relentless reminiscing as a healthy working-through of their separation anxieties, and not to expect an instant release from their depressive moods before the mourning is truly finished. By pointing out to them that previous experiences of loss, particularly in childhood, will have made their mourning more complicated and take longer, they can be helped to mobilize the necessary patience. Helping them reactivate their natural supportive network of family and friends may be another task, as is generally putting their difficult experience into empathic words that will facilitate the telling of their story and may mitigate and help them bear the apparently endless pain. If they need more time for this than the bereavement counsellor can give them, they must be directed to another service or be referred to an experienced counsellor. However, it is necessary to bear in mind that this would be another bereavement, and requires careful processing and holding during the transition.

Once again I want to emphasize that bereavement is a natural process that will always involve long periods of time, the natural healer. None the less, it can also be the trigger that opens up unknown areas of existing pathology, as my last case has shown. This process may lead to repeated relapses into mournful states, particularly in the case of severe trauma, of suicide, of holocaust survivors, or of parents when there has been the death of a child. It can cause persistent depression, even suicide, and lead to resignation and meaninglessness, particularly in the aged. Each of these complications need competent professional help. The bereavement counsellor has to make a realistic assessment of every individual case and learn to curb the temptation of omnipotence. It takes extensive diagnostic experience to tell normal mourning from complicated grief states, and this is particularly so in cases of suicide, accident, or a murder crime, when there are no farewells and many unanswered questions remain as to the why and the what, which leave anger and guilt in the survivors. In traumatic and sudden death there is no chance to be prepared, there is no "good death" that can easily be shared with relatives and friends, and accepting that one will never know the motives and causes is another almost impossibly difficult dimension of the mourning work.

Suicide always carries a stigma, and the bereaved are shunned because people cannot possibly conceive of how they feel unless they have had similar experiences themselves. The same applies to murder, which provokes a reaction of disbelief, confusion, and vengefulness. The usual question is: how could this happen and why was it done? Counsellors without any knowledge of such serious bereavements will be unable to understand what the bereaved are going through, and may then be tempted to reassure them like relatives who expect that after the funeral the bereaved should be back to normal, when in fact they may feel even more lonely then. The painful stage of mourning often only starts properly after the first stage of shock and numbness is over. These types of untimely, unnatural, and shocking death are experienced like a psychic attack that cuts into the self, and they leave a wound that takes a long time healing.

Abortion is a type of loss that involves death of a different sort— intentional and self-inflicted, it is a step often taken for the best of motives, but immensely difficult to live down once it has happened, because its real implications often only become known long after the event. It can become severely disabling, because it is both unconsciously repressed and unconsciously active in the psyche, returning sporadically as a memory, as a guilty secret, as remorse and regret, often forgotten for years, and then suddenly popping up at anniversaries or by free association, when the person meets a child of the age the aborted child would have been. Counselling an atypical bereavement like this requires empathic skill and a non-judgemental attitude that can be difficult for women and mothers. There is an unborn child that is grieved as it can go on growing in the mind of the person, who could have been a mother, causing painful pining and guilt feelings. Similar feelings occur in connection with dead children, whose lives have come to an end before they had a chance to grow up, and who will be remembered forever as young and full of promise, particularly when they have been murdered or violated. Nothing can be worse than experiencing innocents suffering, when all words fail and the mind is unable to grasp the horror of it.

It has been said that the best bereavement counsellors are widows, as they have been through the process themselves and should therefore be able to empathize with the client's experience. But there is always a danger of confusing their own experience with the client's and of expecting their mourning to be paralleled by the client's. This is not accurate empathy, but identification, a distinction that has to be borne in mind in all counselling. Another danger is erosion of sympathy, as the counsellors' sensitivity can become blunted when they are exposed to too many variations of one theme. And when the client's complaints go on for a very long time, as they did for a full year in a case of mine of a client bereaved by her husband's unexpected suicide by hanging, it is very difficult to keep one's interest alive and to remain patient. In that respect, time-limited bereavement counselling seems more pragmatic than open-ended work, particularly when the counsellor has been taught how to do brief work effectively by focusing on the psychodynamics of the case.

Serious loss can be experienced as a bereavement similar to death. For instance, when one loses one's home as a refugee, by fire, or by accident, this takes months or years to get over and is experienced as very traumatic. An adapted form of bereavement counselling can be very helpful in such cases, but it requires a counsellor to be empathic to the particular circumstances of the loss, which may have many layers, as it can be accompanied by experiences of war or persecution.

Another major hazard is the fear of death—one's own fear as much as the client's. It is easy to advise acceptance when one has not been able to accept oneself that universal fear which waxes and wanes with the eventualities of life and with the approach of old age. I do not believe that anyone is ever without anxieties about dying, nor that daily exposure to stories of death and dying can inure one entirely to the natural fear of death. Even clergy find it difficult at times to get into the right spirit for conducting a funeral, particularly if it is that of a stranger. I believe that the bereavement counsellor, therefore, always needs supportive supervision in which this aspect of the work can be aired, and the counsellor's absolute honesty on that score will be essential.

I also believe that it is necessary to vary one's counselling work so that there is a balance between difficult cases and rewarding ones that provide sufficient gratification to feed one's healthy narcissism. That's why I would advise against concentrating on bereavement work alone—it can easily lead to burn-out.

There is another aspect to bereavement counselling, which relates to the counsellor's existential relationship with others and to the effect that other deaths will have on him or her. This is to do with what Martin Buber called the "I–thou relationship"; in other words, it relates to the ideas contained in a passage written by the Elizabethan writer John Donne in 1623, when he was suffering from a serious physical illness:

> No man is an island, entire of itself; every man is a piece of the continent, a part of the main; if a clod be washed away by the sea, Europe is the less, as well as if a promontory were, as well as if a manor of thy friend's or of thine own were: any man's death diminishes me, because I am involved in mankind, and therefore never send to know for whom the bell tolls; it tolls for thee. [1839, pp. 574–575]

This reality of the self being diminished by another's death is always active in the background when one counsels the bereaved, it is the heart and the life of the matter, the acknowledgment that every human being is both unique and irreplaceable to the whole of humanity and that there is thus a deep spiritual meaning in every death which highlights the fragility of human life.

CHAPTER SEVEN

The selection of candidates for training in psychotherapy and counselling

Introduction

This chapter deals with the selection of training candidates for counselling and psychotherapy, and establishes the criteria and requirements I look for in the selection interview, which in many respects resembles assessment interviews with patients. I look for the patient in the helper, using the concept of the wounded healer to make my choice. Drawing on Paula Heimann's classic paper "The evaluation of applicants for psycho-analytic training" (1989), the assumption is that "the therapist does not have to be an extra-ordinary personality", yet needs to have an ability for "learning from experience" and three indispensable requirements: empathy, intuition, and the capacity for thinking. The chapter is illustrated by vignettes of candidates who have chosen to train because they "feel summoned by an internal voice, a call from the super-ego which forms the basis of any vocation". The conclusion drawn is that the wish to help is rooted in an experience of suffering.

Selection criteria

What difference is there between the initial assessment of patients for psychotherapy and the selection interview of candidates for training in psychotherapy or counselling? In both situations a stranger presents reasons for wanting to start an activity, which involves learning and change of self. Learning, in the case of the patient, why there has arisen a need for assistance to explore incomprehensible anxieties that are disabling the patient's functioning and will not go away by themselves. Learning, in the case of the candidate, how to become a therapist helping troubled people overcome disabling emotional states of mind. Surely, the former are disturbed and lost, while the latter are guided by a desire to repair broken lives. There seems to be a qualitative difference between them, the difference between the helper and the helped, which is true on the surface, yet, when one looks beyond the roles to the unconscious motives and narcissistic wounds in both, one discovers a striking similarity in the desire to understand psychic processes, to explore internal conflict, and to heal wounds that are revealed in the narrative of a life story pieced together in both interviews to reveal its meaning and its traumas.

As an interviewer, I find myself looking for the helper in the patient and for the patient in the helper when I try to establish their suitability for the task they intend to take on. The patient will have to show evidence of a capacity to make use of the therapist and enter into a working alliance in which he or she will learn better self-management and self-reflection. The candidate will be examined for evidence of a self-reflective capacity and of a willingness and ability to put himself into someone else's shoes, both of which will be the result of life experience, suffering, loss, or mourning. It is a truism in the profession that the therapist cannot take the patient further than they have come themselves, and that the empathic understanding indispensable for therapeutic work depends on reflected experiences of having been where the patient is. The essential difference between them, which the interviewer will look for, is whether the patient has the genuine desire to understand and change, and the would-be therapist the capacity to acquire a professional identity, a "working ego" rooted in psychodynamic theory of how the human mind works, that can be the basis for constructing a working model of the patient.

I went back to Paula Heimann's classic paper (1989), which helped me rethink the criteria I apply when I interview and select candidates for training and to put the above questions to myself about their striking resemblance to the patients who present for psychotherapy. In other words, I am concerned with the ancient truth of the "wounded healer". Candidates often say that their motive for training as therapists is that they want to give others what they (or their mother) did not have when they needed it. It is the unconscious reparative drive that underlies the desire to help and to revisit with another an area of pain, of unfinished mourning, or of unresolved conflict that resonates with something familiar in oneself. This is one of the rewards of this difficult work, the explanation for the interest in other people's life stories. One constantly finds echoes of, and solutions for, parts of one's own narrative, and thus learns from the patient (Casement, 1985). The unconscious processes of identification and internalization that go on in the intermediary space of therapeutic dialogue promote the healing and integration that is the goal of therapy for the patient and of the therapist's ongoing individuation in the course of doing therapeutic work. Images of wounds and scars are natural symbols for the traumas inflicted by life and their recovery attempted through relationships and therapy. Therapeutic learning, at its best, is through mutuality: learning of the patient, learning from the patient, learning by the patient, remembering, repeating, and working through (Freud, 1914g).

When selecting candidates for training, there are important issues around safety and boundaries for the interviewer to look for in order to make sure that the would-be therapist has the capacity to hold and contain the patient and to manage the powerful fusional forces that arise in therapeutic relationships and can prevent thinking. She will use her countertransference to test the strength of projections and identify the candidates' defences, resistance, and anxiety, in order to check whether their wish to help is prompted by healthy desire rather than immature narcissism. The helper who derives and expects gratification and narcissistic supplies from the patients' idealizations may use them as self-objects rather than treat their transference projections as diagnostic evidence, which would need to be interpreted and handed back to the patient in manageable form. Abstinence is essential to the holding of secure

boundaries, and thus an ethical absolute for the professional counsellor, as is a self-critical handling of intuition (Heimann *ibid.*), to
stop it from overwhelming the integrity and common sense of the
dedicated practitioner. The wish to help and the passion to repair
damaged internal objects are essential ingredients in the counsellor's
motivation, yet they always need curbing in the interest of safe-
guarding the analytic space and relationship against a narcissistic
infringement of it.

How can the interviewer become sure that the candidate is a safe
bet? She will use her intuition and make links in the candidate's life
story, which contain the clues to unresolved conflict, developmental
blocks, and unattended breakdown likely to reappear in crisis situations later on in life. Identifying the transference situation obtaining
in the interview, she will be able to flag up potential dangers of
boundary-breaking in the dyadic situation of therapist with patient.
These attach to moments of identification and psychic overlap, to
the emotional storms in which the two partners merge and become
one to the extent that the counsellor loses the capacity to reflect,
which would create space for reverie and act as a protective skin
separating the two self identities.

> The dyad may even become locked in what Lacan (1988) refers to as
> the seesaw relationship in which it is quite difficult to sort out who
> is doing what to whom. A frequent rapid reversal of opposites may
> leave analyst and patient alike feeling that the other is driving them
> crazy. [Goldman, 2003, p. 487]

The conscious analytic attitude necessary for hearing and metabo-
lizing the patient's unconscious communications can become
eroded, and the consequence may be an infringement of the patient's
fragile self, a likely repetition of what happened in infancy.

Example

I have a client who had to take care of her mother after her parents'
separation and divorce, and also had to share with her the caring for
a handicapped brother. She later became a youth worker and found
work with children who were carers of parents. She had been fiercely
independent all her life, and had used anger and irritation to defend

herself when vulnerable, a behaviour that increasingly served her less well and affected her social functioning. She came into therapy with massive guilt about the decision to emigrate to Australia with her fiancé, which would enable her to leave her mother with the handicapped brother, and release her of the duty to care for them. So far she had avoided therapy and had acted out her need to be cared for by caring for others (who cared for their parents!). In the transference with me she turned into the distressed child she had ignored, and felt inconsolable and abandoned. It was an epiphany when she realized that she had used her job to seek out her irreparable childhood trauma in others, and was now trying to escape from it to Australia. Her work had been a manic reparation of others that kept repeating her trauma and prevented her from working it through. As a hobby, she was writing a children's book in which the heroine used magic to overcome her adversaries. This was a way of omnipotently defending against distress, another form of acting out and resolving her own dilemma in fantasy, like Harry Potter, who becomes powerful as a magician. The moment when the self-possessed client broke down and was transformed into a weeping heap of misery felt as if a window was opened and light let into a darkened room. It needed firm containment from session to session to let her fall to pieces for the space of fifty minutes and put herself together at the end of it to face the outside world and its demands on her ego.

The case illustrates how the helper can remain trapped in an unresolved infantile conflict with a demanding mother out of pride, which is a narcissistic defence against rage and guilt. It also demonstrates an ongoing repetition compulsion, until she can allow another, e.g. the therapist, near her pain and vulnerability and feel safe enough to drop her angry defences. Many of the candidates I have had to interview for selection have been in this situation, and are finally "summoned by an inner voice" (Heimann, 1989, p. 240) to help others in order to help themselves. Those who have had some therapy already have usually valued it, while others discover that they chose to get trained because this is a safe option and gives them the legitimate chance to go into training therapy. The training then becomes a therapeutic experience in itself, apart from offering the chance to do fulfilling work, and it helps them to realize that this is what "the wish to help" was partly about, i.e., a denied wish to be helped themselves. By the time they graduate as therapists they will have been able to put two and two together and to fully acknowledge their own wounds, which allows them to own the wounded healer in themselves, who will then be able to identify and treat the wounds in others, in full consciousness of why they have chosen this vocation, while respecting other persons' individuality. Or they are freed to do something else, like my client, who thinks she will no longer need her work with these children and now wants to become a writer of children's stories.

In the selection interview of the candidate, which structurally resembles an assessment interview with the patient in that it includes the patient's or candidate's history, their significant relationships, their goal and their motivation, and the reasons for presenting themselves for interrogation, the interviewer will have to link the wound and the wish, and to make conscious the unconscious mechanism connecting the helper with the helped, so that he or she becomes able to establish and maintain good contact with his or her childhood. Therapeutic activity for the candidate will then no longer be the acting out of unfinished business, but a meaningful use of the gratitude felt for the therapist who had helped and facilitated self-understanding and a job in which they can use themselves creatively.

The therapist's personality

What is important is that the training therapy will be thorough and can become a model for how the candidate will conduct himself or herself in the professional life with others, while the interview itself will endeavour to become a trial therapy, which tests the candidate's aptitude to tell a coherent life story, to reflect on it, and to maintain a working alliance with the interviewer, who will be holding the frame, to test out ego functions, identify the transference, the defences, and anxiety levels, and bring the meeting to an end that is satisfactory to both participants. Heimann's selection criteria included integrity, psychopathological aptitude, and "unusual sensitivity, personality and character" which boils down to reliability, dedication, and patience. To which I would add curiosity about what makes other people tick, self-discipline, to hold the frame, practise abstinence, and reflect on the process. When I was a greenhorn, I accommodated my first therapist's chronic unpunctuality as eccentricity rather than call it pathology, which was wise, as it did not interfere unduly with the ongoing process, though later on I questioned the wisdom of not challenging it, as it was an avoidance of conflict and anger, characteristic of my dealing with authority, while she failed to model the self-discipline necessary for the scrupulous attention essential to the demanding work of deciphering the patients' unconscious communications.

Heimann insisted that the therapist who "fulfils his function as his patient's working partner . . . does not need to be an extra-ordinary personality, and we need not attribute to his character more than the ordinary human decencies". In order to establish this, she quoted the remark of a colleague who said "no matter how sophisticated our concepts of ego pathology have become, what we really expect in a psychoanalytic candidate is that he should have a good heart and that he should have gone through some suffering without denying it" (Heimann, 1989, p. 249). And she concluded by emphasizing categorically "Indeed analysts have not become better persons than those who have not experienced analysis. What they have achieved as a result of undergoing the process of being analysed is that they have acquired a new dimension of their thinking" (*ibid.*). This is beautifully put, giving the lie to any form of self-satisfied idealization, while emphasizing that "Freud's discovery of the unconscious psychic world represents an event to which the status of an evolutionary step must be allocated".

I want to return to the statement of the "necessary suffering without denying it". It is conceivable that someone wants to become a counsellor because they are what Andrew Samuels has called "a natural counsellor", someone who is born with the capacity for communication, with an empathic perception of intrapsychic processes, a good ability for constructing narratives and the capacity to slip into the skin of others. In time to come, scientists may isolate a gene that predisposes its owner to practising the psychodynamic craft of counselling and the healing of other people's emotional wounds. They will need to have a highly developed imagination and an uncanny understanding of situations unknown and strange to them, which would also predispose them to becoming writers of fiction, who invent characters, or actors, who play characters other than themselves. Once again, it would be a question of which kind of narcissism would motivate their wish to be therapist or thespian, but the main point I want to make is in favour of reflected life experience. This has baffled literary critics when it comes to Shakespeare's writing and its wealth of human experience, way beyond what the native of Stratford-on-Avon could possibly have had. He was indeed an evolutionary step forward. But there is no doubt that the therapist has to have suffered, *without denying it*. And that he has to be able to make experience and suffering meaningful by conceptualizing and interpreting it. The capacity of finding the right word at the right moment, of surprising by articulating something well, is essential in a therapist.

Learning from experience

Bion's notion of learning from experience, i.e., by not denying but transforming it, is another way of saying it is necessary to live *consciously*, or to be helped to do so. The counsellor's metabolized life experience, be it of suffering, trauma, or loss, is the bedrock from which he or she will practise, and facilitate the patient's changing and growing. In a recent batch of candidates selected, there were two whose parents had divorced in their childhood, one, who had been brought up by what André Green has called a "dead" mother (1960), who was depressed due to the death by drowning of a son, another one whose father had killed himself in her childhood, and another whose father had died when she was six months old, so that she had never known him. In their training applications, all had mentioned these events as significant facts, and some of them had underplayed their emotional significance, probably in order not to be considered too disturbed for the training. But, when we focused on the deaths and divorces, they turned out to have been pivotal in their emotional development. In some cases, the relational capacities were severely affected—difficulties in partner choice or in constructing stable partnerships, in trusting others, or with intimacy in relationships. In the case of the suicidal father, whose motives for killing himself were obscure, the daughter turned to philosophy in order to understand the "workings of the human mind" and motivated her desire to train as a wish to "put the theory she had learnt to practical use". Interestingly, she had written a thesis on Jung's breakdown, and it was easy to see that this could have been a vicarious attempt at understanding her father's breakdown, and thus a creative intellectual defence against strong feelings about this traumatic childhood event.

A different case was the woman who had been raped in early adolescence and felt she had had her innocence stolen. She was abandoned by her unempathic mother and then had a breakdown later, when a secret sexual relationship ended in another abandonment as the man in question chose to marry someone else. The desire to train arose when she went into counselling for this, and the experience of feeling contained and understood made her want to learn to do it herself and for others. Having previously been a nurse and having left the profession because she did not like to do "management", this way of holding rather than controlling appealed to her unsatisfied need for being of help to others.

Many patients nurse a wish to train because of an identification with their therapist, which makes them both incestuously merge and compete with them. Envy and gratitude come together in the desire for, and the idealization of, the therapist, which leads to an oedipal challenge to become a professional rival. There are many such cases in the history of psychoanalysis, which has always tended to run in families. Incest, projective identification, oedipal conflict, and sibling rivalry lie behind the wish to do it. There are many different avenues into psychodynamic training, and most of them lead through effective training therapy. The doing it and the receiving of it are somehow inextricably intertwined and interchangeable.

The candidate's previous profession and work experience is another factor in the development of a professional identity, as attitudes and behaviour connected with this will inevitably influence the way he or she will approach their new work. The ex-teacher may retain didactic features, the doctor a bedside manner, the clergyman a pastoral flavour in language and gesture. The sooner this is made conscious, the better for the integration of the particular tendency into the personal therapeutic style.

The wounded healer

I want to return to the notion of the wounded healer (Samuels, Shorter, & Plant, 1986, p. 65) and to the problems associated with this paradoxical condition, which is for good as much as for bad (Guggenbuhl-Craig, 1971). When the Ancients said "physician heal yourself", they gave a warning to the helper that he was not to presume that he was omnipotent and that he needed humility when practising his art. Experienced psychotherapists do well to remember the limits of their power and effectiveness, and are constantly reminded of how often they fail and how much uncertainty they suffer in doing their work. In their excitement about the encounter with a brave new world, candidates presenting for training tend to forget how difficult it can feel to be confronted by unmanageable, unintelligible, and intractable conditions like anorexia, suicidal ideation, or borderline symptomatology, and the assessor is wise to point out to them the impossibility of helping others unless they help themselves. There is neither cure nor salvation; there is desire and striving. Of those who have suffered, and then experienced the consolations of empathic listening, of being with another in the depths of despair, many are inspired to take on the arduous task of being the listener and the sharer. "We must be mad to do this", colleagues often say, usually adding that they have chosen to go on, even though it can feel like drowning, or falling forever with the patient, waiting for something to happen, when words fail to contain the unnameable, catastrophic fears projected on to them by a desperate patient.

Most of the time the challenge of each session is to make contact with the patient and to make sense of what he or she brings. The quality of patience and the ability to tolerate frustration and disappointment are crucial in a candidate. Much of the time rewards can seem few and far between, but when something transformational happens, it feels that it was well worth waiting for, and then the desire for doing the work is strengthened by the hope that more of this will happen. Meanwhile, there is no shortage of people, particularly women, who have raised a family, who are struggling to equip themselves for psychotherapy training by doing voluntary work with special needs children, in hospices, in bereavement, alcohol and abortion advice centres, or even in vets' practices. They have to raise the steep training fees when they are taken on, and then they toil for years with training patients and training therapy until they qualify and can set up in private practice, which is another long struggle in itself to get referrals, consulting rooms, supervisors. Always, too, there will be the need for continuing professional development, for keeping one's theoretical knowledge up to date, for constructing a safe place where the work can be done. It is not for the money that we do it, but for the love of it, and out of the desire to help that cannot be described except as a passion—or a vocation. Paula Heimann said,

> Such need expresses the feeling of being summoned by an internal voice (the superego) and it forms the basis of any vocation. It is this concept of a profession as a call from the super ego that lent to the picture of the analyst a quality of idealization and even of mysticism. [1989 p. 240]

I used to have a colleague who described the moments of transformation as occasions when she felt privileged, as if she was walking on holy ground, and when she wanted to take her shoes off, because she felt overawed. In her book *Jacob's Ladder*, Josephine Klein (2003) writes about the "experiences of the ineffable" that happen in psychotherapy, and that make the therapist feel privileged, struggling with language like the mystics when the universe becomes transparent to some deeper reality. These experiences are the parameters between which the therapist works and which make the work so special and rewarding to its practitioners.

After I had done my last batch of assessment interviews, I sat down and reflected what I had learnt over the twenty years of meeting dozens of candidates, hardly any of whom could be dissuaded and of whom most of those I turned down had proved unstoppable, went to other training institutes, got taken on, and managed to enter the profession, which is now bursting at the seams. There are few jobs as fulfilling and appropriate for people interested in people, for women who suffer from the empty nest syndrome, from unsatisfied maternal and nurturing instincts, and from the burning desire to relate to interesting others. They are indefatigable object-seekers, story tellers, and communicators, who feel they have at last found themselves in this profession. This is barely a hundred years old, but it has produced a vast body of writing and theorizing that is endlessly fascinating and beckoning to be read and reread, particularly its psychoanalytic texts.

This brings me to my last point, to another quality I am looking for in candidates for training: a capacity for reflection, conceptualization, and thinking, which will enable them to read and draw on theory, to use it creatively in formulating diagnostic hypotheses, and to adjust these in the light of new material emerging during the therapeutic process. Together with empathy and intuition, thinking is the third indispensable factor in the therapeutic endeavour, which aims for psychic change and for the transformation of unconscious processes into conscious ones, into better ego functions and the self-management of emotional conflict. This could be Heimann's category of "scientific creativity", which enables the therapist to contribute innovative ideas to the existing literature, "securing the future of psychoanalysis" or, more generally, of psychotherapy and counselling. It is indispensable for the training to be a therapist, for the reading of theoretical papers, for the preparing of seminar presentations, the writing of qualifying clinical papers (Spurling, 1997), and the contributing to professional discussions and journals.

PART II
CLINICAL AND OTHER MATTERS

CHAPTER EIGHT

The stifled cry, or Truby King, the forgotten prophet

T his chapter presents some research into the activities and influence of the New Zealand psychiatrist Frederic Truby King (1858–1938), in relation to a clinical case where Truby King's baby-feeding methods played a crucial role as major pathogenic agent. Truby King is seen as the product of his time and of his biography. The pros and cons of his ideas are examined in contrast to D. W. Winnicott's thoughts about babies and mothers, which explicitly overturned his predecessor's influential dogmas.

One of my patients called himself a Truby King baby. This was his laconic way of blaming the particularity of his early feeding situation for a crippling emotional disorder he suffered from. He alerted me to the fact that there were other "Truby King babies" among my patients. This poses the question: what is a Truby King baby?

> Truby King babies are fed four-hourly from birth, with few exceptions, and they do not have any night feeds. A Truby King baby has as much fresh air and sunshine as possible and his right amount of sleep. His education begins from the very first week, good habits being established which remain all his life . . . After he has gone through his regular morning performance of bathing and being "held

out" and has had his breakfast, he sleeps all the morning. If he wakes
a little before his 2 p.m. meal all one knows about it is a suddenly
glimpsed chubby little leg and foot waved energetically from his cot
for exercise and inspection . . . Altogether he is one joy from morning
till night to himself and all the household . . . The mother of such a
baby is not overworked or worried, simply because she knows that
by following the laws of nature, combined with common sense, baby
will not do otherwise than thrive. [King, 1937, quoted in Paulsen
1967, p. 192]

The infant who is fed regularly, put to sleep and played with at definite times soon finds that appeals bring no response and so learns
that most useful of lessons, self-control, and the recognition of an
authority other than his own wishes. [King, 1918, p. 52]

Clearly, my patient and the writer of these lines hold different
views on the matter. The latter's rosy picture and dogmatic attitudes convey certainty and optimism about baby care and baby
needs. By contrast, the former used the label sarcastically, indicating that he was bitter about this style of child rearing and he blamed
it for his difficulties in later life. He suffered from a deep sense of
being unacceptable and unlovable, and was plagued by the constant
fear of being overwhelmed by strong feelings that acted like an ongoing depressive undercurrent, tugging away at him inside. He had
been brought up in the stiff-upper-lip ethos to deny all feelings and
to consider their public display as unmanly. Yet his experience was
that they would not go away and that they were an inseparable part
of his inner world, persistently bothering and overwhelming him
unawares. He was trapped and ashamed and felt emotionally
isolated, maintaining that his stern upbringing was responsible for
a stubborn independence, a childish pact with the devil, as he called
it, against the parental authority he had experienced as harsh, withholding, and non-accepting.

In therapy he would occasionally allow himself to experience the
hidden feelings he so feared, and they made him feel weak and limp,
uncomfortably at the mercy of an uncontrollable primitive force,
which rendered him speechless, as if choked by rage, and disconso-
late, as if abandoned and left to hopeless despair. After a while,
when he had recovered from the force of their impact, he invariably
chided himself for "being silly", as if in the voice of the parent or

teacher who had told him off for being a "wimp", and then he felt ashamed that he had been seen by me in this state, and he had to denigrate me as "merely a woman" in order to re-assert his adult masculinity—a cycle which repeated itself inexorably and unchangeably over the many years he was in therapy and which clearly constituted his particular repetition compulsion, his "core complex" (Glasser, 1992). In the helpless moment of the "stifled cry", as he came to call it, he seemed to re-enact his baby experience of being hungry and physically and emotionally abandoned, a state well beyond the angry protest that accompanies a baby's frustrated waiting for the breast in the expectant knowledge that it is still to come. His longing would never be stilled and would never leave him alone. Like Sisyphus in the Greek myth, he would endlessly and hopelessly carry his burden uphill, and nobody would ever come to relieve him of it.

The other picture of a Truby King baby is the reverse of what I have just described. It stems from an age and a class that believed in teaching babies self-control from the moment of birth (breaking their will, as some would put it), and that did not pay any attention to their feelings; the same age and class in which parents sent their children to boarding schools from the tender age of five in order to form their character and prepare them to be the leaders and rulers of their country. This school system freed the mothers for other tasks and forced the children to take responsibility for themselves while repressing their dependency needs. It taught them to despise feelings as signs of weakness, which led to their denial, splitting off, and projecting, and hence to rigid defences against alternating states of depression or persecutory anxieties. "Grin and bear it" was the motto of the stiff-upper-lip ethos. Punch, in Rudyard Kipling's *Baa Baa Black Sheep*, undergoes this process of traumatic separation and sadistic education, and the story describes how his "character" was formed, or rather deformed, as a result of constant disciplining, a poignant study of the origin of neurotic conflict (Kipling, 1888).

My patient had been subjected to this draconian kind of schooling too, which meant that the rigid regime of his first years at home had been continued and reinforced by an equally rigid system of primary education in "exile" from home. The sense of being banished for unimaginably long spells of time was pervasive throughout his childhood, embodied in painful memories of anguished farewells on railway station platforms, fighting back the tears little boys did not allow themselves to show in public and knowing full well that appeals for reprieve would not be heard, as the only people he could direct them to were telling him that it was "all for his best". He clammed up, told himself he could do without them, became sulky, withdrawn, and passively aggressive like Punch, forever nursing a narcissistic "grudge" (Symington, 1993).

In the therapy, the core complex was gradually identified as it was enacted, and then attempted to be worked through in the transference. In the presence of the primitive infantile feelings constellated by the client's early experience of abandonment, the task became first and foremost one of containment: murderous rage, profound despair, deep longing, alternating with and followed by shame and contempt, created a tense emotional climate in which empathic holding was of the essence. It felt as if suddenly a demon rose inside him or, clinically speaking, as if he regressed to the earliest moments of his life, and his facial and bodily expressions were like a baby's, arms gesticulating wildly, face crumpled piteously, eliciting a maternal urge in me to pick him up, which, when interpreted, was invariably rejected by a spluttering, angry baby response, just as the mother would have got when she came to feed him "too late". He tended to spit out my interpretations like bad food, and to rubbish my words as "dogmatic" or "feminist", indicating that he would never let a woman rule him or tell him anything about himself. Having to be with a female therapist was bad enough, though he had to admit that he would never allow these feelings out in the presence of a man (and indeed his previous male therapist had said to him "you need a mother"). With men he enjoyed being competitive, playing physical games, going to the pub, talking politics, and with them his stiff upper lip remained in place, making him feel separate and isolated in order not to be considered "wimpish" or like a woman.

The fifty-minute hour was a straitjacket that seemed to mirror the rigid feeding schedule. He always came on time; I could have set my watch by him and he always checked my clock, ticking me off when it was a minute or two fast. When he was late or cancelled, it was because his wife had asked him to do something for or with her. He came to therapy secretly, without telling his wife or anybody else. He talked about needing a "psychological whore", drawing a parallel to his secret visits to prostitutes when the tensions and frustrations of the schizoid condition became too much. He often compared the two settings: the man hands himself over to a woman and shows himself in need of her; he allows himself to be weak and to be cared for in a safe setting of anonymity and confidentiality.

Anything I said was stored and then reproduced in later sessions, chewed over and distorted, like food that is hard to swallow or is spat out with mother made to watch. The spitting could be venomous, with delusional overtones of persecution, and the words seemed to be used as paranoid triggers for blind hatred of the bad mother, the uncaring, cold, withholding female who dominates and dogmatizes the relationship, who remains unaffected by appeals for nurture, and who is unable to become attuned to his needs. He seemed to fight a tight corner, hoping for retaliation, for confirmation of his fears. He was a big man, and in the moment of delusion I was his bad mother. All I could do was to "hold the fort" and survive.

Earl Hopper's (1991) concept of "encapsulation as a defence against the fear of annihilation" seems to describe accurately the defensive structure that momentarily collapsed in these states of regression, revealing unbearable anxieties of annihilation and hopelessness that normally remained concealed and split off from his psychic life. Inevitably, these incidents happened just before the end of the session and had to be cruelly cut off, producing reproachful protest and momentary clinginess, followed by a meekly obedient rising from his chair, gathering himself together by wiping his eyes and blowing his nose. I was left feeling guilty for not making it last and realizing that the analytic frame was experienced as a poignant repetition of the four-hourly feeding stint. A longing for and a fear of fusion was enacted and understood. But there was no lasting satisfaction and no "corrective emotional experience" as the shame destroyed the goodness and by the time he came for his next session he was back behind his fortress wall. He could not internalize me as a good object, and was unable to restructure his petrified inner world. All he was able to do was use me as a lifeline, getting temporary relief from great unhappiness and isolation. It seemed too late for anything else.

Alerted by him to the Truby King method, I discovered that two other patients of mine had been raised in this manner and that their emotional problems could also be usefully traced back to this mechanical way of feeding babies that had enjoyed such a fashion between the wars and well into the 1950s. They, too, used schizoid mechanisms and described their mothers as narcissistic, smothering, and withholding simultaneously. With both of them narcissistic transferences were predominant, but there were substantial changes over the years and by termination big improvements in internal integration had occurred. Patient A was unable to do any work on herself between sessions as she switched off the process until the next instalment/feed; patient B had to be given once-monthly sessions because of her work commitments, which made her do most of the work in between sessions—two variations on the same time theme of avoiding intimacy? The former was compulsively "obedient" to the schedule, was always dead on time, never cancelled except a week ahead, and was initially tortured by an overwhelming need to be "special" and "good". The latter always used the hour to the full, and the weeks in between for creative working through, as if the monthly ration of food that she received could be made to last. Apparently, the Truby King feeding regime had been supplemented in various ways by enough good experiences for both of them to make reasonably satisfying marriages, though the former had to have secret extra-marital affairs to get her regular narcissistic supplies, while the latter had difficulties with sexual penetration that could not be overcome and she miscarried many babies, eventually choosing to adopt three Indian children from the same family (her father was Anglo-Indian, a well-kept family secret).

It seemed important to find out more about Truby King and the regime by which these clients had been raised. The name had suggested a woman, yet on consulting the *National Dictionary of Biography* I found an entry: "Sir Frederic Truby King (Kt. 1925), Director of Child Welfare, Dominion of New Zealand, 1858–1938". It proved very difficult, in fact impossible, to find any of the works listed. He was not in the British Library Catalogue, and the Royal College of Nursing had two titles in their catalogue but the books were missing. "Sorry, it's too long ago", said the librarian, after looking up the publication dates. Finally, I found a biography of Truby King by his daughter, Mary King, at the Wellcome Institute Library (King, 1948) and, through an advert in the *Spectator*, got hold of a well-thumbed copy of the *Mothercraft Manual* (Liddiard,

1938) containing his ideas on the "Feeding and care of babies" (the title of his most influential book (1923)).

The Jungian analyst Paulsen (1980) had found the same difficulties when she tried to trace Truby King's writings to understand patients who had been raised by this method, and she had had to settle for another book by Mary King (King, 1937) commenting wryly: "I could not get hold of one of his books at a public library, which may be a sign that he has gone out of fashion". Gone out of fashion, but not before he had left his mark on a whole generation and class in England between and after the wars. Now apparently repressed and forgotten, his books had vanished from the library shelves as if he had never been, or as if they were a shameful and guilty secret.

It was intriguing to discover that Truby King's dates were almost identical to those of Sigmund Freud (1856–1939), that he too had studied medicine, had visited Professor Charcot in Paris (1880), and was a passionate believer in the scientific method. But here the similarities end, because Truby King, though a psychiatrist, was not interested in neurology or in the workings of the human mind. He concentrated solely on the body and on preventative physical health care, whence he believed mankind's salvation would come. His motto was "*mens sana in corpore sano*", which had dominated the thinking of educators of the ruling classes since Dr Arnold of Rugby. His own fateful contribution to infant care was that he stressed the importance of the first year of life for laying the foundations for a human being's physical health, implying that mental health would automatically follow:

> If women in general were rendered more fit for maternity, if instrumental deliveries were obviated as far as possible, if infants were nourished by their mothers and if boys and girls were given a rational education, the main supply of population for our asylums, hospitals, benevolent institutions, goals and slums would be cut off at source . . . a great improvement would take place in the physical, mental and moral condition of the whole community. [King, 1918, p. 15]

This belief puts him squarely into the tradition of the great hygienists and nutritionists around the turn of the century: the

Virchows, Listers, and Pasteurs, who were conducting medical research on a scientific basis. Some of them he had encountered as a brilliant medical student in Edinburgh as they gathered for the university tercentenary celebrations in 1884, admonishing their captive audience "to follow the spirit of the experimental scientific method". He became inspired by their work and their beliefs.

But he also had his personal agenda for his career choice and for the lifelong obsession with the health of mother and baby. Bad health was a family theme. His father had emigrated to New Zealand at the age of nineteen on account of his delicate health; his mother was "not a strong woman" and had developed TB as a governess; his oldest sister died of TB aged eighteen; and he himself suffered from TB as a young man, which made him lose the sight of his left eye while a student in Edinburgh (remaining one-eyed in more than one sense of the word).

Most significantly, like so many of his contemporaries, he suffered from infantile diarrhoea. In his case this was contracted on board ship while sailing from New Plymouth to Nelson when mothers and children had to be evacuated owing to outbreaks of hostilities among the Maoris. The doctors then used purging and bleeding when treating diarrhoea, and the story goes that Truby King was prescribed once-hourly purging by a young doctor. His father stopped the treatment "in order to let him die peacefully". He survived, and was later to contribute decisively to the dramatic reduction in infant mortality due to gastro-enteritis.

Following an unconscious vocation, he decided, aged twenty-two, to give up banking, his father's profession in which he had already made great strides, in order to become a medical student and, although he trained and graduated as a surgeon, he was offered the post of Medical Superintendent at Seacliff Mental Hospital, New Zealand. There he stayed for thirty years, rigorously reforming treatment methods along hygienic lines, encouraging physical exercise and improving the diet, and there he also found his second true vocation as a "scientific farmer" (Mary King's words). Half a century later, the writer Janet Frame (1984) described in her autobiography the strict regime at Seacliff Hospital, where she was given ECT treatment.

One wonders what Truby King would have thought of this method of treating mental disorders. Truby King came to his mother-and-baby work by way of his hobby, the rearing of plants and animals in the hospital grounds. He observed his calves during an epidemic of "scouring", and realized that it was the bucket-feeding that undermined their resistance while suckled calves were immune to diarrhoea. This proved to be an important discovery, which made him experiment successfully with a new feeding formula to equate bucket milk (i.e., skimmed milk in which the butter fat had been replaced by cheaper fat for economy) with full-fat cow's milk. It was only a step from this to the observation of human feeding and to a comparison between the artificial feeding of calves and the bottle-feeding of babies that had become almost universal in the "civilized" world, having replaced breast-feeding for reasons of comfort and fashion. From there he made the link to the discovery that cow's milk was unsuitable to the newborn baby's nutritional needs as it did not contain the right mixture of ingredients, was often TB-infected, and did not give the immunity that mother's milk bestows on babies.

On a visit to Japan in 1904, Truby King was impressed by the universal custom of breast-feeding among mothers and became convinced (using the analogy of the bucket-fed calves) that the prejudice against breast-feeding in his country (and in Europe) needed to be reversed. After his return from Japan (with an adopted baby daughter as his marriage had remained childless), this idea became an obsession, a mission, and the subject of intensive scientific experiment. As a result he became firmly convinced that there were

> fundamental laws of nutrition, of growth and reproduction common to all living beings and that the fundamental law that obtains among mammals is that each according to its kind has specific qualitative and quantitative milk requirements in the suckling stage. [King, 1948, p. 155]

Truby King seems to have had superhuman energy. While running a large mental hospital, he still found time to go round the country lecturing about his discoveries and ideas and endeavouring to put them into practice, first on a nationwide, then on an international, scale. Together with the wife of Lord Plunket, the then Governor General of New Zealand, he founded a society for the promotion of the new "mothercraft" and the training of nurses and advice-givers to mothers, first in New Zealand, then in England and the USA. This led to the establishment of Mothercraft centres and to an untiring campaign against much initial resistance to realize his scientific programme and his vision. He put this into Darwinian language: "We have bolstered up the unfit instead of giving attention to the fit" (*ibid.*, p. 156). His mission led to appearances on the international scene as a child welfare expert, first in 1913 and then towards the end of the First World War, when public health had become an important international issue, owing to the realization, during medical examinations of soldiers, that out of every ten men only three were healthy, three were unfit and unhealthy, three were infirm, due to failure of development, and one was a chronic invalid. Infant mortality in England stood at 102 out of 1,000 babies, while in New Zealand it had been drastically reduced, due, apparently, to a decade of campaigning for breast-feeding by Truby King and his followers.

It must be said, in fairness, that he was not the only lonely figure on the international stage who advocated breast-feeding—there was a strong movement in France in favour of it, and in Germany and Austria doctors had been making use of feeding tables and of regular weighing of babies in order to monitor growth and physical development in relation to diet. Truby King took due notice of these, and the *Mothercraft Manual,* written by the nursing director of the Mothercraft Training Society in England, includes instructions for weight charts among "Elaborate explanations and instructions relating to artificial milk formulae broken down into constituent parts and quantities with the admonishment 'measure carefully—never guess'" (Liddiard, 1938).

All this took account of mothers who could not breast-feed their babies. Truby King (knighted in 1925 for his work as a "benefactor of mankind") established his own factory to produce the fat emulsion that he had developed resembling mother's milk, a product he sold all over the Empire in powder form. He eventually achieved what had been part of his mission—soon no small babies were given cow's milk any more (much of which was infected with TB), and those mothers not able or willing to breast-feed learnt to "make up" their bottled milk by using his formulae. The "nursery hygienist" had not toured the world in vain . . . Yet, strangely, all this seems to have been forgotten, and Mary King's leading question at the end of the biography of her adoptive father (1948, p. 302) will receive a different answer from what she hoped: "Fifty years hence, what will the rising generation of New Zealanders know of Truby King, one of the greatest humanitarians of all time?" Precious little, I gather, and that probably inaccurate.

What is remembered, however, by people who were brought up in an upper-middle class nursery, perhaps with a nanny or a nurse, is something he did not invent himself, but a Dr Thomas Bull fifty years before him, who wrote in 1850, "the great error in the young is overfeeding", and insisted:

> It may be easily prevented by the parent pursuing a systematic plan with regard to hours of feeding, three hourly in the first month, four hourly afterwards, with no night feeding . . . This is the only way to effectively prevent indigestion and bowel complaints and to secure to the child healthy nutrition and consequent strength of constitution. [King, 1918, pp. 20–21]

The erroneous ascription to Truby King of authorship of the four-hourly feeding schedule is one of the ironies of history, where benefactors tend to turn into villains with every new generation of historians and of ideologues. He must have approved of Dr Bull's ideas, otherwise the Mothercraft manuals would not have endorsed the feeding schedule, but to go down in history for somebody else's *idée fixe* instead of being credited with his own beliefs or achievements is unfair, if not uncommon, as much "knowledge" is shot through with prejudice and inaccuracy.

What it proves, however, is that the achievements of one age can look like disasters in the next, and that bright ideas often cast long shadows. In spite of his approval of Froebel's ideas on education ("to slowly bring out and develop in their due order and proportion all the latent powers and faculties of the pupil, physical, mental and more"), despite also his disapproval of the English examination system, which together with forceps deliveries and the use of the dummy was another of his favourite bugbears, Truby King was at heart a Victoria disciplinarian and an obsessional systematizer. Dr Bull's recommendation and the "overfeeding" argument appealed to his belief in "rational education" and his Mothercraft nurses turned this into an institution. He is now remembered for their strict feeding and babycare regime (which enabled them to manage their anxieties and their envy), which are rightly lumped together with the discredited paternalism of his age, which knew and cared nothing for children's feelings or their emotional development as long as they "behaved", and which laid down strict rules for mothers and women in general to conform to.

The emotional harm done by its enforcement took some time to be discovered by a later, psychologically-minded generation, who had become aware of the unconscious and instinctual processes of the infantile mind and were learning to pay attention to the interaction between mother and child. Meanwhile, Truby King's rational regime enabled many ignorant and anxious mothers to hand over the responsibility to the experts, using the argument my mother-in-law gave me when I asked her about her son's early life: "I handed him over to people who were trained and knew better than I how to look after him". Paulsen has an interesting quote from Mary King's *Mothercraft*, which came directly from the horse's mouth. Like Anna Freud, Mary King was a devoted advocate and faithful guardian of her father's system, and totally identified with him (Paulsen 1967, p. 192):

> Were the secretion of milk and the feeding of the baby functions of men and not of women, no man inside or outside the medical profession would nurse his baby more often than five times in the 24 hours if he knew that the child would do as well or better with only five feedings. Why should it be otherwise with women? Mothers have too much to do in any case, why should they throw away time and leisure by useless frequent nursings?

Paulsen comments that "this argument appealed to the rigid father concealed in the mother, herself over-influenced by an unrecognized slavery to her father's dogmatism". It also appealed to the nurse or nanny who was trained to follow "man-made" rules and routines, which took care of her primitive anxieties stirred up by the baby's crying. It also allowed them to control the mother, who was experienced as an envied rival and was treated like a child in defence of this envy.

The denial of feelings in the service of reason (called discipline) goes back a long way in the history of childhood (see de Mause, 1974), and Truby King's efforts at rationalizing childrearing are in some respects more enlightened than many others. These patriarchal attitudes were, however, decisively changed in the second part of our century by a number of men whose scientific observations derived from paediatric practice (Dr Winnicott and Dr Spock), or from their dissatisfaction with psychoanalytic theory concerning the first months of life (John Bowlby and Daniel Stern).

Truby King had a theory and a vision that is summed up in the statement: "Bring back to women faith in themselves" (King, 1918, p. 9). Working away for "mankind", however, the individual was being lost sight of. Like many a painter of madonnas, he idealized the nursing couple, probably out of an unconscious need of his own. Yet he was also the traditional father who was largely absent from the day-to-day business of the nursery, occupied with grand schemes and expecting high standards while neglecting practicalities and realities. He was remote from the tears and the tantrums, the playing and the cuddling, the anxieties and the difficulties, disregarding and ignorant of the natural and necessary ambivalence of baby and mother (Parker, 1995). He had intended his nurses to act as mothers' friendly advisers, in fact, they became mothers' tyrants, thumping the book of rules and chiding them for any anxious involvement. Man-made rules and scientific reason distrusted and overruled the maternal instincts ("measure—never guess"), while paternalistic attitudes forbade primary maternal preoccupation, recommending the nurse caretaker's "common sense" to rule the nursing couple. Characteristically, it was said of Truby King that people never contradicted him because he was usually right!

The work of Winnicott and Bowlby, the former inspired by discoveries he made in his consultations with mothers and babies, the latter by the studies of animal behaviour done by ethologists like Lorenz and Tinbergen, concentrated on closely *observing* the mother–child relationship that Truby King had dogmatically *prescribed*, focusing on the instinctual and unconscious processes within the couple and their development in health or illness. Winnicott (1964) seems to acknowledge Truby King's work and to refute him categorically at the same time. As he puts it in his inimitable way:

At any period of the world's history a natural mother leading a healthy life must easily have thought of infant feeding simply as a relationship between her baby and herself, but there was at the same time the mother whose baby died of diarrhoea and sickness; she did not know it was a germ that had killed her baby and so she must have felt convinced that her milk was bad. Infant diarrhoea and death made mothers lose confidence in themselves and made them look for authoritative advice. [Winnicott, 1964, p. 30]

It is only because of the great advances in knowledge of physical health and physical disease that we can now return to the main thing, which is the emotional situation, the feeling bond between mother and baby. It is this feeling bond that must be developing satisfactorily if feeding is to go well . . . if the relationship between mother and baby has started and is developing naturally then there is no need for feeding techniques and weighings and all sorts of investigations. The two together know just what is right better than any outsider can. [*ibid.*, p. 31]

The real trouble is that so great feelings of pleasure belong to the intimate bodily and spiritual bond that can exist between a mother and her baby that mothers easily fall a prey to the advice of people who seem to say that such feelings must not be indulged in. Fancy starting off feeding a baby by the clock before he has gained the feeling that there really is anything outside himself and his desires at all. [*ibid.*, p. 32]

The pendulum has swung to the other extreme, and nature is now defined as instinct and "primary maternal preoccupation" (Winnicott, 1958). Here is a man who is not rigid, authoritarian, envious, or omnipotent, and who assigns the back seat to experts like doctor and nurse, "who should be aiming at so managing the physical side that nothing can disturb the delicate mechanisms of the developing infant–mother relationship". The abstract rationalism has been replaced by clinical experience that led to the concept of the "ordinary devoted mother" and the "good enough mother", avoiding the defensive male idealization that was the shadow of Truby King's theorizing.

An important distinction was made between the clinical infant and the observed infant by Daniel Stern, who, like Winnicott, stresses the importance of the face-to-face contact for "emergent relatedness", and takes on Truby King by using his own methods, quoting from relevant observational studies:

Among mammals one can predict the frequency of feeding for any species from the ratio of fat, protein, and carbohydrates in the milk. On the basis of the composition of human milk, human newborns should be fed every twenty to thirty minutes, as was once the custom, rather than every three or four hours, as is present practice. [Stern 1985, p. 237, fn.]

Much evidence about the feeding patterns of existent primitive societies and historical evidence on patterns in pre-industrial societies suggest that throughout most history infants were fed very frequently, on the slightest demand—as often as twice an hour. Since most infants were carried about with the mother, against her body, she would sense the infant getting even slightly restless and would initiate short and frequent feedings, maybe just a few sips to keep the level of activation low. [*Ibid.*, p. 237]

The import of this perspective is that the drama of feeding today is in part the product of our system of creating a great deal of stimulation and activation in the form of hunger build-up, followed by a steep fall-off of activation. Satiation becomes a phenomenon of intensity and drama equal to that of hunger, but in the opposite direction. It may well be that constant experience with exaggerated peaks and valleys of motivational and affective intensity is an adaptive advantage for the infant who is to enter the faster, more stimulating modern world. [*Ibid.*]

Stern here emphasizes an aspect of "regular" feeding that may lead us back to my clinical material. Demand-feeding, as practised in primitive and pre-industrial societies and advocated by Dr Spock, may follow the baby's need for instant gratification and satiation as described by Winnicott, but it also aims at "keeping the level of activation low", while a more regular feeding schedule by "exaggerating affective intensity" may prepare the infant for "the faster modern world". He thus indicates that there are pros and cons to each method and that the recourse to "nature" (taken by Truby King and by Winnicott) is not "scientific" enough, leaving out the social and environmental changes rarely considered by clinicians.

My patients' upbringing fitted a template contingent on certain social circumstances: they were middle or upper-middle class; two of them had fathers absent because of war, one a mother traumatized by becoming a displaced person at the end of the war. These mothers may have used the four-hourly feeding regime for their own containment of depressive anxieties. The demand-feeding mother of other cultures may have followed a tried and tested traditional system that left the initiative to the baby, letting him find his own rhythm. But it may also have been used by the mother for protection from a baby's annoying needs and wishes for stimulation and activity and for containment of her anxieties. How the mothers' needs and circumstances affect their feeding choices!

CHAPTER NINE

Some thoughts on sibling rivalry and competitiveness

This chapter is a revised version of a paper presented at a conference on envy twenty-five years ago. I chose the theme of sibling rivalry because it has always been a burning personal issue for me and at the time surprisingly little had been written about it. I hoped it would be interesting for a change to think about an aspect of envy that is a universal experience and yet different from the primary envy that Melanie Klein located in the mother–baby relationship and the stage of object-relating. Rivalry and competition begin in the later developmental stage, when the infant has achieved unit status and when the two-person relationship has expanded into three- and multi-person relationships where the issues are loss, exclusion, and inclusion. Then the experience of difference and otherness has to be mastered so that socialization can take place.

Since that time, there have been many studies on sibling relationships (e.g., Coles, 2002; Mitchell, 2000), but I believe that what I wrote then is still worth putting forward, in particular the argument that relations with siblings are primary, as siblings are present as significant others in the infant stage, influencing the primary environment with their needs and demands for relating and sharing. In his book *The Plural Psyche*, Andrew Samuels (1989) argues that

> The fascination with the numinous image of mother and child has led to a tendency to regard subsequent relationships mainly or solely as redolent of mot–infant dynamics, implying that people tend to repeat patterns of relating and that the mother–infant relationship being the first has unusually great influence in this respect, characterising all other dyadic relationships. [p. 21]

But, he also says,

> Two-person relating depends, in a way, on three-person relating, for only when another person is experienced as being in relation with a third person does the individual have to face the fact that he or she is not that first person and does not own or control them. [p. 19]

Thus, the discovery that mother has a relationship with father, which thwarts fantasies of having him or her exclusively to oneself, is as momentous as the birth of another baby, which requires mother's undivided attention and shifts the dynamics in the family. The infant has to learn to adapt to triangular and multi-personal relationships, abdicate uniqueness and the sense of being special, bear frustration and ambivalence, and cope with disillusionment. The still precarious sense of self is severely threatened. Strong defences are called into play to deal with the new situation: omnipotence, denial, devaluation, and avoidance. The destructiveness that displacement engenders is turned inwards and can produce a profound sense of worthlessness and emptiness. To avoid the jealous feelings, there might be idealization or reaction formation. Altogether, this is a critical situation that takes much trial and error to work through and master. It is an important stepping-stone on the way towards mature personhood.

Infant observation and twin studies are two areas where sibling relations have been studied in *statu nascendi* rather than being inferred analytically from adult patients' reports. The observers have found them closely linked to the quality of mothering (and fathering) that is modified by the presence of more than one child. The rivalry that develops round the mother's or father's attention is mirrored in the rivalrous feelings that clients experience when first confronted with the knowledge that there are other clients who claim our time and attention, and their phantasies as to who is better or more favoured will relate to their original relationship with siblings. Thus, there are aspects of the transference and countertransference that relate to this.

But there is also a much wider field into which sibling relationships and rivalries of the nursery get translated where they are constantly re-enacted. In fact, whenever there is a peer situation with or without an authority link, competitive feelings relating to the childhood scenario of interpersonal relationships are likely to be evoked and thus the original scenario of the family of origin will unconsciously be activated. Our whole society is based on peer competition—school systems, industry, and the professions.

There are people who purposely have only one child, as they attribute hate, envy, and rivalry to the sibling situation rather than seeing it as a natural and necessary development on the way to socialization, or as something innate in the individual. This is, of course, naïve, as man cannot live by love alone, yet there is still considerable disagreement on the origins of our affective and emotional responses. Some writers, like Searles (1958), claim that

> lovingness is at its most pure in the newborn infant with an inevitable mixture of cruelty and destructiveness ensuing only later, being deposited on top of the basic bedrock of lovingness, as a result of hurtful and anxiety-arousing interpersonal experience. [p. 228–229]

Here is the notion of a paradisal state, the oceanic bliss of primary narcissism, which Searles shares with the early Freud. Yet, around the same time, primary envy was pronounced by Melanie Klein to be an elaboration of the notion of a primary state of hate and love. Winnicott, who left the Kleinian camp because he disagreed about this new departure in her thinking, speaks of the baby's ruthless love, and sees this early form of aggressiveness as movement, activity, and motility rather than possessing destructive or envious content. Envy can be seen to need a conscious awareness of object existence, of differentiation, and to arise out of the painful realization of separateness, thus indicating a regressive longing for fusion and incorporation. When this is thwarted, and thus proves impossible, envy becomes the destructive response to the knowledge of separateness and difference.

Initially, it is probably not the baby but the older sibling who feels rivalled, rivalrous, and murderous towards the displacing new arrival. Yet, with the passage of time, there comes a jealous reciprocity of aggression with the competition for food, toys, approval, and attention. Winnicott says that hate of sibling precedes love of sibling, with the mother performing the task of mediating the two until the nascent ego can take over in ambivalence. As the object of rivalry is similarly immature as the subject, however, the pitfalls of this situation are, of course, numerous, and therefore all adults have to live with the many scarred wounds of their nursery experience while trying to manage the competitive situation they find themselves in and moving from self-centred narcissistic rivalry to the creative and cooperative competition that characterizes the interpersonal relationships of the mature adult.

In health, the containing environment of the family and its members and the satisfactions derived from their company, from the shared playing and learning experiences gained through identification and emulation with them, keep the natural rivalry between siblings within bearable limits, so that hate and love are brought together and ambivalence can be managed. Yet most people retain some grudges, grievances, or guilt feelings towards their sibling as a result of unresolved envious conflicts in childhood, and these early rivalries simmer on into adulthood, when they tend to spill over into competitive peer situations where competencies are compared, activating anxieties of rejection and failure, and defensive mechanisms against these. Shyness and arrogance, ambition and self-denigration, and the constant need to win are evidence of some of these defensive attitudes and reaction formations, which range from primitive omnipotence, denial, and splitting to the more sophisticated competitive games that are part and parcel of the educational and professional goals cherished and promoted in out society.

What I am trying to say is complex and difficult. It revolves around the notion of healthy competition that is sibling rivalry in action, harnessing its aggressive and aspirational aspects in the service of work achievement, which emphasizes differences and rewards results. Erikson (1950) speaks of the ethos of prevailing technology and, thus, of sanctioned and regulated competition. This starts in childhood with competitive games in the nursery where there are winners and losers, and continues with school performance,

whether academic or athletic, moving into professional and voca-
tional life, where the goals are position, prestige, or money. It is also
present in the competition of mothers who compare their children's
developmental achievements, making late developers seem like
freaks or failures and the management of developmental tasks a
system of semi-public exams that allow little individual leeway in
terms of being rather than doing. The fathers who, consciously or
unconsciously, place expectations on their children that relate to
their own successes or failures in life and education, rather than
respecting the children's own individual endowments and wishes,
also add their share to the rivalry among siblings. There is no doubt
that the well-contained and integrated child with enough ego
strength, secure attachment, and a strong sense of self will attempt
competitive hurdles eagerly and competently, yet excessive parental
expectations make for anxious performance rather than creative
achievement and comparisons with better (or worse) siblings are
negative incentives that foster hate and envy.

As a basis for relating, working, and being, rivalry is not very
secure or ultimately satisfying, since fortunes can at any moment be
reversed and the fear of failure, disappointment, envy, and hostility
that always accompanies it is taxing. Unless tempered by job satisfaction, competitiveness is an empty shell, as is winning a game
against another child when there is no enjoyment in the playing of it
because the ambition to win is setting the players against each other
and spoiling the atmosphere of mutuality.

In the small child, where strong feelings of hate and envy are easily aroused in relation to siblings receiving favours or winning prizes,
the transition from rivalry and competition to mutuality and cooperation is a difficult, seemingly endless, and often hopeless struggle. I
would like to speak of brotherliness and sisterliness alongside mutuality which the *OED* defines as "interchange of acts of goodwill, intimacy", but I also found, under "mutualism, biological", "a condition
of symbiosis in which two associated organisms contribute mutually to the well-being of each other . . . philosophically: the doctrine
that individual and collective well-being is attainable only by
mutual dependence", stressing the interdependence among human
beings and the fact that we are "deeply social beings from the moment
of birth", as the eminent child observer Daniel Stern stresses in his
book *The Interpersonal World of the Infant* (1985): "in the sense of

being designed to engage in and find uniquely salient interactions with other humans".

We use mutuality alongside peers in a manner that indicates equality, though the *OED* lists the word "peer" as synonymous with rival as well as equal, companion, mate, and, of course, it also denotes "a member of one of the degrees of nobility in the UK". There is, thus, no absolute equality, and even peers have to live with difference, as do siblings, who cannot be equal though they have the same parents.

In interpersonal relations there is a multiplicity of negative and positive responses relating to difference, dependence, and interdependence, and the processes of negotiating these are complex. They resemble a piece of music in which the interplay of instruments and notes produces alternations of harmonies and dissonances. The achievement of mutuality and the transition from sibling and peer rivalry to this desired state are continuous processes in which more narcissistic, aggressive, or envious states alternate with the cooperative and loving interactions by which "two organisms contribute mutually to the well-being of each other". This is the state of biological symbiosis, not to be confused with the symbiosis described by Margaret Mahler (1975) as forming the early mother–child bond, before separation–individuation is achieved. Siblings live together, and their very separateness has to be constantly negotiated so that they can contribute to the well-being of each other rather than vie with each other, threaten each other, or, at worst, wish each other dead.

I would like at this point to tell Schopenhauer's story about the porcupines, as this illustrates humorously the peer situation of the good-enough kind offering a reasonable solution to the perennial problem of living together amicably. I am quoting from Freud (1921c):

> A company of porcupines crowded themselves together one cold winter's day so as to profit by one another's warmth and save themselves from being frozen to death. But soon they felt one another's quills, which induced them to separate again. And now, when the need for warmth brought them nearer together again, the second evil arose once more. So that they were driven backwards and forwards from one trouble to the other until they had discovered a mean distance at which they could most tolerably exist. [p. 65]

Here is the prickliness of hostility and the separateness of the human condition, but also the need and willingness to adapt spatially to others' needs that is the minimal requirement for the peaceful coexistence of mutuality and cooperation. Our natural need for each other and our natural hostility towards each other, Schopenhauer indicates, are not mutually exclusive, yet they have to be constantly negotiated. Self-interest and the territorial imperative are as active as is the "overriding human need for inclusion in the human group", of which Daniel Stern speaks. It would be interesting to examine sibling rivalry in the group as well, but as I am not a group therapist I shall confine myself to Bion's statement "that the individual cannot help being a member of a group even if his membership consists in behaving in such a way as to give reality to the idea that he does not belong to a group at all" (1961, p. 90).

Myths and fairytales abound in stories of envy and sibling rivalry, centred around the mother (when the culture is matriarchal) and the father (when the culture is patriarchal). The most obvious one is, of course, the story of Cain and Abel, where murder is the compulsive response of the first-born child to the successor and displacer who wins the father's favour. The mother, Eve, who greeted her first-born ecstatically with the words "I have gotten a man from the Lord" (Genesis, 4.1) is not further mentioned, but we know that she was a temptress and probably quite narcissistic. When Cain finds his offering neglected and is told that he would have been accepted if he had done well, i.e., had done the same as his brother, he feels rejected by the parent, killing his brother in order to kill the envy and the hate. He is punished by being cast out from the face of the earth, marked forever by the stern judgement of the talion law. His offspring, by implication, are our ancestors.

The developmental stage is, of course, the pre-depressive position. The story of Joseph and his brothers takes a different turn, as it involves love as well as hate, and the concern of the envied gives the enviers a chance to learn and let go of it. It is a story of favouritism and of the need to acknowledge difference. Father Jacob loved Joseph more because he was the son of his favourite wife and of his old age. He demonstrates this by the gift of the coat of many colours: "And when his brothers saw that their father loved him more than all his brothers they hated him and could not speak peaceably with him" (Genesis, 37.4). Naïvely, Joseph shows pride at being favoured and asks for trouble when he tells them his dream, in which their sheaves of wheat stand around his sheaf making obeisance to it. After this, of course, they are even more envious and they plot to murder him. He survives because of one brother's concern, is sold into slavery, and continues to prosper abroad, while the envious brothers are punished by lack of achievement in life, eventually having to serve him as in his dream. The reality principle triumphs and the depressive position is reached when Joseph reveals himself to his supplicating brothers in Egypt after some cruel testing-out and gives them corn, weeping at the reunion with Benjamin, whom he loves more than the others as they are the sons of a different mother.

But what about that other Old Testament story of sibling rivalry that tells of the reversal of fortunes by cunning: the story of Jacob and Esau? Jacob solved his sibling feelings by resolutely getting his own needs satisfied and by confusing the traditional principle of primogeniture. It must be noted that he is favoured by his mother Rebecca, who clearly conspires with him against his twin Esau and father Isaac. In her womb the twins had struggled for priority and Esau had forced his way out first, with Jacob holding on to his heels. The prophecy of the two nations in Rebecca's womb and of the elder serving the younger is set in motion by Rebecca when she encourages Jacob to cheat the blind Isaac, making him bless him instead of Esau. This reverses the birth order and shows that what really matters is mother's love. Jacob is clearly more creative and lovable than Esau. Yet he has to struggle, in the fight with the angel and while he serves seven years for Rachel, as if in reparation for his offence towards father and brother, making up his quarrel with Esau much later. When it comes to his own children, however, he shows an unconscious bias against first-borns. And thus the sins of the fathers are visited upon their children!

What do these stories tell us about the many forms sibling rivalry can take, about the management of envious feelings towards other siblings and about the parents' role in the struggle of their children at the beginning of their lives to come to terms with each other's differences, with their feelings of hostility towards each other, and with the need to bear frustration and curb destructiveness? They certainly confirm the primitive force and the archaic universality of these feelings, while relating them in origin to parent figures who themselves are or have been plagued by them, so are inclined and perceived to be partial.

Thus, the role of the parent, particularly the mother, can be seen as vital in the handling of the powerfully destructive feelings characterizing sibling rivalry and envy. And so are the unitedness and consistency of the parents. Splitting the parents, as the Jacob and Esau story tells us, is a way to triumph and to achieve satisfaction at the expense of the sibling.

Yet one would suspect that the separation from mother cannot have been easy for Jacob. This is, of course, one aspect of the Oedipal situation that leads to developmental failure and difficulties in relating to peers emotionally and sexually, manipulation remaining a neurotic way of functioning that prevents the maturing into more cooperative, reparative, and intimate relationship patterns. There is also the familiar pattern set up by the narcissistic mother and/or father who favour the more interesting or compliant child with a view to getting needs of their own fulfilled against the child, or children, they find less congenial, useful, or simply too difficult to manage.

They may cast their children into roles; for instance, splitting them into good or bad when there are two. This creates a situation where envy is rife, has to be denied, and cannot be managed, because the parent's confusing self-centred behaviour does not help with the overcoming of it. Children, as Jung has observed, are driven unconsciously in the direction that is intended to compensate for everything that was unfulfilled in the lives of their parents. We know from our work that the good child has quite a task in life to keep the performance going, often suffering bouts of inexplicable depression or unaccountable temper tantrums when the split-off badness breaks through, while the bad sibling has a hard time struggling with feelings of envy, inadequacy, and hostility, and often remains unseparated from mother, moving from badness to madness.

There is another type of narcissistic parenting that tries to deal with sibling rivalry by forestalling it: the scrupulously fair parent who assures the quarrelling siblings that they will always be treated exactly the same, get equal amounts of food, presents, hugs, punishment, etc., on the assumption that this eliminates envy, that bad feelings can be treated as unreasonable, and that justice can always be done. Mothers adopt this stance when they cannot live with difference and need to curb their own feelings of inadequacy. It gives them rules and a disciplinary framework in which to deal with a situation that is experienced as chaotic. This, too, encourages denial of envy and leads to sneaky and secretive behaviour instead of open hostility and jealousy.

This is demonstrated in the case of a client whose marriage was on the rocks due to his constant premature ejaculation. His mother had operated the tit-for-tat system of ostensible fairness with him and his somewhat older sister, thus lining them up against each other in a competitive situation where winning became a constant goal. Conversely, if this was not possible, the goal became not to allow the other to win, if necessary by sabotage. For my client the problem became envy of his wife's orgasm, as she demanded orgasm as her fair share of the deal. If he finished before her, her anger was devastating. Yet they could not make it together; she wanted to win. With denigration on her part, sabotage and withdrawal on his, it was a stalemate situation, resolved only after he developed an insight into this no-win pattern of perpetual castration, which resulted in an outburst of rage, a retaliatory acting-out in the form of a short-lived affair, and a return to base, like the prodigal son, now ready to work out a relationship of mutuality and cooperation in which grievances were worked on openly. Needless to say, his wife also went into therapy, though this was not merely in a spirit of tit for tat. As they had also had a Relate counsellor it took three therapists to move them into a more mature way of marital interaction.

The recalcitrant patterns of sibling rivalry are not easily changed in therapy.

Here is an example of transference interaction, when the envious controlling could be examined in action: John was late by ten minutes due to no fault of his own. As the patient after him had cancelled and he had much to say, I offered him some extra time at the end to make up for what he had lost. He accepted gladly and we carried on after the hour. Ten minutes later he stood up and left. He had slotted my gift into his system of fairness and when I pointed this out to him, it seemed only natural.

It would be interesting to pursue this application of fairness to child-rearing in terms of the litigious aspects of the psyche and the sense of justice, but that is a subject for another time.

For Freud and the Freudians, sibling rivalry implies castration anxiety and penis envy. The gender issue and traditional preference of boys over girls are certainly rich sources of envious feelings among siblings, yet penis envy has, of course, its equivalent in the male envy of women's ability to give birth and to nurture. The rivalry among brothers and sisters is further complicated by the parents' envy of the children of the same sex that complicates the intricate field in which the developing individual tries to shift into a position where he or she can play creatively, can identify and compete constructively, and eventually mature and individuate. Cross-identifications are, of course, rife in families with mixed-sex siblings, and it would be most interesting to examine the development of feminism in this light, as a resolution of sibling rivalry in which the envious feelings of the girl in the face of her brother's preferential treatment by mother leads to identification and competition with him or with father, rather than with the sisters or mother. We know about Mrs Thatcher's father, but what do we know about her mother?

The *locus classicus* of sibling rivalry is, of course, the story of Cinderella. It is a rich source of omnipotent and narcissistic fantasies produced defensively by the hurt and displaced child in order to survive the unhappy situation of having to share with siblings in the family. Bettelheim's discussion of Cinderella in *The Uses of Enchantment* (1975) contains some profound insights into the painful situation of the child who considers herself abandoned and degraded in relation to siblings preferred by the mother, and therefore seen as stepsisters. He says:

> As long as the child is little, his parents protect him against the ambivalences of his siblings and the demands of the world. In retrospect this seems to have been a paradisal time. Then, suddenly, these older siblings seem to take advantage of the now less-protected child, they make demands, they and the mother become critical of what the child does. [p. 237ff]

He refers to the beginning of separation anxiety, the now consciously experienced awareness of exclusion and hostility that is fantasized as all-out persecution and defended against by omnipotent fantasy, alternating with experiences of helplessness. Devaluation of mother and siblings is performed by splitting the good mother, who is dead or lost, and the bad stepmother and step-siblings, who are experienced as persecuting and envious. Forced to do the dirty work and living in the ashes (of depression and worth-lessness), Cinderella suffers and endures until the prince discovers her beauty and carries her off. A magical solution to the split of love and hate is found. It is also implied that without parental mediation and management there is no possibility of healing the split.

Patient A, reminds me of Cinderella when she tells me of her childhood relationship with her mother and brother, in which she felt abused and rejected. It has the melodramatic flavour of the fairytale. She was told that she was an enchanting baby and changed out of all recognition when her brother was born. She was also told that her mother brought her up by the Truby King method of four-hourly feed-ing, though she found her crying in between feeding almost unbear-able. She remembers being horrible to her brother because he became mother's favourite, and once when he sat on the windowsill behind a drawn curtain he "disappeared", and it was never clear whether he fell or was pushed by her. Father was a busy doctor and it was diffi-cult to get his attention when he was at home, because he always hid behind his paper and talked to mother while Ann waited for him to come up and say goodnight. He died when she was eleven and she found that she could not grieve, struggling with confused feelings of anger, loss, and guilt As her mother was devastated by grief for a long time and had to support herself and the two children, Ann had to be a good girl and look after her, while the brother was sent off to board-ing school, where he apparently enjoyed himself. Ann became prema-turely independent, developing a competent false self, and became very competitive. Her mother always criticized her and made her feel bad like Cinderella, worthless, rejected, and punished for having wished father dead while her brother, who later took up the father's profession, was held up as a shining example of goodness and appar-ently could do no wrong in his mother's eyes.

Ann's story taught me the intricate connection of sibling rivalry with inadequate parenting. In health, the way leads from the good enough mother to the resolution of oedipal rivalry and of the worst excesses of sibling rivalry, to the maturity of relationships in which difference can be tolerated and experienced as an enrichment rather than a threat, can be valued instead of being envied and destroyed. Never having been lovingly contained, Ann was struggling to solve these conflicts, and in the transference alternated between competing with me as sibling, putting me down as therapist, and confronting me with challenges in which I found myself in competition with colleagues. Originally, she had chosen her mother's trade, becoming the better and more sophisticated practitioner of the two; then she had outdone the brother by marrying a rich business man and producing two daughters; eventually she worked as a counsellor in an agency.

The therapy revolved constantly around competitive issues that were used as resistance and to avoid intimacy. It was also around notions of being a good client, if not my best, around comparisons of therapeutic styles and abilities, around entanglements with peers, and fantasies of almighty analysts, all of which were used to make me feel useless and envious. While she was thus attacking me and trying to involve me in games of professional exposure, I sometimes felt in the presence of an implacable evil force, and overwhelming feelings of hate in the countertransference were hard to manage. I was definitely the bad stepmother.

I remembered what Francis Bacon had said about envy in one of his essays: "He that cannot mend his own case, will do what he can to impair another's". At the same time I became intensely aware of the reader, quite fearful in anticipation of his or her critical sibling reaction. Ann sometimes made me fear my supervisor when I presented her clinical material incoherently, as it was so difficult to convey the coldness that pervaded the transference and the shameful entanglements I found myself drawn into. All of this reflected the intricacies of the case and played directly into the patient's ingenious competitive and narcissistic manoeuvres of staying in control.

In Bible story and fairytale the extent to which sibling rivalry unleashed murderous hate is spelt out plainly for the primitive developmental stage at which it originates. In life, as defences and superego prohibitions build up in the course of growing up, it usually expresses itself more cunningly and subtly, being channelled into ambition, power, and control. Yet, while hatred and envy remain at its roots, producing bad and guilty feelings of worthlessness and fantasies of omnipotent destructiveness, everything turns to ashes.

For A., the prince, her husband, had not brought happiness ever after, as her envy of his potency, both as breadwinner and possessor of a penis, made her withhold herself. During intercourse she clammed up and became angry—no penetration was possible. In the transference this scenario was repeated, with the envy experienced as hate in the transference. I was told that a similar version of this was played out between her and her former therapist. He had asked her to bring her dreams and then amplified them skilfully with the help of his knowledge of mythological literature. She felt abused and cheated, felt he was not interested in her, only in her dreams, using these to feel potent and powerful. In the end she terminated with him unilaterally. The anal origin of this was plain to see, and the hurt child reaction could be spelt out as: "I don't need you. I won't play with you. I'll keep it all to myself". It was also a case of negative satisfaction: "I can do as well as you if not better. But it really is not worth having".Thus, sibling rivalry in the transference was complemented by sibling rivalry in the countertransference. The first therapist played an important role in our work together.

In any competitive game involving two players, such as tennis, it is more satisfactory for the learner to play someone who is better and it may also be satisfactory for the latter to play a teacher. By analogy, siblings can emulate each other through identification and then learning takes place by introjection. Envy and hatred, by contrast, block introjection and learning, as there is projection and evacuation. Favouritism and the establishment of a pecking order inhibit the former process and encourage the latter. The larger the family, the more difficult is the parents' management task quantitatively, yet qualitatively the outcome depends ultimately on the parents' own experience of parenting, and on the quality of their internal parents. If they need their children to make up for their own deprivations and shortcomings and to fulfil narcissistic needs of love or hate, the prognosis is bad.

Our own sibling rivalry with each other—counsellors, psychotherapists, analysts—should be acknowledged here. The struggle is sharpened by our constant dealings with our patients' rivalrous envious and competitive feelings, all of which produce a veritable greenhouse effect. At the agency where I worked as a supervisor and tutor, this could be observed every year during the time of assessment, when the place became a hotbed of competitive and paranoid anxieties, and even murder was mentioned by a trainee whose paper I had once to fail.

As in any business, it is a matter of personal survival, of professional identity, and of self-esteem. We always compete against each other, alternating with sharing and belonging to each other. In assessment, this is about the parent body's approval and recognition; in professional practice it is around patients, money, jobs, popularity, publications. As men compare cars, salaries, positions, sexual conquests, and women compare looks, clothes, or children, we therapists compare prestigious trainings and prominent therapists, and as we cannot measure therapeutic success, we have to measure job satisfaction, fees, and referrals taken up or turned down.

As there is always identification with our own therapists, there must also be a degree of sibling rivalry and hostility towards them. If this is acknowledged rather than deflected by projection on to colleagues of other schools, there is positive emulation and gratitude. Kenneth Lambert's (1981) concept of the therapist who is motivated to a large extent by gratitude towards his or her analyst is, for me, a realistic ideal for the profession. For this to be realized, however, the therapeutic experience has to have been good enough, rich and real, resulting in a satisfactory ending with enough good experiences to internalize the therapist as a good object. If the ending has been premature or abrupt, because of death or other external forces, the sense of loss may hinder internalization and there may remain an envious grievance, not gratitude. If the experience has been bad, I do not need to spell out what happens.

To sum up my thoughts, I shall restate my position. Whether envy is seen as innate, or a development out of primitive ruthless aggressiveness in the course of early object relating and object use, it is an aspect of our continuing and developing narcissism and, thus, a fact of life. It becomes pathological only if denied, but needs constant monitoring and management, at first by good enough parents, then by the maturing individual himself or herself; and the conscious awareness of its recurrence in situations of rivalry and competition is essential for the development of good enough relationships with others and with oneself.

Culturally and morally, this position has been difficult to maintain, since envy carries a heavy stigma of sinfulness and its denial has been encouraged by religion and conventional morality and by traditional methods of childrearing. To admit to the deadly sin in an atmosphere of disapproval is difficult, and in the consulting-room it easily assumes an air of pathology; for instance, when Melanie Klein talks of "excessive" envy, does this not smack of a value judgment? I treasure a remark my therapist made to my supervisor in reply to his saying that he envied her. She frankly and emphatically said "Good". We like to be envied when we have achieved something or done something well, but this has to be admitted. Then there can be admiration, identification, and, ultimately, creativity. Joseph wept when he met his brothers again in Egypt. Starving in Canaan during the seven year drought, they came to ask for food. He must have felt good enough in himself, probably due to job satisfaction, to forgive them their past hostility and to feel pleasure at seeing them again. Blood, as they say, is thicker than water. But the tears indicate that there was something more, something, I think, of pity and compassion, of *agape*, as Lambert (1981) calls it in relation to the therapist. He forgives them because they did not know what they were doing, in their narcissistic primitive way denying and destroying the goodness they were craving for themselves.

In therapeutic terms, denial is the real sin, not the impulse of envy, which is natural and recurrent and part of our aggressive and assertive humanity. It cannot be analysed away forever, because it is forever waiting in the wings ready to spring. What matters is what happens to it, whether it is acknowledged as potentially negative and destructive and transformed creatively into learning and acceptance of difference. Good management, to use a fashionable word, is of the essence for the survival of wildlife, the growth of business, the living with difference and with our strong contrary feelings of good, better, and best. It is difficult to endure the devastating feelings of badness and the loss of self-esteem that accompany envy when it rears its ugly head or, more accurately, sprouts, Hydra-like, one ugly head after another. Once acknowledged as being closely linked with admiration and the love of good things it becomes more manageable, and the narcissistic urge to destroy their possession by another can be curbed.

Paula Heimann (1975) made the distinction between naïve narcissism, object-hostile narcissism, and creative narcissism. She stated that these three "can develop through life into a mature form that does not interfere with mature object relations, making for positive enjoyment in encountering another self with different qualities felt as enriching, complementary and congenial to one's self". This can also be said with reference to the resolution of envy in oedipal rivalry, including rivalry with siblings. I want to end with words by Freya Stark, that explorer extraordinaire of strange and different worlds: "Not the thing itself, but the sense of others and contrary things makes reality" (1991).

CHAPTER TEN

The absent father and his return: echoes of war

In Homer's *Odysseus*, the eponymous hero returns from the Trojan War after ten years' absence to find his wife besieged by suitors and his son Telemachos desperately trying to protect her. Together they defeat the intruders, and Odysseus establishes his claim to his palace, to his wife, and to his place in the family and in the community. This story sums up the legendary image of the hero as man and father, of the woman as faithful and patient consort, and of the son as modelled on the father whose image was kept alive for him by his loving mother. Over the centuries this story has assumed an exemplary moral force, and it has been a template for masculinity in male patriarchal society.

There is, however, another Greek story that is its shadow and is told as tragedy: the return of King Agamemnon from the same war and his murder by his wife Clytemnaestra, who had taken a lover in his long absence and was revenging herself for his sacrifice of their daughter Iphigenia and for his abandonment of the family. Elektra and Orestes, their two surviving children, are driven mad by the horror and by their divided loyalties, which require the son to kill his mother. The hero as protector of the family and the hero as its destroyer—these are the two faces of war, the heroic arena of men from time immemorial.

Freud based his developmental theory about the role of the father in the sexual development of male children on another Greek myth, the tragedy of Oedipus, which led him to his hypotheses about infantile castration fears and incest wishes. I would like to speculate on the basis of some clinical material how psychoanalysis might also have used the stories of Odysseus and Agamemnon to supplement and enrich the theorizing of oedipal conflict. I want to do this, in particular, with a view to the two great European wars of the last century from which so many fathers returned after years of absence to their wives and children, like Odysseus and Agamemnon, while millions of others were killed, leaving their families fatherless. This is a historical fact and a psychic reality that has affected generations of Europeans, many of whom were brought up on the Greek stories of heroes and tragedies. How are we taking notice of this in our clinical work?

Over the years I have been involved with a group of patients whose stories show severe disruption in their infancy due to the absence of their fathers in the war, which left them in full possession of their mothers well beyond the oedipal age and then exposed them to a shocking experience of being bereft when the fathers suddenly returned. Unlike Odysseus, these fathers seemed to take little loving notice of their sons (and daughters) and made them feel unable to fulfil impossible paternal expectations or to form good relationships with their father as well as with their mother as Telemachos had been able to do.

These fathers settled back into civilian life with difficulty and behaved like tyrants in a domestic set-up that required them to adjust and shed their warlike behaviour. In some cases, as in Agamemnon's, the wives punished them for their abandonment, or took them back with bad grace, unable to mediate between father and child, which led to severely dysfunctional family situations in which violence and splitting were rife. In others, the child had been used by the mother for comfort and support in the absence of her husband, and this had led to premature ego development in the child, characterized by false-self structures and splitting-off.

My hypothesis of developmental damage, due to this situation, is based on two sets of trauma and maladaptation: the child's traumatization, on the one hand, when the dyadic relationship with the mother is suddenly disrupted by the appearance of a stranger father who claims her for himself and banishes the child from his symbiotic paradise, making him feel excluded and confused. On the other hand, there is the father's war trauma, and consequent brutalization, which renders him, temporarily or lastingly, incapable of civilized behaviour towards women and children, baffled in his object relating and slow or incapable to reconnect and readapt to a life of domestic decision-making and civility. The mother, in her turn, having fended for herself under conditions of uncertainty, fear, and deprivation, is forced to readjust to an intimate relationship with a man who may have become a stranger and is demanding his conjugal rights, requiring her to shift back into a shared scenario that has become unfamiliar and in which he reassumes a dominant role without negotiating a transition. The child's difficult readjustment complements this oedipal situation, sometimes beyond repair and without possibility of its resolution—which has severe implications for his future life, his sexuality, and his relationships.

Let me give three examples, all focusing on a particular moment in childhood when the father returned from the war, which may have been a screen memory of a real event or a retrospective reconstruction. The first of these stories was told by a woman patient, born in 1941, who shared her mother's bed and bath for years until one day there was a strange man in the house who told her that he was her father and her mother's husband and that he would be in bed with mother tonight. Early next morning, feeling abandoned and confused, she got dressed, filled her basket with toys and food and left the house, intending never to return. She was, of course, apprehended and brought back. But from then on she daydreamed that she was leaving home in a horse-drawn cart that took her to another world where she had heroic adventures. Her relationship with her father was one of bullying and fear and only after the parents' divorce did they form a sort of truce, while her relations with her mother remained complicated by feelings of anger, guilt, and dependence.

My second story concerns a gay man, also born in 1941, who had his mother to himself until his unknown father returned from the war, and who remained inseparable from his mother until she died of heart failure when he was a teenager. Apparently unacceptable to his father, who constantly taunted and humiliated him and showed no interest in his gifts for story-telling and play-acting, with which he entertained his mother, he withdrew into a world of fiction and the theatre, grew up to become an actor and lived in a series of gay relationships, always plagued by periodic urges to pick up men for one-night stands in public toilets, until this ceased with the help of therapy and he managed to establish a long-term relationship.

The third patient is a gay priest of similar age who also remembers his father's return from the war as a first encounter early one morning, when he came into his mother's room to get into bed with her and was pounced on by a stranger from behind the door, apparently as a joke. He hated this father, who was cold and sternly demanded obedience, prayer, and godliness, for whom he could never do anything right, whom he despised as a grown-up and whose death many years later he described as the happiest event in his life, nothing but pure relief. He sought therapy in his mid-fifties because he had become haunted by fears and nightmares that one particular affair he had had with a young boy twenty-five years ago might, in the new climate of paedophile exposure, cause him harm in his successful public career of a visionary project manager in various inner-city charities.

An absent father returned from the war and then experienced as a childhood tyrant was the connecting link between these diverse clinical narratives, whose individual complexities demonstrate an array of rigid defensive structures employed as a protection against sadistic attacks. Exerting a detrimental influence in the child's object relations and sexual development, this father can be constructed as a castrating parent, following Freud, or as a non-facilitative parent, following developmental and object-relations theory. He became a persecutory internal object for the child in a process of projecting out his own traumatic war experience, of primitive anxieties, castration fears, and helplessness. In each case the mother's behaviour was similar in that during the father's absence her anxieties and needs had been projected on to the child—inappropriate closeness, demands for protection, and selective neglect. Individual constitutional factors explain the difference in defences and outcome, while the trauma of father's return seems to have had a similar significance in all cases.

The emotional conflicts presented by the demanding child were experienced as frustration, affront, and disobedience. Authoritarian attitudes became confused with authoritative assertiveness, which could have modified the oedipal child's rivalry into necessary identification, admiration, and emulation of the bigger male. Mother's anxious and aggressive mediation may have been experienced as an unhelpful weakening of what was conceived as the male's disciplinary task, and as an interference and alliance with the child that inflamed rather than encouraged reasonableness. In consequence, her ongoing role as the child's "protective shield" and auxiliary ego was diminished, and the father–child relationship led to a situation of "cumulative trauma" (Khan, 1963) in the oedipal three-person constellation. For the boy, this meant problems of gender identification, for the girl, a conflict between compliance and defiance, and in both cases there was a splitting of "father hunger" and "father hatred". The separation from mother became complicated and frustrated, an impossible developmental task.

I am aware of a danger of generalized hypothesizing from a social reality which was inevitably complicated by the psychic reality that may have predated the parents' war experience and the child's dyadic experience with mother in the absence or father. Traumatic life experiences are particularly merciless for those who are already troubled. In the clinical examples I have focused on the representation of a particular childhood scenario—absence and return of the father—for an inference of specific pathological elements in these patients' psychosexual development and their object relating. These showed interesting common features for the male as well as for the female patients, with some striking gender differences. Not surprisingly, they developed schizoid character structures and in my sample there was a marked tendency for withdrawal into pathological retreat (Steiner, 1995) and day-dreaming.

I have already mentioned the woman whose nocturnal heroic fantasies enabled her to survive the traumatic loss of her mother's undivided attention. She developed these further into identifications with orphaned children, persecuted gypsies, and separated identical twins, while living a seemingly intact middle-class life. In her marriage she was emotionally and physically unable to have children of her own, but with her husband's agreement she adopted three children, which satisfied her identificatory orphan fantasies as well as the strong maternal urge that had been sabotaged by unconscious fantasies of starving her own babies.

The actor felt emotionally most himself when acting, because, in character, he could abandon himself to strong feelings otherwise unavailable to him, and he was at his most sensitive when he was able to direct a play, omnipotently peopling a stage with actors and conjuring up a make-believe world in which he had absolute mastery over the set, the story, the characters, and the dialogue (like Shakespeare's Prospero in *The Tempest*). Taunted by his father as a child for his lack of masculine interest in football and other sports, he had developed a talent for entertaining his mother (and later his therapist) by transforming everyday events into vivid stories. He later realized that this was a manoeuvre to seduce her away from the hated and humiliating father and to triumph over him imaginatively, while in his intimate relationships he conducted an unending search for the ideal father, acting out his split-off rage and hatred in periodic bouts of "cottaging".

In the third clinical case, creativity once again was the survival strategy that enabled the patient to endure years of paternal humiliation and retain omnipotent control in the most adverse psychological environment. Unable to satisfy the father's impossible demands for perfect behaviour, and all his life extremely gauche in his social behaviour, he survived by the lonely child's retreat into make-believe, and developed a grandiose narcissistic sense of self by becoming the creator of an entire world with towns and villages imagined in vivid details in his parents' garden, conducting a solitary obsessive game of town-planning, of constructing an "obedient" environment in which he felt potent and in control. There are uncanny parallels to this infantile creativity in his adult professional life, in which he started out as an organist, progressed to priesthood, charismatic preaching, and imaginative inner-city project-planning for the "underclass", which enabled him to see himself as powerful and to channel his anger, while his ongoing (but no longer acted out) paedophiliac urges indicate a split-off identification with the aggressor, with the sadistic rejecting father, and a perverted urge for reparation in the sense of revisiting his own and unloved child (Khan, 1963).

He showed no remorse, only fear of being found out, and uses child porn videos for "self-regulation". Following a heart operation, he started to cry, and he has discovered that he always tried to impress his father by becoming powerful himself, while attempting to do without close relationships and dependency on others. This is not the place to enter into the paedophile's perverse sexuality, but I would like to flag up its possible aetiology being due in part to a sado-masochistic father–child relationship.

The fact that all three of my patients found creative solutions of a sort to their pathological problems may account for their capacity to use psychodynamic psychotherapy for understanding themselves. If they had not, they might have been much more severely incapacitated by mental illness. This says something about the possibility of sublimating the development of creative potential in the most adverse circumstances, but their ability to become creative in therapy might also indicate that their good enough mothers offered them a facilitating environment and a potential creative space that was internalized and not destroyed when the father returned. In the transference this enabled them to access their maturational processes, to achieve some integration and also to become increasingly more creative in their work, while their problems of relating to others were more difficult to change. Interestingly, none of them had children of their own. And I found their sexual problems and patterns impossible to shift, with the women frigid or afraid of penetration and the men insecure in their masculinity, incapable of object constancy, and opting for same-sex or under-age partners.

Heroes and cowards

In Shakespeare's *Henry V* there is a passage where the king addresses his troops before the battle and exhorts them to be valiant in their duty to him, promising them remembrance and fame if they "steel their hearts". Returning home, the hero will then be able to share his experience of the battle on St Crispin's Day:

> Then shall our names
> Familiar in his mouth as household names
> Be in their flowing cups freshly remember'd
> This story shall the good man teach his son,
> And Crispin Crispian shall ne'er go by
> From this day to the ending of the world,
> But we shall be remember'd

We few, we happy few, we band of brothers,
For he today that sheds his blood with me
Shall be my brother, be he ne'er so vile
This day shall gentle his condition.
And gentlemen in England now a-bed
Shall think themselves accurs'd they were not here,
And hold their manhoods cheap whiles any speaks
That fought with us upon St Crispin's day (Act IV, scene iii: 51–67)

This is the heroic vision of war and of man's honour and duty to fight for his ego ideal that also reverberates in the story of Odysseus and Telemachos. It speaks of the taming of retaliatory murderousness and primitive violence when there is comradeship and meaningful purpose. Shakespeare's king endorses the Roman motto *Dulce et decorum est pro patria mori*, while he is eloquent in grief and pity when confronted with his dead nobles. In Wilfred Owen's poem of that title, by contrast, the heroic motto has lost its meaning in the face of the horrors of trench warfare.

Thus, the vision of the heroic soldier breaks down when the realities of war are overwhelmingly ego-destructive, as demonstrated by American studies of Vietnam veterans. These show that the trauma of combat exposure occurs, in particular, "when violent death can no longer be rationalized in terms of some higher value or communal meaning", and they demonstrate that in the Vietnam war "lasting psychological damage" was incurred due to "demoralization, participation in atrocities, loss of faith and connection" (Herman, 1992). In modern warfare the hero is exposed to prolonged periods of meaningless combat; and the condition of "shell shock", so lovingly demonstrated in Pat Barker's *Regeneration* trilogy (1991), could be said to be a condition of "cumulative trauma" that had eroded the "protective shield" of these higher meanings (Khan, 1963).

Rereading Bion's autobiographical *The Long Week-End* (1982) in combination with Barker and Sebastian Faulks's *Birdsong* (1994) is instructive, as it describes the author's memories of his First World War frontline experiences in a tank regiment as an officer, aged eighteen. Particularly poignant are the passages that relate to his being awarded the DSO and the Légion d'honneur, in the earning of which he felt there was nothing heroic, rather a sense of unreality and "animal mindlessness", as he had learnt how to avoid pain by economizing thought . . . a state which was not nightmare, not waking, not sleep. It was an animal existence, in which the eyes held sway. One did not think; one did not look; one stared. [p. 205]

For the rest of his life Bion's memory retained this trauma, the fear and terror of the moments in the trenches under bombardment. And he described in particular the frozen, out-of-body experiences that are also reported by victims of rape and child sexual abuse. Later, as a therapist, he revisited empathically such traumatic scenes with his borderline and psychotic patients, and his war experience must have enabled him to understand and to conceptualize their inability to think, and their attacks on linking.

As an autobiographical writer in old age, Bion seems to have had total recall, as if the terrible past was again in the present. There are no heroes in this hell, only casualties or survivors. He writes sardonically about the absurdity of training for tank battle, for instance: "as I discovered later, map-reading remained useful to meet the requirements of the fiction that we were going somewhere". And he remembers a sarcastic ditty (Bion 1982, p. 204):

> Heart ache, belly ache, shell shock, death,
> Head wound, leg off, blinded, death,
> Rich man, beggar-man, thief . . . OK?

In his memories, the whole gamut of emotional experience is graphically described, most convincingly in "going mad":

I got up and quickly crawled out of the hut. I felt it would drive me mad if I stayed there another minute. It is peculiar that so many people felt they will go mad—in another minute! If the baby won't stop yelling, the dog barking, the telephone ringing—and now if the damned guns won't stop banging. No good telling them I would go mad if they didn't stop. I felt I couldn't stay there another minute! [*ibid.*, p. 209]

The memory of trauma, like wounds that leave a scar, remains encapsulated in the psyche until some emotional trigger reveals its ongoing painful embeddedness in the depths of the mind.

There is a fine line between heroism and sadism, and the hero can be a ruthless killer. Like Odysseus, who teaches his son to be heroic like himself in the battle with the suitors, and demonstrates martial skill, calm strategic thinking, and fearlessness, so Shakespeare's Henry V, when he exhorts his men, while the Pistol sub-plot shows the other side of the coin: braggadocio, sadism, and cowardice.

Diana Birkett (1992), in her analysis of war, quotes Freud's perplexity about why "collective individuals should despise, hate and detest each other" (Freud, 1915b). She offers a Kleinian explanation of "the individual's readiness to go to war", in Glover's (1946) words: "springing from the repressed sadism and masochism". The paranoid splitting into enemies and comrades, which makes war into a "cure for madness", becomes the basis for heroism—or for cowardice—depending on the ability to channel rage into the "lust to annihilate" which Eli Sagan (1979) identified as the underlying principle of heroism in ancient Greek culture. Bosnia, Somalia, Rwanda, Kosovo—*plus ça change, plus c'est la même chose.* The rules of war seem quite different from the rules of peace in that what is encouraged in one is banned in the other. Yet the psychology of projection and introjection operates in both, as does the instinct of competition and of grandiosity, while the rules of the game are much more finely tuned in peacetime.

I have come across the "modern hero" most poignantly in the clinical material of a woman patient whose father had been decorated for bravery as a naval officer in the Second World War, and who had a persistent longing to be back in the situation where he had proved himself a man. He never let his family forget this. As his oldest daughter, my patient remembered vividly being dropped as a child by her mother the moment her father claimed mother's attention and being constantly told by her that "your father comes first". She became combative, defiant, and hostile to him, and their relationship was an interminable series of violent confrontations, exacerbated by the fact that she started her periods early and culminating in scenes when he followed her into the bathroom, which she now interprets as sexual harassment. To this day she is terrified of being alone with him and, inevitably, her relationships with men have suffered, fraught with hysterical outbursts on her part when she feels slighted or opposed, the former due to mother's neglect and the latter to father's tyranny. All her life she wanted her mother to leave her father. "I cannot understand what she sees in him", she said, which indicated an inability to let go of mother and to accept and relate to the man who took mother away by claiming his superior conjugal right and who never attempted to relate to her appropriately in her own right—particularly in her early teens, when he was experienced as predatory. His hero status was used to dominate, not to influence or invite identification, and it left her no room for manoeuvre because she feared its potential erotic base.

In legend and in history, the hero is the defender of women, but he also claims the right to rape and enslave the enemy's women. My patient's father demanded total submission, as demonstrated in the story she often tells from her early teens when he asked her to cut her long, painted fingernails and, when she refused, bound her, made mother hold her hands, and brutally cut her nails himself. It is a memory as of being raped, and it shows the hero as thug, getting his own by force. My patient never learnt to tame or to suffer him as her mother and sister did in different ways, and this has prevented her from developing non-confrontational relationship skills. She is aggressively demanding, identified with the paternal aggressor, and castrating of her partners, including myself as her therapist, and she feels little concern or compassion for her now ailing father, as he could not feel concern for her as a child.

The unconscious connection of sex and violence in the hero's libidinal make-up during his warlike arousal gets played out in the oedipal struggles of the domestic situation. The myth of Agamemnon culminates in the unbearable oedipal dilemma for Elektra and Orestes, as their father has been cuckolded and killed by their mother. Revenge is the only means to avenge humiliation. The paranoid–schizoid position reigns supreme, until the Gods of Greek legend, or therapeutic intervention in today's family constellations, open up the embattled scenario to a more hopeful, redemptive pattern of concern and forgiveness. My patient is as implacable as her father, unforgiving and hence unable to make peace with him. She wants to stop her destructive pattern, but finds herself rising impulsively to the slightest offence. Like father, like daughter. The female therapist feels helpless in the face of such fury.

The couple or the family as battlefield is a metaphor that has more than a ring of truth in such cases. War is the past that finds echoes in the present, the transmission of a father's unconscious memories of triumphant victories to the helpless child who becomes the contemptible enemy. Or the echoes may be of his defeats. The consequences of his failed fatherhood are ineradicable, as her defence is an unconscious identification with him as the aggressor. The meaning of paternity has become perverted into a pattern of ongoing warfare.

To complete the picture, I want to mention another common war scenario. Many of Homer's heroes remain on the battlefield, and their children, like Hector's boy, are orphaned, forced to live with an image of father that becomes idealized and remains eternally young. In my childhood, our dining room walls were dominated by two life-size sepia photographs of young soldiers—two of my mother's brothers, who were killed in the trenches of the First World War. Their constant presence during our meals was felt, but rarely mentioned. It was an integral part of my childhood and of my personal existence in the world into which I had been born. One of my brothers was considered a replica of the older uncle who had been my mother's soulmate. The other brothers were each given the name of one of the dead. What a disturbing legacy to grow up with.

The period between the two wars was dominated by the memory of millions of young men who were killed on the battlefields of Flanders and France, and the family portraits and war memorials allowed no one to forget them. My personal experience dates me, as I belong to an older generation than the patients I have been talking about. They were born during the Second World War, which claimed even more casualties worldwide than the First World War. For some of them the absent father became a dead father, and there was no return. One patient's father was killed at the end of the war, which led to her and her younger brother being sent to an orphanage while their mother tried to get her life together again. She lived with an image of him as an angel "gone to heaven", while her stepfather assumed truly Luciferian dimensions—a splitting that ran like a fissure through her whole life and produced a complex system of schizoid defences for survival, great difficulties in relating to men sexually, and much angry acting out in the family. Married to a man who was impotent, she decided in her forties to have a child by IVF, using an unknown donor, which meant that her daughter would never know who her father was and she now has severe difficulties as a pubescent girl, just like her fatherless mother in her puberty. The real event of her father's death became a central clinical fact and was unconsciously carried over into the next generation as planned fatherlessness. Fortunately, the daughter had a reasonably good relationship with her stepfather and knew the facts about her planned one-parenthood, but how would she cope with her fantasies of who her real biological father was? Similar patterns can be found with adopted children.

To be born in order to fulfil a woman's wish for a child by an unknown father is an emotional complication that the invention of IVF has made physically possible. It is another version of the "absent father", but it is also a destiny that could be a life-long burden rather than the intended life-giving blessing for the chosen child. However, whichever way the father is lost, an object called father is always internalized.

Summary

To conclude, I consider that the war experiences of our parents and grandparents must have had a significant influence on the emotional development of those generations who could only relate to the wars in their imagination. The stories and the silences of the parent generations are alive in their children and grandchildren, in the intangible ways in which projection and introjection travel transgenerationally and, as the Bible says, "the sins of the fathers are visited upon their children", until there is a possibility of redemption and regeneration.

The trauma of the past, the echoes of war—how do we become aware of these in our work with individuals who suffered as children the consequences of their parents' war experience, and how do we conceptualize the damaging effects of the parents' emotional wounds inflicted on the second or third generations? Much work has been done with Holocaust victims and the second generation, and the studies of Vietnam veterans (Lifton, 1973) became the first systematic research into the psychological after-effects of combat exposure (Herman, 1992). But it took seventy years and a work of fiction (Barker, 1991) to remind us of the beginnings of therapeutic treatment for shell shock in the First World War and fifty years to commemorate and confront the full reality of the Second World War, especially in Germany, where rebuilding a devastated country became the manic defence against mourning (Mitscherlich &

Mitscherlich, 1975). Steven Spielberg's film *Saving Private Ryan* was made by one too young to have been there himself, but it was a realistic re-enactment of the horrors of war for the next generation to see, be shocked by, and immersed in—minus the feelings of the perpetrators and the victims, however.

Pat Barker's description of Dr River's original therapeutic efforts and findings in *Regeneration* demonstrated the havoc wreaked on soldiers exposed for lengthy periods to frontline fighting. But for Rivers there was an ethical dilemma: the purpose was to rehabilitate and return them to combat (where most of them consequently died, like Wilfred Owen). Most of my patients' fathers returned home, where their shell-shocked behaviour was inflicted on wives and children, as they tried to get rid of nightmares by acting out and making their next of kin experience them.

Once I had become aware of these transgenerational patterns of the post-war generation, I encountered them everywhere. I took into account that it was something in my own story that made me focus on this particular dimension in my patients' clinical material, but that did not seem to make it less legitimate. I became interested in their parents' stories and mental functioning and found the characteristic symptoms of traumatization in the fathers' behaviour, which led to rocky marriages, domestic violence, and family breakdown, causing the children to fend for themselves in dysfunctional ways.

None of the patients I have mentioned enjoyed truly creative, loving relationships with their fathers that would have enabled them to cross the oedipal threshold and to perform their age-appropriate developmental tasks, acquiring good ego-functioning and secure selfhood. In therapy the task is arduous, as the healing of wounds and splits requires lengthy working through of unbearable anxieties, disidentification, and major restructuring of defences. As mentioned earlier, I found the sexual problems and patterns most difficult to shift, encountering frigidity and fear of penetration in women and in men insecurity about their masculinity, inability to achieve object constancy, and a tendency to choose same-sex or under-age partners. I was tempted to hypothesize that the far-reaching changes in sexual roles and gender images of the past sixty years may have had their origins in the social upheavals caused by the war as much as in the post war developments in feminism, education, and society as a whole.

My rough sketch of intergenerational warfare is, of course, a somewhat simplified version of psychoanalytic trauma theory, which ascribes arrested development to real events in childhood as much as to fantasized internal causes. These complex psychic structures require much remembering, repeating, and working through in therapy to produce effective change in the personal narrative of patients. There are, of course, countless other war scenarios that I could have focused on, such as the large-scale evacuation of children, the bombings of civilians, deportations, and other war-related catastrophes, all of which could be traced in individual case stories as pathogenic material that is transmitted to the next generation. The recent resurgence of trauma in therapeutic theory may also have been a consequence of research in these areas (Garland, 1998).

On the other hand, there are many men and women who maintain that they had "a good war", and who emerged from it, like Odysseus, strengthened, mature, and well equipped for the civilian tasks of government, management, and parenting. They came back from the war with the knowledge that they were able to overcome hardship; they had got to know themselves as firm in difficult situations, and could rely on themselves as strong and able to build on these strengths. They and their children are rarely met in the psychotherapist's consulting room, as they possessed the ego strength to recover and to adapt to the changes and different challenges in their civilian environment.

CHAPTER ELEVEN

Fatherhood today: variations on a theme

After one hundred years of psychoanalysis it seems reasonable to re-examine Freud's version of the father's role in the light of some fundamental changes in family structures and parenting practices which have occurred since he formulated his psychosexual theories. Patriarchy was then still largely uncontested, and the father as master, provider and law-maker ruled supreme, demanding obedience and expecting submission to his authority. The bearded faces in yesterday's family photographs inspired respect and fear, bestowing rights and duties on their wearers that were considered unshakable. The image of God the Father was their prototype and his supreme authority was universally acknowledged.

How far the world has moved in the meantime, and how different is our social reality today, when many fathers do not live with or even know their children, are divorced from their children's mothers, act as part-time fathers, step-fathers or mere sperm donors, and occupy a secondary role to that of the mother, who may never have been their wife or a member of their family. We may still live in a largely male-dominated society, but the role of the father in the family and in society has changed dramatically and has become diversified in a way that was inconceivable in 1900 when Freud published *The Interpretation of Dreams,* in which dreams about his recently deceased father formed the basis for his observation of unconscious processes and for the psycho-sexual theories formulated in the course of his self-analysis.

It seems at first paradoxical that most of the followers of Freud (with the exception of Lacan) shifted their theorizing from his focus on the father's role to the mother's function of holding, feeding, and facilitating her child. Yet this trend clearly parallels the fundamental social changes following on the two world wars, in which many women had to assume the dominant, breadwinning, and masculine role in the family and at the workplace. This resulted ultimately in the liberation of women, the rise of feminism, and the establishment of women's studies as a serious academic subject.

Yet there is an essential question to ask here: what has happened to the notion that the unity of the parental couple is an essential prerequisite to the healthy sexual and emotional development of the human infant, and that the capacity to think and to relate, to love and to work, depends on the quality of joint early parenting? In an age where many children grow up with single parents, where divorce and remarriage are increasing and where temporary step-parenting is becoming more and more frequent, the task of mothering and fathering has undergone such major changes that the patriarchal family structure is no longer the norm; even the nuclear family is now less of a reality than it was when the phrase was coined a few decades ago. This is due as much to the women's movement's redefinition of the rights and duties of mothers and fathers as to the emancipation of women from their largely domestic role. Women expect to be able to have a career and, like men, to be able to divide their time between family and work with the help of caregivers and technical gadgets.

One could say that as women gained from their equality of opportunities, so men lost in this restructuring and re-evaluation of family roles. The centrality of the patriarchal father no longer obtains, since in the wake of the Second World War families have become fragmented and marriage is less of a bulwark then it used to be. The modern father comes in many different forms, some more difficult to define legally than others, and he cohabits much less often with the mother or mothers of his children than he used to do a hundred years ago. There is now the divorced father, for instance, who has regular access to his children, or shares the parenting with the mother, quite often on an equal basis. There is the step-father, who takes on a substitute parenting role when he remarries or marries a woman with children by another father; this is a version of fatherhood that is difficult to define and fulfil, since step-children often resent their lack of choice and treat the substitute father as an unwanted intruder, an attitude that is aptly expressed in Hamlet's phrase "a little more than kin and less than kind" (Maddox, 1975).

And there is the "natural" or unmarried father, sometimes partner of the mother, more often absent and in some cases not much more than sperm-donor for single mothers, IVF babies, or gay couples who want to parent children. He may have to pay child support, have shared custody or regular access to his child or children; he may remain unknown to the child or disappear altogether. When the child is adopted or is the product of IVF, the biological father has no legal right or duties, yet he knows that he has fathered a child and that the child can ask for him to be identified or contact him by mutual agreement.

Though relatively rarely distinguished or examined as to the influence on the participants, these different forms of fatherhood have an emotional significance for parents and children that is of paramount importance. Psychoanalytic theory, in contrast to systemic family therapy theory, has sadly neglected the subject by sticking to classical theories, which postulate two parents, without considering the sweeping changes of contexts and family structures in which parenting takes place today, and which determine the quantity and quality of parenting. Just as the triangular Oedipal relationship has rarely been opened up to the reality of siblings or of the extended family, so it has never been adapted to the possibility and the reality of single parenting, and to the ubiquitous splitting that is prevalent in step-parenting.

My intention is to examine some of the therapeutic implications of those irreversible changes in parenting and fatherhood that are characteristic of our age. Politicians go on talking about "family values", as if nothing had changed, and therapists struggle with theories that were constructed when marriage and monogamy were still taken for granted. This dilemma is the result of the social contradiction succinctly described by Margaret Mead:

We have constructed a family system which depends upon fidelity, lifelong monogamy and the survival of both parents. But we have never made adequate social provision for the security and identity of the children if that marriage is broken, as it so often was in the past, by death or desertion, and as it so often is in the present by death or divorce. We have, in fact . . . saddled ourselves with a system that won't work. [Mead, 1971, p. 41]

Here is a demographer's overview of how this unworkable system has become modified over the last decades:

Half a century ago we could limit our families, indeed, were already expected to. But we could not without embarrassment, difficulty or even without legal sanction divorce, cohabit, procure an abortion, live with a member of the opposite sex without being married, have children with someone not a spouse, marry but choose not to reproduce. Now changing attitudes have muted criticism and diminished stigma, and welfare arrangements have removed some of the material impediment to the new arrangements. The result has been a new diversity, maybe transient and unsustainable, in the way we live our lives, which distinguishes countries as a whole and individuals living next door in the same community. [Coleman, 1998, p. 6]

In a previous work (Mander, 1999), I speculated on the basis of clinical evidence that one of the legacies of the two recent European wars was a far-reaching change in the role of the father, and that the traumatic war experience of two generations of fathers led to an undermining of the patriarchal image that seriously threatened the stability and survival of the patriarchal family. Overnight, women had to get used to single parenthood, and children had to live without their fathers who, when they returned, had become strangers. There was a weakening of family bonds and the creation of new family arrangements, which required flexible forms of care-giving. John Bowlby's attachment theory, which strongly emphasizes the importance of a secure base in early childhood, was the result of his post war research for the World Health Organization, and recognized the close connection between maternal care and mental health (the book was later called *Child Care and the Growth of Love*), while significantly omitting the father's role in the world-wide social changes affecting families and children, and, more significantly, choosing to speak of "care-givers" instead of parents, mothers and fathers.

It is a fact that the father has radically shifted position and that his active role has become weakened, diversified, and even shrunk to insignificance. How can we insist seriously on the continued validity of the Oedipus complex, when many children have never experienced their parents as a couple and had their mother and/or father to themselves without experiencing the rivalry, the fears of castration, the envy, jealousy, and guilt that are postulated as inherent in the situation? It has become quite natural, usual, and apparently possible for children to grow up with one parent into adulthood, and, though this will have consequences for their future sexual orientation and gender choice, their individuation and emotional development will continue apace, while the separation from the care-giving parent will possibly be very complicated and certainly affect their sexual relations.

Oedipus or Zeus?

Should we therefore put aside classical Oedipal theory and find another Greek myth to symbolize and conceptualize the changed inner and outer worlds of our own and of future generations? For instance, we could abandon the patriarchal scenario of Greek tragedy, with its emphasis on the family, and focus instead on the Olympian god Zeus, whose obsessive promiscuity led him to impregnate innumerable goddesses and mortal women and to scatter his sperm ubiquitously, in the service, one could say in Darwinian terms, of "reproductive success". This allowed him, omnipotently, to people heaven and earth with his offspring. His manic penis activity could easily be interpreted in the light of Freudian libidinal theory or of post-Freudian notions of identification and internal objects. Then it would be possible to say that two great nineteenth-century patriarchs, Freud and Darwin, were behind the far-reaching changes in parenting and fathering that occurred in the twentieth century and are carried on into the new millennium. Like Zeus, the modern male seems no longer committed to monogamy, nor fully committed to "family values", and he seems to use his penis as freely for entertainment purposes as for reproduction, without fearing the law or social disapproval.

As for his complement, the modern mother, she would, like Hera, Artemis, or Athena, pursue her dual goals of motherhood and self-fulfilment by using men as sperm-donors to father her children, perhaps bringing them up single-handedly (with paid help) while successfully pursuing a career in a "masculine" profession. The children's fathers would be involved in their upbringing by paying child support and maintenance, fulfilling their access duties and generally sharing the parenting without necessarily cohabiting. In this way, the parents might be good and active parents without forming or modelling a stable couple and the children grow up secure and well protected without experiencing or needing the benefits of a nuclear family. The postmodern parenting scenario in the image of the Olympian gods affords women sexual opportunity and reproductive success in a self-determined semi-matriarchy that has liberated them from the opposite self-effacement of patriarchy. They are now shielded by law-given rights and duties fought for and gained by feminism, while both sexes have shed the bonds of strict monogamy and are more or less practising what has been called "progressive monogamy": marriage, partnership, divorce, re-marriage, step-parenting. One could see this development as a return to the mythical sexual freedom of the Olympian gods and goddesses in whose likeness we now create our relationships and procreate our children.

We have come a long way with the help and under the influence of those revolutionary theories about sex and reproduction originating with Darwin and Freud. But it does not look as if growing up has become any easier for the children of these liberated men and women, who are practising self-gratification and self-actualization in a climate of infinitepossibilities than it was when people had to stay together in marriage because of poverty or social disapproval. In spite of the avowed child-centredness of our time, the liberation has not properly worked for the offspring of these unions consummated more or less briefly for the purposes of sex and reproduction without firm commitment to secure parenting. The reason, I suspect, is an increase in narcissism, because the parents, mother and father, are caught in a situation of multiple choices where there is no binding convention, and the temptations are irresistible.

How do present-day fathers affect their children psychically and share the parenting with their mothers, in contrast to previous generations, and how can we prevent the situation of the disintegrating

family from getting out of hand? Some observations from the therapeutic consulting room may offer some answers.

The father as rival to the mother

An American article in the 1960s (Forrest, 1963) traced the "paternal
roots of male character development", in an interesting updating of
the Oedipus complex, to the father's facilitating and modelling role,
which enables the child to "dissolve the symbiotic bonds with the
mother in order to develop a separate identity generated by his own
powers". This prime need is seen as complemented by another, "the
need to relate as a contributing member to the social world he inhab-
its". Thus, instead of being Freud's "frustrating parent whose incorporation strengthens to boy's weak ego, affords him a structure for
masculinity and teaches him the master frustration by relinquishing
mother", he is the first stranger in the boy's world, the first represen-
tative from the outside world who can help him enter this world and
become an adult. Sullivan (1953) confirmed the father's role as a
model for the boy's imitative identification, and maintained that
"the boy learns to be a male by playing at being father".

As the father engages in motor activity with his son, the boy
acquires physical skills and mastery of his aggressive energy that
enhance his self-image as a male. The concept of we-ness, communicated by father's inclusion of the boy in masculine behaviour, interest, and responsibilities, enables him to relate to other males and
prepares him for masculine participation in society. Because fatherhood, unlike motherhood, cannot be established with certainty,
except by DNA testing, fatherhood must be confirmed for the child
by the action of the father. Ideally, then, Forrest continues, in
infancy the father's necessary function is to create a family unit, to
stabilize the mother, to balance the mother–child relationship, to
relate the psycho-biological unit of mother and child to the objective world, and, finally, to penetrate the infant's world, bearing the
pleasurable stimulation and interest of the outside world (Forrest,
1963, p. 84).

This idealized picture of a family where the father still has a
leading role links to theories of Bowlby and Winnicott, which
postulate a secure base and firm holding as the primary maternal

task, before the infant develops self and ego functions that allow him or her to individuate and separate from the mother, moving from dependence to interdependence and independence.

There is no disagreement about the maternal function being primary, whether it is object relating (Klein), containment (Bion), attunement (Stern), holding and playing in the potential space (Winnicott, 1965), or being with the transformational object (Bollas, 1986). But father has an important supportive role (with Winnicott) and, as necessary, he supplements or substitutes for the mother (Bowlby, 1965, 1988) as care-giver. The bond between the parents, however, so vital for the resolution of the Oedipus complex, seems no longer essential as long as the mother functions well in her self-altering and facilitating maternal task and is adequately supported by others, not necessarily the father. And this is, in fact, what has happened as a result of the push towards sexual liberation of the individual, in particular of women, because of the easing of divorce and because of a notable increase in single parenthood due to desertion or lack of commitment on the part of the father.

In fact, Forrest's idea that the father needs to separate the boy from his mother is not based on a notion of strong paternal bonding, sexual unity, or jealousy, but on the assumption that the father cannot trust the mothering to be altogether good for the growing boy in the long run and that there comes a time when the mother definitely has to be left behind. Forrest also does not believe in the ubiquity of Oedipal sexual rivalry, though stressing the importance of the father's emotional stability for the performance of his parenting task. The idea is that, as long as the boy is helped to let go of his need for fusion, to progress to separateness and to identify with the father's "authority and his mastery of Problems in a socially acceptable way" (Fromm, 1956, p. 43), his character development will continue satisfactorily and he will achieve the desirable maturity and integration into the society of his peers.

What Forrest does not consider is the possibility that the father might be motivated by suspicion of, and competitiveness with, the mother, particularly when he and she have fallen out with each other over the upbringing of the child or are no longer in love with each other and cohabiting. She also omits to mention the absent father, so ubiquitous a phenomenon in our time of over-working men (and women), and does not consider the part-time father who may be loving and eager to perform the paternal role she outlines so beautifully, but is unable to do so, either because the mother restricts his access or is hostile to and suspicious of his influence.

In fact, the perspective of the Oedipal triangle may have been shifting dramatically in the course of the easing of divorce and the sexual liberation: from the tensions Freud diagnosed between child and father to the tension between the parents, which can either result in the break-up of the parental bonding postulated for the resolution of the conflict or in an ongoing rivalry between the parents for the child. In both cases the child will experience a clash of loyalties, and, instead of getting on with the task of growing and developing, perhaps become a mediator between the parents or withdraw angrily into a fantasy world of his or her own, both of which will impede the ongoing emotional development towards achieving a firm identity and secure attachment behaviour.

Let me use the clinical example of a man who worked as an industrial negotiator between unions and employers. His father had remained married to his wife (i.e., not the patient's mother), while his mother was resentfully hiding the fact of her "illegitimate" status, which made him feel torn between his parents and withdraw into his books or to his friends' houses. He was full of self-doubt, became an avid gambler and eager to succeed in his industrial negotiations, while at the same time his relationships with wives and children were insecure. He realized that he was acting out his personal problems in his professional life as well as in his gambling, and that the creative solutions to these were only partially working. Interestingly, reading Forrest's paper produced important insights into his behaviour as well as a change in his relationship with his ageing father, whose neglecting of his parental task in the past now became an object of discussion and reconciliation between them. Almost predictably, he confidently conducted and won some important professional negotiations around this stage of the therapy and then managed to remarry and start another family.

Let me now consider the father's role in the character of the girl child, which is quite different and perhaps even more complicated than it is with the boy. While the girl's separation from the symbiotic mother is equally necessary, it is more difficult for her than for the boy to disidentify with the mother and identify with the father, as she needs to grow up into a woman. Also, the father's role is complicated by their sexual attraction to each other. There is a danger of domination and incest, and a difficulty of eventual separation from the father, too, equal to that of separating from the mother, particularly when the mother is denigrated and repudiated. The identification with father, on the other hand, enables the girl to gain self-confidence, to form sexual relationships, and to play a masculine role in the world like the boy.

There is much feminist literature on the subject and an ongoing controversy about the Oedipus complex in the psyche of the girl in which writers like Janine Chasseguet-Smirgel (1970), Juliet Mitchell (1974), Carol Gilligan (1982), and Jessica Benjamin, to name only the most prominent authors, have been imaginatively engaged. Benjamin (1990) speaks about the split between "the mother of attachment" and "the father of separation" and bemoans the loss of mother "as the source of goodness", while the father becomes a saviour from a mother who would pull us back into limitless narcissism. The incipient split between mother as source of goodness and the father as principle of individuation is hardened into a polarity in which her goodness is redefined as a seductive threat to autonomy. There seem to be only two ways out of this dilemma: identification with father, adoption of "masculine traits and of the masculine ideals of autonomous individuality, which leads to gender polarity", or regression and a return to identification with the primal mother. Benjamin recommends the recognition of difference and mutuality in relationships. Is there a possible middle way? An example of the resultant splitting of love and hate was for me the case of a woman whose father died when she was five and left her at the mercy of an immature and envious mother with whom she was unable to identify. The dead father remained the unknowable ideal, on whom she modelled herself, while she dedicated her professional life to repairing couples and families.

Another patient, whose parents broke up when she was an adolescent, was left to shuttle from one parent to the other, torn between unconscious incestuous fantasies of the seductive father and murderous anger with the demanding and abandoned mother, unable to settle into femininity, independence, and adulthood. She craved her boyfriend's penis, felt guilty about her split loyalties, and was unable to resolve her ambivalent feelings—clearly, a suitable case for treatment, but also a vivid example of the great problems of growing up with divided parents, postulating the need for joint parents.

Forrest's idealized picture of the facilitating father who helps the boy separate from his mother does not address the issue of single parenthood, in which the mother needs to be both father and mother to her child and also somehow release the boy child from the safety of her embrace to risk the openness of the wider world, in which he would have to perform a role she could not model for him. The big question is whether this is achievable without the involvement of a male to identify with and whether the longing for the initial symbiotic fusion with the mother postulated by psychoanalysis (Mahler, 1975) is an unalterable fact that always leads to developmental complications when the time comes for the required move towards individuation and differentiation.

Attunement

In order to answer this, I shall draw on Daniel Stern's theories on the development of the infantile self, which contradict Mahler's notion of primary symbiosis and presume a separate, though immature, self from the beginning, with symbiosis or fusion as a pathological rather than normative state, a defence against either maternal abandonment or maternal deficit (or, applying Forrester's theory, against paternal abandonment or deficit). Instead of the "clinical baby" constructed in analytic theory, Stern's "observed" babies progress through various self states from an emergent self, by way of the core self, to a subjective self and a verbal self with the help of sensitive attunement adapted to different requirements at each stage of the process. Instead of the need to progress beyond fusion to separateness, of which both Mahler and Forrest speak with conviction, Stern concentrates his attention on a "sense of self" as a developmental organizing principle in which the sense of self-and-other has as a starting point the infant's inferred subjective experience (Stern, 1985).

Then, the child, boy or girl, does not necessarily have a symbiotic early relationship with mother; rather, he or she seeks this out as a result of a deficit or lack of stage-appropriate attunement, which may be maternal, paternal, or parental in the widest sense (including care-givers).

This means that adopted babies or step-children will equally proceed from one developmentally required self-state to the next when they are part of an adequate and appropriate attunement process. As this is always individualized, it may not be necessary to split the parental tasks in the way Freud, Mahler, or Forrest did, but rather to concentrate on the individual, the stages and the quality of attention, response, and imagination that characterize this process and its continuity.

> The sharing of affective states is the most pervasive and clinically germaine feature of intersubjective relatedness . . . Interaffectivity is what is meant when clinicians speak of "mirroring" and "empathic responsiveness" . . . First, the parent must be able to read the infant's feeling state from the infant's overt behaviour. Second, the parent must perform some behaviour that is not a strict imitation but nonetheless corresponds in some way to the infant's overt behaviour. Third, the infant must be able to read this corresponding parental response as having to do with the infant's own original feeling experience and not just imitating the infant's behaviour. [Stern, 1985, pp. 138–139]

In this model, it is the accurate observation that counts; the attention given to the subjective experience and to the ongoing and unfolding processes of intersubjective relatedness with the baby, the infant, the growing child of either sex by mother, father or any other "ordinarily devoted" care-giver, which includes facilitating, containment, modelling, identification, and other functions considered paternal, and the more of these there are the better for the child, as long as the parents are not quarrelling over his or her exclusive possession.

Of course, this parental attunement will always happen in a particular social context and for this child-centred, intersubjective developmental process the particular parental context, environment, and constellation are significant and influential. So, instead of speaking normatively of the role of the father, it may be more helpful to speak of versions of fatherhood that differ because of their context. I believe that it matters in the case of a child's father, boy or girl, whether he is the legitimate father, the natural father, the adoptive father, or the stepfather, to name but a few versions of fatherhood, because the subjective experience of both partners differs with each context as with individuals. We can speak of traditional or cultural

paternal functions and roles, instead of insisting on constrictive definitions; this would allow a woman to fulfil the paternal role as well
as allowing a man to fulfil the maternal role, if not both roles simultaneously, alternately, or interchangeably. What needs to be held in
mind in each case is to realize the possible permutations and variations and their consequences, in health and in pathology.

Dilemmas

In the following, I concentrate on some novel versions of fatherhood
that I have observed in my clinical practice and consider symptomatic for our time; they are important in their implications for the
children involved and for the future of their parenting of, and relationships with, others.

The identity of the father may be withheld from the child because
the mother cannot or does not want to disclose it for personal
reasons or because he is an unknown sperm donor. Here is the case of
a woman whose mother was a prostitute and had become pregnant
after an involvement with a married man who apparently forbade
her ever to mention him to anyone. When the patient came for therapy, she was tormented by memories of an unhappy childhood in
which she was constantly beaten and abused by the mother and her
clients. She was quite promiscuous, sleeping with every man who
wanted her sexually. Unable to form stable sexual relationships,
while longing to have a child and considering every new lover as a
potential father, she seemed to act out an obsessive fantasy of
searching for a father (ostensibly for her own child, but also for
herself), for her own unknown father, who remained forever a
tormenting uncertainty. The unconscious longing for a child did not
involve any realistic notion of motherhood or of pleasing her
mother, but rather, as Dinora Pines (1993) wrote in relation to
women without good enough mothers,

> an attempt to establish an object relationship which will compen-
> sate for an earlier lack of internalization of a satisfied and satisfy-
> ing child–mother relationship which is doomed to failure since all
> they seek is the infantile omnipotence of the baby. [p. 99]

She was unable to experience her sexual partners as real people with
emotional needs of their own, and none of them, sensing this,

wanted to be the father of her longed-for child. She carried on repeating her compulsive sexual pattern until she became aware of what she was doing, and, in working in the transference with me, matured sufficiently to establish a sexual relationship in which the wish for a child was not uppermost.

Another patient, whose father had died in the war, acquired a violent stepfather when her mother remarried. She had a difficult adolescence and then married a man who became impotent with her, which made her seek sexual satisfaction with other men. None of these extra-marital relationships prospered, and, as she desperately wanted a child, she resorted to having a baby by IVF. The treatment was successful, and as the sperm donor was unknown, it pleased the husband to have a ready-made daughter. In therapy, we connected her wish for a baby with her need for a father, and the anonymity of the sperm donor with her lack of memories of her own dead father. The daughter accepted the mother's husband as a father, but her stormy relationship with her mother could well be an unconscious rebellion because of not knowing who has really fathered her.

Yet another patient's mother withheld from her daughter the identity of the man who had made her pregnant, but married someone who was willing to act as a stand-in and be called father by her daughter, who remained in ignorance of her real parentage. Once again there seems to have been an ongoing unconscious search for the unknown father and no realization that she was passing on a problem of her own to a daughter who had to grapple with its emotional consequence in later life. As this kind of scenario happens quite often, presumably to spare the participants unnecessary "trouble", it has not yet entered all the textbooks that such secrets might be unhelpful to the offspring, who sooner or later find themselves confronted with the truth, or with an inkling of the truth, with perhaps shattering consequences (Pincus & Dare, 1978).

Even professionals think that occasionally it might be better to hide the truth, for instance, when the father is a criminal, or elderly, or has a family already, as was the suspicion of my first patient. Does this mean that we sanction secrets in the family when it seems convenient? I hope not. Yet, when I protested in a discussion with a colleague that everybody should be allowed to know the truth, I was told that Freud himself did not want to know the truth about his own father, as indicated by a dream on the eve of his father's death

in which he was told to "close his eyes" (Freud, 1900a). He interpreted this command as an order not to probe into his father's past,
and, for fear of discovering that his father might have been abusive,
he obeyed the order, abandoning the seduction theory soon after for
a theory according to which most abuse happens in unconscious
fantasy.

Now that the actual scope of sexual child abuse by fathers, step-
fathers, and even mothers is known (de Mause, 1991), we find it difficult to accept the step that Freud decided to take because, in the
climate of the time, he could not persist. However, it certainly does
not sanction the continuing practice of withholding the knowledge
of patrimony or keeping convenient secrets in the interest of the children whose continued uncertainty might cause them emotional
damage in the long run. It has been a development in the right direction that everybody nowadays can meet their birth mother and can
ask for a DNA test and establish their father's identity, whether
they were adopted or produced by IVF.

There are some difficulties, however, about this openness. Many
adoptees discover in therapy the rage and terror experienced at the
point of their adoption caused by their temporary abandonment.
They can be helped to work through this traumatic early experience,
which can be deeply encapsulated in their psyche. An adopted
patient of mine discovered that his continued denial of any effect his
adoption might have had on his emotional development may have
been mistaken, and he decided to start working on this, since he had
been unable to be a person in his own right, always merging with
others and relating symbiotically with his homosexual partners. He
reached a watershed when his fusion with me could not be maintained during a break and we managed to survive, despite some
angry outbursts. This put him in touch with strong feelings about
having been abandoned by his natural parents, and having been told
by his adoptive mother that it was "only for his best". There is no
adoption without an experience of abandonment.

Not much is known, however, about the emotional effects of IVF
on the children born with its help, as voluntary sperm donors are
usually chosen through a system of physical matching and there has
not been enough thought about the possible emotional effects on the
test-tube homunculus. Already, there are predictions that, with the
help of genetic engineering, designer babies will become possible

and, in the words of one genetic scientist, that "in the future sex is going to become recreational and reproduction to become clinical".

In some respects it is like one of the ingenious scenarios dreamt up by science fiction writers like Mary Shelley in *Frankenstein* or Aldous Huxley in *Brave New World*. The sperm donors also seem to be affected by their experience, brief and painless though it may be. They have, after all, fathered a human being and are aware of this. Some of them develop obsessive fantasies about the unknown offspring they are now, by virtue of recent laws, allowed to search for. For instance, there was the case of a man who did not want to have children with his wife, but was proud to have successfully fathered a number of IVF children, which assured him of his potency and reproductive capacity. This may seem unnatural, but it is not perverse in the light of Darwin's evolutionary theory to feel like this. And impoverished college students who earn their college fees through donating their sperm or offering themselves as surrogate mothers may pride themselves on giving a useful service to society and to mothers who are unable to conceive and carry their own babies.

Consider also those men who ask for their sperm to be frozen when told they have a life-threatening illness: they believe that they have a right to fatherhood, though they may not be there to experience its living proof. Once again, however, it is the children who have to bear the burden of their father's decision: they will not be technically fatherless, but will be deprived of ever knowing their fathers in the flesh. They will grow up with the ghosts and the phantoms of the men from whom they sprang and will never experience what it is like to be brought up and loved by the men whose features and talents they may have inherited. Instead, they might be angry with the mother, who exerted her right to have a child and with the father who did not consider what their feelings might be about being produced by mechanical means. Living with the lack of a real father may not be as bad as losing a father in childhood, yet it is a lack and a deficit that has to be acknowledged and lived with.

All this has come about because of the contemporary notion that the right to have a child as well as the right to choose one's sexual partner and to abandon him or her, is one of the inalienable rights of all human beings—whatever means are used to bring it about and however much damage or hurt it may cause to others. Let us pause to consider where this notion has brought us: to a planet whose population has increased fourfold within a century and a world in which half the population is under thirty. The likelihood is that many of the latter have not been parented consistently by two parents who live together and love each other, and that their visions of families and fathers are patchy or unformed. Is it time to consider a revised version of the marriage laws, in which parents are under a legal or moral obligation to stay together until their offspring are grown up, emphasizing again how important it is for people to feel responsible for others rather than concentrate on their selfish interests and on self-gratification?

Therapy cannot take the place of good enough fathers and mothers; it can only attempt to do some symbolic re-parenting.

CHAPTER TWELVE

Abuse and recovery

A ttending this year's Winnicott Memorial lecture, given by Lloyd de Mause, was an experience that had a powerful impact on a professional audience which is used to the subject of child sexual abuse, but was startled by de Mause's statistics, proving that this country has a much higher incidence of childhood trauma due to parental beating than most other countries in Europe. The shocking details of de Mause's talk made me go to the Internet, from where I downloaded two papers of his, "The universality of incest" (1991) and "The history of child abuse" (1998). Both of these had an equally profound effect on me, though I realized that the impact of de Mause's opinions is due to there being a continuing scream sent out from the Institute of Psychohistory in New York, which does not receive much recognition from among his colleagues, who simply do not believe what he has been telling them for thirty years. How can this be explained?

Going to a website on child sexual abuse I read that

> this has only recently become a subject of interest in particular countries and cultures, where it is seen as a social problem and a main source of many people's suffering and personal problems. . . . For the first time in history we are beginning to face the true

prevalence and significance of child abuse, but . . . there are contro-
versies about definitions among experts who claim that there is
nobody who is without bias. [de Mause, 1998, p. 11]

And further, "official government statistics are merely the tip of the
iceberg, as they only include cases which have been reported" (*ibid.*).
So, whom should we believe and how can we respond?

I was reminded of the reception that Freud received when he told
the world he had become convinced that the ubiquitous repression of
sexuality in contemporary society was responsible for the high incidence of neurosis among its urban population. If we believe de Mause,
then Freud's withdrawal of the seduction theory (in 1897?) was
unjustified, as he would have been right about the prevalence of child
sexual abuse in the Viennese society of the time, which he had encountered in his early cases, but misinterpreted as fantasies. De Mause
calls the history of childhood a "nightmare" and points accusingly to
the family bed of previous centuries as the scene of constant incest
among children and adults, who slept there crowded together, abusing each other and being abused, without anyone objecting or complaining. This is plausible, and so is the other claim he has made: that
melancholia first came in at the turn of the seventeenth century, with
Hamlet as its first dramatic impersonation, indicating that Melanie
Klein's "depressive position" may finally have been reached by someone. The vast literature on melancholia—from Burton via Montaigne
to the Romantics—would then be the expression of a big step forward
in the civilizing process of humanity, which had previously been
emotionally primitive and predominantly paranoid–schizoid, with
everybody splitting off and projecting their badness on to others, particularly children, thus harming their relationships with significant
others.

Here I shall explore some of my own professional experiences
of working with child sexual abuse, and describe some of the
most poignant clinical cases I have seen in order to develop some
thoughts that came to me as a consequence of their narratives. In all
of these cases something could be shifted, and helping patients lift
the veil of secrecy became therapeutically creative, though only after
years of patiently remembering and working through, and of facing
much pain by patient and therapist.

I first encountered clinical material of sexual abuse one year into
the work with my first training patient in the late 1970s. She had

first told me the story of her parents' embattled marriage, which had ended in divorce and in the disappearance of her father, whom she called a monster. Her attitude to me had so far been characterized by firmly holding me at arm's length, but after this confession she started to open up, telling me about the secret relationship she had with her stepfather during her childhood. He had initially behaved like the loving father she had always craved, and then turned into a controlling abuser who showed her pornographic pictures and held her captive in the evenings with the connivance of her mother, who always sent her to his room after he returned from work.

She was covered in embarrassment while telling me these painful memories. We never went into them in detail, as I did not want to be intrusive and she did not divulge particular episodes, but she was clearly immensely relieved to have opened up a can of worms to a sympathetic listener who was not scandalized by her tale of buried torments.

At the time of my working with her, the subject of childhood sexual abuse had not yet received the attention it is given now and I initially adopted a careful approach to her narrative, though I was aware of its importance. Deciding to let her tell me in her own time and concentrating on the broad sweep of her anxieties about the subject, I did not press her for details, and this paid off because it led us to the importance of her mother using her for her own purposes, to a description of the abuser's controlling power over her, and to her own defensive controlling of every encounter with other people, including the relationship with me. Her fear was of impingement and helplessness, the defence was a plea for *noli me tangere*. It did not seem to matter what actually happened in the room with the man in it, who behaved in an apparently incomprehensible way. What mattered most was that she was told to go in by her mother, who herself had seemed frightened of him, and that once inside she always felt terrified and abandoned, had to obey and do what she was told, without understanding what it was all about. Apparently, he did not hurt her and may not have done that much to her physically, but he frightened and confused her and it was a traumatic experience that had left an indelible impression in her psyche and had deeply disturbed her. I still remember excitedly telling my supervisor how the case had developed into my being told a shameful sexual secret. His response was that she had reached an important breakthrough, and that I was revealing an emotional reaction he had to contain for me in order for me to contain myself in my patient's presence. This was significant learning from experience, a monitoring of powerful countertransference feelings.

In retrospect, I was able to read this intensely emotion-charged narrative as the typical scenario of sexual abuse in the family. There is the abuser whose dysfunctional sexuality requires the use of a willing and preferably young self-object for its gratification, as this cannot be achieved in sexual intercourse with an adult. There is the emotionally deprived child, who is seduced into participating in a perverted sexual activity and becomes a confused accomplice, unable to extricate herself from the compulsively repeated activity. The child feels guilty for colluding, frightened because she is sworn to secrecy, and unable to tell anyone else, as the mother is also a collusive part of the events. Bollas (2004) describes a similar sequence in "The structure of evil" in relation to the serial killer, and this sequence confirms my clinical experience of working with both categories, abuser and abused. It explains the initial bonding and the ensuing enslavement of the passive victim, including the secretiveness that is an integral part of the "evil' relationship. The serial abuser is after sex, not violence, but he is acting out an unconscious pattern as compulsively and ruthlessly as the serial killer, using force and controlling his victim.

My patient's complex psychic functioning, a mixture of shame and schizoid defences, was a result of her guilt, splitting, and denial. It led to a persistent inability to trust or to establish intimacy, to a need for control and to a simmering aggressiveness that found discharge in aggressive joking and manic defences. Being able to tell and to explore her childhood trauma was a relief, and enabled her to change over six years, but she was never able to enjoy sexual intercourse without anxiety, and control remained a central issue in her personality. Interestingly, after some time she tracked down her natural father and instead of encountering a monster she found him to be a reasonably friendly man with whom she established a good relationship, keeping her mother out of the picture.

Another case of an abusive father—daughter relationship reconfirmed for me the important role of the conniving mother, whose frigidity makes her sexually withholding, using the child as a protective device against the hated husband. This was a patient whose mother was preoccupied with her sick son and stubbornly refused her husband his conjugal rights. Feeling rejected, he came into his daughter's bed at night, usually after a fight with the mother when he had come home drunk from the pub. Here, too, there was an unmanaged oedipal constellation that victimized the powerless child and resulted from a marital impasse. A flirtatious daughter relationship had turned into incest, which shattered the child's basic trust. The adult patient described repeated experiences of terror and dissociation, and displayed a "freezing" defence against unbearable anxiety that could lead to temporary depersonalization and eventually to the construction of a "false self". In the consulting room she never felt safe, and often lay on the couch silently in a rigid position, turning her back to me, unable to speak (as she had been with the father when he invaded her bed). When she was asked in her training to participate in a psychological test that involved associating to a series of diagrams, all she produced were stories of abuse and she suffered crippling anxieties while performing the task.

Her father had been traumatized in the war and had become an alcoholic. When she was seven, he disappeared one day, having been hospitalized for a brain tumour, from which he died soon after. She never saw him again, nor was she taken to his funeral, as the relatives did not believe a child should be confronted with death. Father remained a ghostlike figure, undead and idealized, with mother blamed for his disappearance. Perhaps she had a fantasy that she had murdered him.

My third case is one of persistent sibling incest perpetrated by an older brother, who for many years systematically abused his younger sister, probably in an act of revenge on the mother, who had sent him abroad as a small child during the war. Once again, the patient had at first mistaken the abuser's interest for loving kindness and had been seduced into participating in perverse sexual activities, without penetration, whenever the mother was absent from home at work. For years she had to serve as her brother's captive playmate, sometimes together with a cousin, or alone, her face covered by a sheet while he played with her body. Finally, she made him stop when her periods started. All this was kept a strict secret from the mother, partially from herself, and totally from her husband later, until she came into therapy decades later as a result of having discovered that her two daughters had been regularly abused by her father during the family's habitual Sunday visits. The girls "remembered" this in their late teens, and the older girl, who had always been a good girl, turned viciously against her mother to shift the blame on to her. The younger girl had been anorexic for years and this had been resistant to treatment until the truth came out and shattered the apparent equilibrium of the family.

My patient felt immensely guilty for not having watched her daughters better during the family visits to her parents' house, and was mortified that she had not put two and two together earlier. After all, it was in the very same house that she herself had been abused years earlier, and not only by her brother, but earlier by a bachelor uncle who lived with the family and was always mutely present, ironically, when the little girls sat with their grandfather watching television, which enabled him to secretly touch them up while their mother was talking to her mother in the kitchen preparing tea. The mother had always idealized her father, as she needed to believe that he was loving in the absence of any love from the mother, and the revelation of his betrayal of her trust was devastating. The scales literary fell from her eyes. It had not worked to turn a blind eye to the truth of her dysfunctional family and to keep her own abuse a secret.

When she discovered after her mother's death that the mother had herself had an affair with the man next door, the complex pattern of secrets and abuse was at last revealed, and she became able to share her own dark secret and to use her therapy constructively. The brother's still persisting hold was broken and she found the courage to confront him, to force him to sell the house they had inherited jointly in their mother's will, and to close the door forever on this haunted house that had seen so much abuse. She was then able to get rid of the fear, be free of the bondage she had always lived in and to use this liberating act of revenge and retaliation reparatively and transformatively. She also shed the deferential compliance and the lifelong striving for perfection that she had practised as daughter, mother, wife, and patient. It left an ongoing difficulty with the oldest daughter, who was struggling in her therapy with her own feelings of rage by relentlessly blaming the mother for her abuse, and by cutting herself off from her for years. All this amounted to a complex transgenerational pattern of compliance, secretiveness, and abuse, requiring much further therapeutic work on the biblical theme of "the sins of the fathers are visited upon their children", in the form of primitive defences and repetition compulsions.

Welldon calls incest the pathological solution of a family to the problem of sexual perversion: "Keeping sex in the family" (1992, p. 135).

> The process of incest begins very often with the wife refusing to have sex with her husband. This makes the husband feel insecure and inadequate and leads to the marked regression which is characteristic of the incest perpetrator ... the situation brings nightmarish echoes from their own childhood in which similar cumulative traumas occurred.

My three cases are variations on Welldon's theme of children being used and abused by sexually dysfunctional parents, with the victims struggling to repair their own sexual and psychic functioning and finally recovering from the trauma in therapy.

There are, of course, incestuous mothers, too, and my most poignant example is of a woman patient whose mother used her for comfort while the father was away in the war, making her share bed and bath until well into her early adolescence. While not overtly abusing her sexually, she was impinging by establishing a stifling physical bondage that resulted in frigidity and life-long sexual impenetrability of the patient, the development of a false self, and of an underlying depression that occasionally struck with debilitating force.

Hinshelwood once asked the important question: "When does hurt become trauma?", and answered it by describing sexual abuse as an experience of inside-out exposure, where the particularly traumatic feature is the breach of the private and the public boundary. When a mother's care and attention becomes an intrusion of orifices, it infringes the child's need for the body to be her own private possession, instead of sensitively negotiating this essential need and respecting the separateness of that other psychic world. The therapist can set in motion a conversion process that negotiates the horror of the abuse by containment and helps the patient metabolize their traumatic memories into verbal form, thus putting into words the experience that has created a mental space filled with fantasies of inappropriate sexual relationships.

An essential feature of the abusive experience is the misuse of parental or adult power, the lack of empathy for the other, and of respect for the sexual immaturity of the child. It took centuries for the conceptualization of human rights. First, there was the formulation of individual rights, then of the rights of women, and finally, in the wake of this development of protecting personhood, the rights of children also became recognized. This meant that the traditionally total power of parents and other adults, such as teachers and carers, over children was called into serious question, and finally broken. Power corrupts, and parental power has been no exception to this fundamental rule. But it has been taken for granted for centuries that children could be disciplined and abused by adults for their own purposes, like possessions. It had not occurred to previous generations of parents, who were caught in traditional patterns of feudal thinking, that parental power, like political power, had to be used protectively, respecting rather than exploiting weakness and helplessness, and that parents and adults are accountable for their actions towards children, who are psychologically more vulnerable.

What had also not been admitted was the fact that the sexually disturbed adult seeks a willing victim in the child to satisfy his impulses and that he seeks out situations where his tyrannical behaviour will be tolerated under pressure and threat. The patriarchal father used methods of psychological control that were designed to instil terror and to destroy the victim's sense of self. Mothers, too, were far too often liable to use rather than nurture and care for their children, and even though they may commit fewer sexual offences, they can be equally controlling, impinging on and dominating their children, which results in lasting damage to their self-development and arrests their natural growth.

Most often children are abused by people who know them, who look after them and who use this powerful situation for their own needs, sometimes even blaming children for being seductive, dependent, or manipulative, and claiming that they want and deserve what they get. Because of the passivity and neediness of under-age children, they become easy targets, letting themselves be seduced by kindness and promises, and they can generally be trustingly persuaded to keep quiet.

Once, being touched up by the milkman, who had lifted me up to sit next to him on his cart, I remember asking myself in innocent confusion why he would want to do this and what he would get out of bothering me like this. In those days children were not warned to beware of strangers, because there was such a conspiracy of silence around the subject of sex in general. And this particular version of it was not much talked about, though it was happening ubiquitously in families, in schools, and in children's homes. Even Dickens, the defender of children, did not talk about it explicitly, though there are many hints of paedophilia and of sadistic sexual acts towards children in his work.

When *Lolita*, the first explicit narration of under-age sex, was published in the 1950s, it was banned because it transgressed a literary taboo against explicit description of sexual acts, like *Lady Chatterley's Lover*, rather than because it broke the incest taboo. Humbert Humbert was Lolita's stepfather, after all. Nabokov's ironical style was provocative because it cheekily infringed the age-old convention of being implicit about sexual relations. The outcry about *Lolita* was, thus, not a case of defending an abused child, but of protecting adults from the reality of their sexual perversion.

In fact, Humbert Humbert is portrayed as the principal victim, as Lolita has already lost her virginity before they meet and she is portrayed as seducing him, using her power to finally get him sent to prison. In Thomas Mann's *Death in Venice*, we have another fictional description of an adult falling under the spell of a seductive child, who is aware of his power and is using it artfully. In both books, therefore, there is the assumption that the pre-pubescent child is the seducer and the regressed adult the helpless victim of his imagination and of obsessive infatuation. This is part of the truth, but he is then guilty of an abdication of his adult responsibility, and has lost the capacity for adult self-management.

Fifty years later the perspective had changed, and in Alan Bennett's *Talking Heads* (1998) the child's sexual abuser is not the evil fiend he is so often portrayed as in the media now, but a sad, lonely, and emotionally twisted individual who seeks sexual gratification from a deprived child, being himself the deprived child who probably has been abused. During the investigation the park keeper, Wilfred, tells the young policewoman about the girl he took into the bushes; "It's what I thought she wanted". "That's what men always say", she said. "Choose how old you are."

A patient I once assessed for therapy used the same words about the little girl he had abused, unwilling to consider that he might have shocked her by what he did, after she had trustingly held his hand and snuggled up to him. It is because of this lack of understanding and of the compulsiveness of his actions that the perpetrator needs help. Can he be changed by treatment? Bennett poignantly describes the perpetrator's confusion on being told by the judge that he would be given treatment. On being asked by the doctor, "Did anyone touch you when you were little?" He answered, "No, they didn't. And if they did, it's done. Anyway, they tell you to touch people now. They run courses in it." This satirical approach contains the writer's deep compassion and psychodynamic understanding for the sad plight of the perpetrator who reports, "They haven't given me any treatment. They put me by myself to stop the others giving me the treatment. The piss-in-your-porridge treatment" (1998, p. 57).

Finally, there is the case of a patient who was haunted by a ghost, who terrorized her whenever she was alone in a house, whom she imagined coming into the bathroom when she was having a bath, lying on top of her when she was asleep, or lurking behind the door, after she heard him come up the stairs in the night. Whenever she tried to remember and put into words what happened to her as a child, when her father burst drunk into her bedroom, put his hand on her mouth and abused her sexually by penetration, her legs began to shake, her mind went blank, and she dissociated, terrified of going mad.

I listened to her and held her in my gaze until she came round again from the experience of being haunted and asked me whether I thought she was mad. I calmly interpreted what had happened to her as a flashback. Calling it a re-enactment allowed us to explore how she had tried to deal with her childhood experience, first by deper-sonalizing herself and becoming a yoga nun, then by developing a fantasy of being chosen, turning a secret anxiety of having been the one who seduced her father into abusing her into the resolve of becoming a spiritual healer, someone with a sense of vocation. There was a haunting fear of being evil and responsible for the abuse, of having been the seducer herself. This meant that she was defensively identifying with the aggressor and thus deflecting the attack away from herself on to others.

Making these links was liberating, and made sense of her choice to eventually study anthropology, but the paralysing fear of ghosts and demons remained for some time and she continued to self-harm and somatize, as she did in her adolescence when she developed a long-drawn out form of glandular fever that was ascribed to a persistent virus and recurrent immune deficiency. She had been deeply traumatized and was so haunted by her memories that it took a long time to work through the unconscious material and make her feel safe enough to live alone, to feel free from the crippling fear of a repetition of the abuse, and to have a relationship with a man who was not abusive. Our relationship was precarious, as she reported a great fear before the session of having to face the unbearable trauma, and sometimes she had to be counselled over the phone. My countertransference veered from compassion to helplessness and vain rescue fantasies, when all I could do was persist in holding her through her anguish and offering a safe space in which she could occasionally face her memories, summoning the necessary strength for that.

Needless to say her childhood scenario was similar to some of the other cases. The patient's mother was herself afraid of her husband when he was drunk, and he usually molested her while the mother was either not around or turning a blind eye when he went into her room to say goodnight. The patient remained unable to access any anger with him or with the mother, kept on smiling while she talked, and, because she was terrified of being alone, she continued to seek physical closeness from a male friend whom she also experienced as abusive when he demanded sex, but this seemed to be the choice of lesser evil. It was a vicious circle that could not be broken, as long as the past kept invading the present in the form of flashbacks. When she took up going to Kabbala meetings, she experienced some comfort, and eventually she escaped to Thailand. I heard nothing from her for a long time, but recently I was told that she is now married and having a child. All's well that ends well. I was often reminded of how in previous times priests tried to exorcise ghosts by praying with the victims.

On the subject of abusive priests there is now no longer a conspiracy of silence, and the recent exposure of incidents in Irish seminaries and the Irish Catholic church has opened the lid on a long-festering scandal. The church lost its all-powerful grip and the priests some of their respectability, after generations of young women came out with tales of having been persistently abused, impregnated, and forced to give up their illegitimate babies for adoption. Another aspect of this scenario is the abuse of altar boys by gay priests (Bennett, 2001) and rumours of widespread sexual activities in male religious orders. Nowadays, the churches run their own therapeutic services for errant priests, but the continued celibacy vows are making it difficult to stop and police under-age or same-sex seduction. Working therapeutically with such cases can be counter-productive, as long as there are no permitted sexual outlets for priests and religious leaders. Repression leads to neurotic symptoms or to acting out, and Freud has been proved right once again.

CHAPTER THIRTEEN

Defiant resistance in the service of the impoverished self

Herman Melville's *Bartleby*: an illustration of clinical casework

"About suffering they were never wrong
The Old Masters . . ."

W. H. Auden

Resistance is encountered in psychotherapy in many different forms and can be seen as a survival strategy. This chapter interprets the short story *Bartleby the Scrivener,* by Herman Melville, as a fictional case of defiant resistance, which some patients develop to fend off external demands experienced as intolerable impingements. Clinical material from two particularly intractable cases of narcissistic damage is introduced in the second part of the paper to support the hypothesis that the therapist needs to contain and understand this kind of resistance as a defensive stance in the service of protecting a weak self structure, thereby making the patient feel held and enabled to shed the fear of impingement and to bear what Melville called the "cosmic orphanhood" of man.

Works of fiction are a gold-mine for therapists, as they often describe characters whose behaviour and personalities resemble the psychopathology of clinical cases. Before the invention of psycho-analysis, fictional narratives provided glimpses and interpretations of the unconscious processes in the inner world and of the complexity of emotional conflict, object relations, and individual psychopathology. The life stories of fictitious heroes and villains can help their readers recognize something of themselves in these others, and they demonstrate universal truths about complex psychological structures. Shakespeare, Tolstoy, Balzac, Proust, and many others have peopled their works with protagonists and minor characters who could be diagnosed as suffering from conditions definable as manic-depressive, perverse, narcissistic, self-destruc-tive, or borderline, the likes of whom turn up daily in the consulting room. As it is getting increasingly difficult to publish case histories because of the need for confidentiality, the choice of fictitious char-acters can be a convenient way of presenting clinical narratives and to demonstrate therapeutic points.

To this end, I shall use a short story by the American writer Herman Melville, *Bartleby the Scrivener*, written in 1855, which has long fascinated me because of the tragic fate of its strange and haunting hero, who reminded me of some of my most difficult and perverse patients. The story's first-person narrator says of its eponymous hero that "it was his soul that suffered, and his soul I could not reach". He goes on to say that after knowing him for some time he became persuaded that Bartleby was "the victim of innate and incurable disorder" (p. 18). This is reminiscent of the therapist's situation with a patient, when the diagnosis is of some severe disor-der, the cause of which could be constitutional, developmental, or environmental, and which would require thorough initial investiga-tion in order to find the therapeutics that would promise results. Most probably, Bartleby would be classified as a difficult patient if he presented for help (which is, of course, unlikely); he would proba-bly be considered autistic and untreatable at assessment and be offered supportive work to determine whether he was suitable for some more probing treatment.

Melville's narrative is an attempt at understanding what ails this man, what motivates his mysterious behaviour, and what drives him so inexorably to the tragic end that the narrator attempts in vain to prevent. There is no attempt at explanation beyond the vivid descrip-tion of his strange behaviour that arrests and casts a melancholic spell on narrator and reader, only the fact that Bartleby works in a solitary and exploitative occupation, a law office in Manhattan's Wall Street. Copying documents day in day out requires an obsessional personality, as the task is to check and countercheck manuscripts pedantically for possible errors. This repetitiveness is presented as soul-destroying, as it requires meticulous attention to the fine grain of the writing rather than imagination and creativity. The story has usually been read as critical of a society that cast the individual into the role of a mechanical wage slave and hence destroyed his humanity. This is certainly true, but what is an individual's humanity if not his psychic functioning, which is easily damaged in childhood and can suffer irreparable breakdown, in particular of the ability to form and sustain relationships?

The main characters in Herman Melville's magnificent works of fiction are often paired as protagonists in a way that there is a narrator/observer and a mysterious, hard to read Other: Captain Ahab (in *Moby Dick*), sea-captain "Benito Cereno" in the eponymous story, scrivener (in *Bartleby*), to mention only three works that to me are particularly riveting. Not unlike therapy, Melville's narratives are about two-person relationships in which dependence, fascination, resistance, and the effort to understand operate. Two of these narratives end tragically for the main character, still shrouded in mysteries, only partly understood and unredeemed. The third has a dramatic reversal that turns the narrator's view of the protagonist upside down. Melville invariably describes eccentric behaviour verging on or leading to madness. His characters are elusive and enigmatic, more or less resistant, warped or perverse, driven and secretive. Ultimately, they remain incomprehensible. As a result of their dangerous occupations among brutalized people, they are all involved in complex struggles and plots not entirely of their own making, and the narratives can be read as savage social criticism. As Melville's own life story was full of tragic events and setbacks, his fictitious characters can be interpreted as the unconscious heroes of the theatre of his mind.

Moby Dick is Melville's most famous tale, and it has been analysed and interpreted in many different ways as an obsession, a mythical quest for revenge, or a potent metaphor for the monomaniac's life struggle. I was drawn to *Bartleby*, in particular, because the story's hapless hero strikes me as someone in the grip of a developing and incurable pathological condition, which is crying out to be diagnosed and treated. The first-person narrator, who is his employer, encounters a persistent and defiant resistance that will not yield to empathy, to force, or to understanding. Offers of help, of kindness and persuasion, even bribes, are rejected, and like many a therapist the narrator/employer is defeated in the end, having to fall back on an explanation that is plausible, yet not conclusive and impossible to prove. In therapeutic language, one could say that Bartleby regresses to the level of his basic fault, which Balint has described as "feelings of emptiness, deadness, and lack of pugnaciousness" (1968), tracing it back to "a considerable deficiency in the early formative years between bio-psychological needs and the psychological care, attention and affection available during the relevant times". As the story does not tell us anything about Bartleby's formative years, there is only Bartleby's symptomatology to observe, which is surprisingly similar to that mentioned by Balint. And there is, of course, the unsupportive environment in which he has to work.

The story's pace is relentless and hypnotic, and, as it gradually unfolds, the reader is getting hooked into it, compulsively becoming more and more mystified and involved. The narrator relates how he struggled to keep the upper hand in his uneven relationship with Bartleby, who is one of his three scriveners, and who does excellent copying work in his legal office, yet refuses bluntly to engage in any other kind of work by "mildly" saying: "I would prefer not to". Who could object to that?

The phrase "I would prefer not to" becomes the formulaic leitmotif of the struggle between boss and clerk, which the clerk wins by stubbornly refusing to reveal his reasons, where he lives, and who he is, thus becoming a kind of anti-hero, whose "interiority", (a concept coined by American literary critics to describe Melville's narrative method) remains inscrutably enigmatic. The master (like an unsympathetic parent) is deprived of his mastery, and while trying in vain to coax, persuade, and threaten his recalcitrant employee, he ends up feeling guilty, defeated and rather sorry, as the struggle finally leads to the scrivener's death.

To be more specific: Bartleby keeps insisting that he will only copy manuscripts, but not cooperate in any office team-work, as he would "prefer not to do this". At first he simply seems to demonstrate his right to insist on the letter of his contract, to go on strike by refusing all infringements of it by requests for favours like running errands, for being helpful in small ways, by socializing or conversing with the boss or with the two other clerks (who have developed two different forms of hysteria in line with the hypothesis of a pathogenic environment). As time goes on, Bartleby digs in his heels, becoming ever more resistant and more incomprehensible in respect of why he acts this way. It is an unequal power struggle in which he uses passive aggressive resistance to survive, most probably because he never had any parental "care, attention and affection", which is imperative for healthy psychological development.

It could be said that Melville here describes a rigid and highly defended narcissistic character, whose physical and emotional survival depends on having everything his way, on keeping firm boundaries between his self and others, on defending his private space and his true self from hostile incursions. It is highly symbolic that in the office he has his work place in the room of the boss, secluded by a screen that allows him a view out of the window on to the blank wall of a neighbouring building, while he cannot be seen by the boss or see the boss himself. When he is called into the boss's presence, he emerges reluctantly from his lair, sometimes only after repeated requests, avoiding all eye contact and restricting himself to the laconic verbal response "I would prefer not to". He does not budge, and, though provoking anger and aggressive threats, he remains inviolable. Because he does not cause offence and expects no answer other than a defeated shrug, he disarms the narrator. Apparently, he has no fear, no need for companionship. Nobody knows where he lives, what he eats, where he has come from. He seems well beyond any hope of recovery or redemption.

Gradually Bartleby becomes a menacing fixture in the office. One Sunday morning, the boss finds him there, mysteriously locked in and unforthcoming as to why he is there. Then he stops working, as his eyesight fails, and declares, "I have given up copying". A catastrophe is looming, things are getting out of control. He has become a burden for his boss, who still feels sorry for him, but quite uneasy and at a loss as to what to do, graphically describing Bartleby: "He seemed alone, absolutely alone in the universe. A bit of wreck in the mid-Atlantic". Eventually, the narrator decides to make him leave the office by telling him this in the kindest possible way. "But he answered not a word; like the last column of some ruined temple, he remained standing mute and solitary in the middle of the otherwise deserted room." The narrator describes that "wondrous ascendancy which the inscrutable scrivener had over me", now struggling with "nervous resentment" and an incipient murderousness from which he is only saved by remembering the Christian injunction of loving thy neighbour (p. 24). He finally gathers his resolve "to rid himself from this intolerable incubus", and decides to change his chambers. Yet the incubus cannot be shaken off or made to give way. Bartleby "refuses to budge" and eventually he has to be forcibly removed from the empty premises. The parallel with the therapeutic environment ends here, where many a difficult patient has left uncured or has had to be terminated as untreatable.

Melville's description of the inexorable downward course taken by the story's events is laconic and breathtaking in its speed, ending with Bartleby in prison as he continually refuses to take up offers of help from the narrator, who finally abandons him to his fate. Bartleby's defiant narcissism takes a turn into mutism and logically leads to a hunger strike. Like an anorexic patient, he clings to total resistance in the last act of his particular autistic drama and is eventually found dead, in a moving scene, where the narrator compares the Egyptian masonry of his prison cell to the heart of the eternal pyramids, using a metaphor with which the story assumes a mythical dimension. "Strangely huddled at the base of the wall, his knees drawn up and lying on his side, his head touching the cold stone, I saw the wasted Bartleby. But nothing stirred. Something prompted me to touch him. I felt his hand, when a tingling shiver ran up my arm and down my spine to my feet. 'Eh! He's asleep, ain't he?' asks the grub-man. With kings and counselors, murmured I" (p. 33).

What follows is a postscript in which the narrator tells "a little item of rumour which came to my ear after the scrivener's decease". Apparently, Bartleby had previously been a clerk in the Dead Letter Office at Washington, and the writer muses: "Dead letters, does it not sound like dead men? Conceive a man by nature and misfortune prone to a pallid hopelessness, can any business seem to be more fitted to heighten it than that of continually handling these dead letters and assorting them for the flames? On errands of life these letters speed to death. Oh, Bartleby, Oh humanity" (p. 34).

Was Bartleby chronically depressed, condemned by his perverse condition to passive suffering and a protracted suicide? Dominated by the death wish he "preferred to" die defiantly rather than take the friendly hand offered him by his employer. Because of their social inequality, resistance was the only way he could preserve his humanity in the American labour system in which the worker was no more than part of a cold mechanism. He had become, in therapeutic terms, the victim of an environment in which the vulnerable individual is reduced to narcissistic withdrawal and an unremitting repetition compulsion.

In a society that, in Marxist terms, was exploitative of its labour, the employer of Bartleby was unable to look after his employee, as he was himself also part of the market economy's "disciplinary" regime, which allowed the worker no sense of agency except for the passive resistance, which Melville describes so vividly in this story. At around the same time, Karl Marx conceptualized what he called the alienation of the worker in the capitalist economy. And the nearest literary equivalent to *Bartleby* I can think of are Kafka's stories in the twentieth century, in particular *The Trial*, whose protagonist K dies like a dog in a corner. The social context Kafka writes about is different, but equally inhuman: fascism, labour camps, racial hatred, genocide.

I find Michael Eigen's concept of the "psychotic core" (1993) useful to make Melville's enigmatic narrative meaningful therapeutically as a metaphor for the psychic suffering of two of the most difficult and unresponsive patients I have worked with, both of whom I would consider borderline cases. With them I was up against a similarly defiant resistance, which resembled Bartleby's insistent refusal to be helped, and I struggled for years to understand how they functioned psychically. I was helped by what Greenson (1967) writes about "the threat to the psyche of the Other we need so much when an ego-hostile superego puts itself on the defensive" which he calls "oppressive intimacy, a shared physical and mental state that constitutes a threat to the self". The "ego-hostile superego" is another word for a for an obstructive interpsychic part which contributes to the fierceness of the conflict that obstinately defies analysis.

Defiant resistance modified

For years I worked with a paedophile who appeared never to have had any good enough parenting, having been sadistically bullied by an older sister, ignored by his mother, tyrannized by his religious zealot of a father and having retreated from all this into an omnipotent world of his own, devoid of relationships and intimacy. As a child he played solitary games, roaming the countryside and constructing an elaborate traffic system in the family garden. Later on he learnt to play the piano, was awarded an organ scholarship, and mastered this acoustically most powerful instrument sufficiently to gain employment as an organist. But he remained isolated when he realized that he was sexually attracted to young boys, and after secretly abusing some street children he had a severe emotional breakdown from which he eventually recovered. He remained a recluse, with fantasies of writing a novel, dreaming of a spirituality project, and eventually finding work with the homeless, which enabled him to construct ingenious projects for rescuing lost souls like himself.

I came on the scene when, years later, he was visited by nightmares of being found out and when fears that he might be convicted for his past as a child molester made him seek counselling—not, as he later admitted, because he wanted to share himself with someone, but because he believed this would mitigate his offence in the eyes of the law. For years he came once a week to tell me selected bits of his life story, candidly admitting to having had sex with under-age boys, which he described as "out of order", gradually unfolding the bleak landscape of an inner world that was totally devoid of good internal objects. His nocturnal dreams were of aimless wanderings in empty houses, and he declared in a matter-of-fact way that he found other people boring. Towards me he was politely withdrawn, talking about himself like an object rather than inhabiting himself, and it took years to link up his narcissistic childhood with his present loneliness in a large ramshackle house filled with lodgers who remained strangers passing him on the stairs. Their rents paid his bills. He socialized with the frogs in his garden pond. Like Bartleby, he preferred anonymity to intimacy and kept himself to himself.

One day, however, he discovered a group of equally lonely gay men, and found that in the group he could share something of himself, though not the fears about his past, which he had allowed only me to know. Inevitably, as he had anticipated, he was one day denounced by one of the boys from his past and the police visited him at dawn, confiscated his computer, and charged him with child abuse. He failed in the suicide attempt that he had told me long ago he intended to commit in such an event. And, as happens with many a survivor from botched suicide attempts, this decided him to embrace life again, to confront the charge the police had brought against him, to face the trial, go to prison for six months, and eventually to re-emerge in my consulting room for more counselling.

All this seemed to confirm David Malan's theory of the "Cord of Life", which "comes into action when the patient is close to death and proves that suicide attempts can have a cathartic effect which results in the suicidal impulse becoming greatly weakened or reduced to zero" (Malan, 1997, p. 175). He was spared the tragic fate of Bartleby, perhaps because we had had a tenuous working alliance and he could return to me. My part in all this was difficult to establish, though I felt reassured when he resumed his therapy soon after the dramatic events, showing some relief and gratitude when I agreed to stand by him, though I was never asked for a report to the court. There was, however, a distinct change in the transference from the previous aloofness that I had identified as a consequence of his "dead mother" trauma (using André Green's concept, 1983) to an acknowledgment of tenuous trust and a genuine need of me. From then on he felt more alive, showing a new range of emotions and object-seeking behaviour.

Together we had turned a corner, and his life took off into joining encounter groups, earning his living by music-teaching, and making genuine friendships. Still in many ways a loner, he said goodbye to me a year later and I felt we had done a reasonable job together, though his "psychotic core" was still there, preventing him from relating fully to anyone.

Survival

Bartleby reminds me of another patient whom I also saw for years, and whom I have always compared to Sisyphus, as every session with him began with a burdensome climb up a mountain of abuse, attack, denigration, and sadistic invective, which I had to survive before the atmosphere turned and he was able to describe agonizing emotional pain, collapsing into impotent tearfulness and revealing his psychotic core, a deep emotional wound hiding behind the aggressive defence. Once this regression to a primitive state of help-lessness had been allowed to happen, there was a manful gathering together of facial features and a determined tightening of posture, followed by a sense of grateful relief.

This sequence of events was repeated every week, and every time it felt like a new variation of the same theme. I knew I was needed as a witness, first as a target during the beginning of the session and then as a containing presence during the second part, while the coda felt like a careful preparation for the necessary return to the outside world.

I refrained from interpreting the repeated scenario, though I knew it was a perverse repetition compulsion, enacted in order to remem-ber and to work through something traumatic that had happened in his past. The patient supplied his own interpretation of what was going on and what he needed to come for, more than once telling me the story of a sexual encounter with a friend's wife in which, to his dismay, he had found himself impotent at the moment of attempting to have intercourse. But soon after having suffered this shameful experience his sexual prowess returned, and he was able to perform to an ecstatic orgasm that triumphantly confirmed his masculinity. He compared his weekly session with me to a visit to a prostitute, and when he paid me it was like paying the prostitute her fee, which I felt as an intended humiliation as well as a confirmation of my useful-ness. He taught me much about sado-masochism, shame, perversion, and the dynamics of potency, and the myth of Sisyphus became an image of the wounded narcissist's life struggle.

My countertransference went through various phases, of hate when abused, of pity and sympathy when he cried, of a sense of achievement and closure when we reached the end of the session together. Over the years, these Sisyphean efforts added up to a slowly progressing therapeutic journey in which many things were explored and interpreted—early experiences with a depressed mother who was regularly abandoned by a seafaring husband, a recurrent dream of flying upwards and away from the earth, a persistent stammer that sabotaged his ambition to make a career in the Navy, and the unsatisfactory marriage to a doctor from whom he kept his neediness and vulnerability, while he was deeply fond of his two daughters.

In the end we terminated when the wife retired from her work and he could no longer visit me, as he had never told her about me. One important facet of the outcome for the patient was that he had learnt to trust a woman within the container of the analytic hour, and it was symptomatic that on parting he gave me a long hug, as if to indicate this. I still do not know whether to count this case as a success, because it always remained secret. I have, however, written it up (1996) as an example of a "Truby King baby", which he had called himself in our initial interview, because his mother had followed the New Zealand psychiatrist's rigid child-rearing system. But that is another story.

Apart from *Bartleby*, Herman Melville's *Billy Budd*, his last, unfinished, narrative work, resonated with this case for me. This is the moving story of "Handsome Sailor Billy Budd", who comes to grief for his mutinous behaviour, and who suffers from a stammer like my patient. At the moment when he is called to defend himself, "his vocal impediment", also called an "emotional difficulty of utterance", paralyses him and, "unable to defend himself verbally, Billy strikes out violently against his provoker", Claggart, killing him "in an expression of explosive rage". At the trial he declares "could I have used my tongue I would not have struck him", and when he is executed, his last words are "God bless Captain Vere", in a gesture of naval obedience.

Melville called this story an "Inside Narrative". Nothing is known of what Billy feels and thinks. Melville implies that individual agency is at the inside core of the personality and maintains, like Rousseau 200 years before him, that "unobstructed free agency" is something good and true, but impossible to actualize in a society where military discipline and social rules demand the individual's total obedience. I wonder whether one would now consider the characters of Billy Budd and of Bartleby as anti-heroes, or as patients with an encapsulated "psychotic core" to which they regress in times of "nameless dread".

My patient was subjected from birth to the four-hourly rule of feeding, part of the early-twentieth century method of child-rearing introduced by Truby King that is now notorious for the inhumanly strict feeding regime of babies. He was convinced that his stutter, like Billy's, was an expression of the strong emotions resulting from this discipline, of a constant struggle between acquiescence and revolt, which made him feel paralysed and tongue-tied in the face of parental authority. The repetitive sequence of explosive rage, helpless impotence, and orgiastic triumph that was enacted in our sessions cast me into the role of witness and seemed a re-enactment of this early traumatization and defiance, comparable to the repetitive labour of Sisyphus imposed as a punishment for insubordination to the Greek God Zeus.

We tried to move from repetitive re-enactment to remembering, working through, and integrating, with some success, but it was very late in my patient's life. For decades he had been like a fortress, as he graphically described it, protected by his rigid defences, but also imprisoned in them and impenetrable. He was unable to leave his fortress, but he let me in and felt less lonely inside it.

Resistance defined

On the surface, Melville and Freud may seem to be uneasy bedfellows, but they both believed in and described the action of powerful unconscious forces in the psyche. Rereading Melville's stories, I have come to understand that many of their extraordinarily vivid characters use defiant resistance as a protective shield in the service of a fragile self (Mollon, 1993), as a survival mechanism in a hostile society, as do so many narcissistically wounded individuals in our often equally hostile society. Plants in desert environments grow quills and are thick-skinned!

The lesson about resistance to be learnt from these three stories is that a defensive stance has to be seen as vitally important for the narcissistically wounded individual who feels under threat, and that it should under no circumstances be broken down, belittled, or ridiculed.

> The patient's weak self structure is always proportional to the strength of resistance and an individual's ego fragility is due to unreliable holding, which produces unbearable fears of disintegration. Persistent resistance thus amounts to resisting the very experience that is longed for, not allowing any potency or penetration on the part of the therapist. It is a stance of remaining intact, upright and together instead of opting for compliance, intercourse or longed-for homeostasis. [Lambert, 1981]

The defiance of parental authority is the result of a fear of being devoured, of a fear of intimacy and dependence, and it makes resistance an expression of the individual personality, protecting the true self from impingement, and upholding the integrity of the fragile self. [Mollon, 1993]

Bartleby preferred to die rather than yielding an inch; my two patients held out firmly against my becoming threatening and impinging in order to maintain their autonomy and survive.

CHAPTER FOURTEEN

The burden of being German

One thing is certain: we cannot choose our parents, nor can we choose the country we are born in. In my case of the parents being German and the country being Germany, this means having to come to terms with a past and a history which includes the Nazis, the Holocaust, and two terrible wars, in both of which Germany was defeated and of which the second was started by Hitler. Sixty years later, and after much struggling with my German identity, I feel more at ease with myself than I was when I first came to England in the 1960s and encountered strong anti-German feelings, which I naïvely was not prepared for and had to understand as a widespread reaction to having been bombed, having lost fathers and sons, and having had to make many sacrifices to win the war.

I have tried to live with my German-ness as an ongoing burden and to develop an attitude of admitting a share of collective responsibility by making reparations whenever I come up against the subject of my ancestry. My middle-class liberal parents were against the Nazis; I was too young myself to be responsible for what the Nazis did, but old enough to have consciously experienced the horrors of the war and the bewildering post war years of insufficient de-Nazification. I consider myself a second-generation German, who has had to live with the terrible fact of the Holocaust perpetrated in our name and often had to take the blame for the atrocities and crimes my fellow-countrymen of the previous generation committed. It is a case of "The sins of the fathers are visited upon the children and the children of the children", as the Bible said. Whatever may be the truth of this curse based on a retaliatory philosophy, it is more likely that there was much unconscious intergenerational transmission of hateful and guilty feelings from parents to children, and the only way of going forward was by confronting the past without remaining stuck in self-pity and with a bad conscience. I feel ashamed, but not guilty, and am still ambivalent about Germany because I cannot be proud of its recent history.

Some time during the bombing of my home town, I inherited a library of English books from a burnt-out house, and this became a treasure from which I derived the knowledge that I could change my identity if I learnt the language. I learnt English very gradually, at school to start with, then by reading voraciously, by attending an interpreters' course, by working for the American military government and for the American army, by reading English literature, and finally by marrying an Englishman in Berlin, who took me away to England where I have lived ever since. How much of this was an unconscious or a deliberate effort to get away from Germany and from my German-ness is difficult to say. I have sometimes been accused of trying to escape from, rather than accepting, my German origins, and with this accepting the burden of belonging to a nation of perpetrators and willing helpers. Did I adopt the role of the bystander, like my parents during the Nazi years, rather than actively resisting the regime, choosing a form of "internal emigration" that many German writers used as an excuse after the war? No, definitely not.

In fact, I became more conscious of being German when I first set foot on English soil, because my German accent and my German ways were unmistakable and, rather than allowing me to escape, this made me conspicuous, and I was unable to deny where I came from. Having an English husband did not help, and the company he kept at his job at the weekly journal *New Statesman* made matters worse for me. His friends and colleagues were mostly from the radical Left, many of them Communist fellow-travellers, and all of them notoriously anti-German. Among them, however, were some German-Jewish refugees, like the cartoonist Vicky. I had met some already while working for an American radio station in Berlin in the 1950s, and I soon discovered that I had more in common with them than with the English themselves. This helped me reclaim my shaken sense of German identity, as I felt accepted by the very people who had suffered most from Nazi persecution because I was sharing their culture, their language, and came from the same country, though for different reasons.

This, in fact, made me confront the issue of being German much earlier than I could have done had I stayed in 1950s and 1960s Germany, where the emphasis on reconstruction led to a general silence about the recent past and an inability to mourn (Mitscherlich & Mitscherlich, 1967). In England I met with feelings of dislike and strong hatred of Germany and had to accept their validity, while not allowing myself to hide, and in the end I came out of it all in one piece and stronger, though chastened and shaken and always feeling ashamed for what my country has done to others. I learnt to understand the distinction between shame (for what had been done in my name) and guilt (for what I had done myself), and apologized for the crimes committed by my fellow countrymen, while not accepting the blame, as I had not done anything blameworthy myself. Since then I have understood the full magnitude of German crimes, and have gradually learnt to live with who I was and have become, never denying or trying to shed my German-ness. This now goes hand in hand with feeling European and also English in certain ways of behaviour, thinking, and understanding. Identity is a multi-layered thing—it involves many lived and felt experiences that are added to one's original birth existence and that make up one's complex sense of self—ethnically, culturally, emotionally, and intellectually. I am glad that I have never denied that I am German, even though I was sometimes tempted to say I am Swiss, not to have to face the inevitable silence and embarrassment that has ruined many social situations for me. But I have recently become able to get angry when people make crude jokes in my presence about storm-troopers, German accents, or certain characteristics, like order, pedantry, efficiency, which are connected with "the Germans". What were painful memories immediately after the war have since turned into national stereotypes.

I have become more or less bilingual, but still have a trace of a German accent that some people notice and identify. I now feel more comfortable in English than in German, because I live in an English environment and have taught myself to write in English. My mother tongue comes back instantly when I am in a German context, but it lacks many words that I have since acquired in English and never known in German, and German has developed in my absence in many ways, so that I have not been able to keep up with it. For instance, in my second profession of psychotherapy I am not as fluent in German as in English, and I often find myself groping for words because my mind is switched into English. People often ask me which language I dream in, and I cannot answer this question, as my dreaming self is not usually a verbal self, but a visual self, on the whole.

This does not mean that I feel split, except when I am in Germany and people attack the English, or when I encounter English attitudes that I consider unjustifiably anti-German. Inevitably, I now suffer from divided loyalties, as I identify with the country where I live, have become assimilated, and am grateful to for having become accepted. After some nostalgia earlier on, which I had not been prepared for, I built myself a new life, shaped a new self, and never felt like an exile, as I kept in touch with my family and visited Germany often. There are some things I miss, though, and occasionally I catch myself out feeling somewhat alienated; for instance, by the class system, which has become less dominating than when I first came and felt excluded from it. Or by the English suburban townscapes of identical red-brick terrace houses, the eccentric architecture of which offends me aesthetically. I regret not having been brought up on English nursery rhymes and children's books, though I caught up with these when I brought up my son and read them to my grandchildren now. But I still feel uncomfortable with the English weather and particularly with the greyness of winter and the lateness of spring. What you gain on the swings you lose on the roundabouts. In other words, I no longer idealize England, and sometimes I acutely miss my childhood home and the landscapes I grew up with. But these have changed, and many things are no more than memories.

This is a state of mild ambivalence, of regret and longing intermingled, and there is a new danger that I identified for myself sharply at a recent conference as a sense of belonging nowhere, of living in no-man's-land. It made me think of a poem by Bertolt

Brecht, in which he asks himself, while sitting on the roadside waiting for his car to be repaired:

> I do not like where I am coming from
> I do not like where I am going
> Why am I so impatient?

This feeling of not being settled is experienced by many asylum seekers and refugees, who feel deracinated once the idealization of their new country has faded away and they have become disillusioned. There is no place like home, but what is home? The theme of a group relations conference I recently attended was "Shaping the future by confronting the past", and the participants were Jews, Germans, and affected Others. In my small group a German woman was talking about what she called her *"unstillbare Sehnsucht"* (unsatisfiable longing) for something, she knew not what, perhaps to do with her rejecting Nazi mother. This expression became a powerful theme: longing for some other who makes one feel special, longing for release from the endless struggle of living, longing to be at peace with oneself and accepting where and who one is. People were asking themselves what troubled them and what was problematic about their identities. The Germans were saying that when they are away from home they feel vulnerable and uncomfortable with the recent past and with the unforgivable sins of their fathers, which they still carry, resent, and want to shake off. They were attacking each other in their German group and many of them expressed a wish to join the Jewish group in order not to feel the pain of being German. Were they also longing to be allowed to be individuals, pure and simple, or did they say "enough is enough", stop treating us all as perpetrators and let us go forward together into a different, easier future? Otherwise, the implication was, we all have to commit suicide and wipe out our country. But that would be regressive and an admission of defeat, instead of struggling for a new togetherness in which the violent patterns of the past can be resolved and new ways of relating to each other are constructed.

In a recent book with the title *Easier Fatherland*, the English author concludes:

> One thing is clear, Germany is not about to relapse into the past. History will not repeat itself, as tragedy or as farce. Instead, the

country can perhaps begin to move into a normal, dull future at last.
[Crawshaw, 2004, p. 220]

In other words, we must create a way of living together that is civilized and democratic and no longer hampered by unfinished business from the past. The first attempt for Germany to shed the burden was by creating and joining Europe. There was another attempt, after the Communist state of East Germany collapsed, and the two halves of Germany were politically reunited, to understand and address the enormous problems of difference, recrimination, and envy. There was also the ordinary struggle of economic survival, political stability, and cooperation with others, but there are still two kinds of Germans, East Germans and West Germans, and it will probably take another generation to resolve this uneasy split.

It seems there are many other peoples in the world who now have to create viable identities, to come to terms with their pasts and build stable communities. Perhaps the German task is to assist others in these attempts and thereby demonstrate that they have learnt from experience rather than repeating past mistakes by erecting defences against these.

The lesson I learnt from the conference was that the ongoing process of German introspection is unconstructive and sterile, and as long as the Germans are still suspected of not having sufficiently confronted their past this will not stop. For instance, painful Holocaust memories and powerful revenge-feelings of survivors and second-generation Jews remain understandably active and have to be respected by ongoing generations of Germans as their historical responsibility, but this means thinking of ways to make amends and reparations and does not justify continuing self-hatred. Another lesson I learnt was that I was fortunate in my ability to forge genuine friendships with Jews which have amounted to reconciliation and reparation. Being called an "honorary Jew" by one particular friend of forty years' standing with whom I have shared a love of books and of Berlin has enabled me to feel valued as a German rather than wishing to give up that identity. I know that the doctor who assisted at my birth was Jewish, and I mourn her as someone who died in Theresienstadt. A strong affinity to Jews is thus an important and insoluble part of my German life history. Hence my great interest in Freud.

The German-Jewish poet Heinrich Heine wrote in one of his poems:

> Denk ich an Deutschland in der Nacht,
> bin ich um meinen Schlaf gebracht.
>
> (Thinking of Germany in the night,
> I cannot find my sleep)

This was in the nineteenth century, long before the Nazis and the Holocaust, which has legitimately been called the worst pogrom in Jewish history. It led to Zionism and to the establishment of Israel as a homeland for Jews from all over the world. But it also created a new problem—the struggle with the Palestinians who were living there and are demanding their right to the land that Jewish settlers considered theirs to take. There seems no end to a process that began when the Jews were driven out of their homeland 2000 years ago, and were forced to live in the diaspora, where they were never made to feel entirely secure. Establishing an apparently secure base in Israel, they have not yet managed to establish their right to it, because they are not yet allowed and able to share it peacefully with others.

Heine was talking with concern about the politically ambitious Germany of his time, which was competing for a role in the world alongside England and France, criticizing the Germans as a race of Philistines who liked to make speeches about freedom, but secretly enjoyed their chains.

> There was as little doubt about his Germanness as there was about his Jewish origins, but he was a satirist who was leading his German readers into sentimental moods and then, when their defences were down, confronted them brutally with reality. [Craig, 1983]

He seemed to have had an uncanny foreboding of what was to come, knowing the volatile and aggressive features of the German personality. Now the catastrophe has happened, yet there is still a fear that it might happen again, just as some people who have had a breakdown in the past are afraid that they might be heading for another one, until they realize that this is not inevitable and that they can do something to prevent it (Winnicott, 1971).

210 DIVERSITY, DISCIPLINE, AND DEVOTION IN PSYCHOTHERAPY

These kinds of regressive fears have haunted Jews and Germans since the Holocaust, in spite of the knowledge that history does not repeat itself unless the same conditions arise again. Can Germany be trusted, or is there an uncanny comparison with Cain, who fled after he had murdered his brother Abel, whom God had favoured? There have been serious comments about German self-hatred as if it were indeed a Cain syndrome, a symptom of collective abnormality, which has foiled all attempts at redemption until it is fully understood or changed into ordinary self-belief and erased once and for all from the German psyche. A group of Germans at the conference I mentioned discussed the subject of "Open and hidden hostilities", and in the course of it the group almost tore itself to pieces until they reframed the theme to "Does the German idealization of the Jews lead to their own self-denigration?" The century-old symbiosis and sibling rivalry of Germans and Jews could not have been more poignantly acted out.

Another burning subject is the difficulty with German victimhood. The German writer W. G. Sebald, who was born at the end of the war and lived most of his adult life in England as an academic teaching German literature, raised this subject in 2000 in his book *Luftkrieg und Literatur*, whose English title is sharpened and generalized into *The Natural History of Destruction* (2003). Describing in poignant detail the bombing of German cities, particularly the apocalyptic fire storm of Hamburg in the last year of the war, Sebald, who had thought as a child that "all cities are ruins", asked himself why so few German writers had given the subject compassionate expression. Raising his voice fifty years after the events, he demonstrated the force of intergenerational transmission which has enabled the next generation to speak, where their traumatized parents had remained silent and unable to find adequate words for what they had suffered. Since then, first-generation Germans have been able to think of themselves as victims, too, and though there remains a well-established hierarchy of suffering headed by the Holocaust victims, the "secondary" victimhood suffered by the German population in the final stages of the war has become a subject for writers like A. Beevor in *Berlin—The Downfall*, and Joerg Friedrich in *Der Brand*, which revived old memories and started a process of retrospective mourning for the millions of German victims who lost their lives in 1944 and 1945, when the Allies and the Russians wreaked vengeance on their

defeated enemy. At important anniversaries dead fathers and brothers are now quietly commemorated, the next generation have found
words to describe their difficult war-time childhoods, and others
have remembered their post war sufferings in ruined townscapes and
makeshift homes with little food and inadequate heating.

This collective remembrance is different from what happened
immediately after the war, when people talked of their sufferings as
if they were innocent victims, like those who had been murdered and
killed by the Nazis (for instance the Austrians, who considered
themselves Hitler's first victims, a wording which has since been
withdrawn). Now at last there can be space for all the dead, German
and Others, as long as the responsibility for what happened is
owned collectively by the Germans, which has been a process from
guilt to shame, and to the recognition of responsibility for what was
done in their name by their fathers. And even now, sixty years after
his death, Germans who are trying to find their identity by self-
exploration find "the shade of Adolf Hitler at every turning of the
way", as predicted by Horst Krueger in his memoir *The Shattered
House: A Youth in Germany*.

This also means that the Germans are gradually shedding the
mark of Cain and becoming ordinary members of a wider humanity.
This does not amount to forgetting or forgiving, but to a recognition
of the fact that the past remains active in the present, and needs
continually to be acknowledged in the present until it can make way
for the future. But what remains is mourning and memory, and the
commemoration of important anniversaries has been an important
feature of this continuing process. There will always be the paradox
that the country that has produced triumphs in science, literature,
philosophy, and art has also produced Hitler and the Holocaust. In
Gordon Craig's concluding words: "They are romantic and conservative, idealistic and practical, proud and insecure, ruthless and
good-natured. They are, in short, the Germans" (Craig, 1983).

German history has been difficult for many Germans to live with,
as it took so long to become a unified country after devastating religious wars and centuries of fragmentation into dozens of princely
states. Napoleon's victories over Prussia (and Austria) promoted
some of the principal rulers to kings, and the rise of Prussia under
Bismarck finally brought together all the warring factions. But this
led to the arrogant ambition to become an imperial state, to rival

France and England, and it produced the terrible world wars of the twentieth century, the rise of Nazism and its defeat. Germans have much to apologize in their turbulent history.

Finally, I want to quote Klaus von Dohnanyi, the son of one of the conspirators against Hitler who was executed. The occasion was the International Conference of Psychoanalysis in Hamburg in 1985, which was opened by him. He was looking squarely at the issue of owning the past:

> It seems we Germans remain a nation in danger, always fearful of being left behind, of being unloved, of not being appreciated sufficiently. It is probably not by accident that the great innovators Marx, Freud and Einstein all spoke German as their mother tongue. But then it is also no accident that they were all driven out of their country and regarded English as a language of liberation. Whoever says, our Bach and our Beethoven, must also say: our Hitler! [Frosh, 2005, p. 1]

CHAPTER FIFTEEN

The fear of death

"Who knows
If life is not death
and death life?"

Euripides

I well remember the moment in my childhood, when I first realized that I would die one day and would cease to exist, entering,
as Shakespeare's Hamlet says "the undiscovered country / from
whom no traveller returns". It was a sudden shock, an experience of
the unthinkable. Trying to imagine what it would be like my mind
boggled and I had to give up. Then I tried to think backwards in the
knowledge that there was a time when I did not yet exist. This was
equally unthinkable; but it eased the first anxious thought of my
certain death to argue that it would simply be a return to the state I
was in before I was born. It stilled my anxiety and helped me to get
over the shock, but it seemed a bit like self-deception and the knowledge that I would have to go one day always remained as an
uncomfortable certainty. Now that I have reached the biblical age

and am much closer to death, it has returned to trouble me and it seems timely to face it squarely.

In his "Devotions upon Emergent Occasions", the poet John Donne says, "it is the going out more than the coming in that concerns us" (1929, p. 539). As I discovered as a child, we do not remember the "coming in", the first stirrings of consciousness in the womb or the moment when we are born, but the conscious fear of "going out", the fear of death and dying increases with the passing of time and becomes alarming in serious sickness, as Donne described graphically in his "Sonnets" and "Divine Poems", and it is omnipresent in old age, when time is running out and the body is beginning to suffer all kinds of ailments.

Poets have tried to express the experience of time running out. For instance, Andrew Marvell, when he wrote: "but at my back I always hear / time's wingèd chariot hurrying near; and yonder all before us lie / Deserts of vast eternity" ("To his Coy Mistress"). This was deliberately shocking, a call for *carpe diem*, and not at all consolatory, as is the Christian notion of "rest in peace". It is as urgent and admonitory as Donne's famous passage "For whom the bell tolls", which emphasizes the ubiquitousness of death:

> No man is an island, entire of it self; every man is a piece of the continent, a part of the main; if a clod be washed away by the sea, Europe is the less, as well as if a Promontory were . . . Any man's death diminishes me, because I am involved in mankind, and there-fore never send to know for whom the bell tolls, it tolls for thee. (Donne, 1929, p. 538).

The universality of death could not be better described. There is no getting away from it—if it is not me, it is someone who is like me, condemned to die without reprieve, and there is no fudging of the issue by throwing in the bit about "everlasting rest". Ron Britton (in *Sex, Death and the Super-Ego*, 2004) pointed out that "rest" denotes a life activity, denying the emptiness and nothingness that we experi-ence when somebody close to us dies, which is often euphemistically described as "passing away". Where? "His soul is gone, whither?" asks Donne, and again, "who saw it come in and who saw it come out?" (*ibid.*, p.539). Hamlet also ponders the conundrum of eternal rest, when he asks himself "for in that sleep of death, what dreams may come / when we have shuffled off this mortal coil / must give us pause". Pause to think and feel, but what?

Most religions have resorted to some sort of belief in another life, whether in heaven with God or on earth through a reincarnation or a transmigration of souls, both of which would preserve the self/soul, while sloughing off the mortal coil of the body. Over the centuries many people have been enabled to die "in peace" with the help of these beliefs, managing to let go of the fear of death, as it would not be the end but perhaps a new beginning. But what about those who cannot believe what the religions teach? Hamlet's last words are "The rest is silence", and King Lear, cradling his dead daughter, cries "never, never, never, never" . . . expressing the finality of her death. It would be so much easier to believe something without knowing, than not knowing and simply "going out"!

Almost everybody has been bereaved of friends and family before they themselves die, and everybody knows that ultimately they cannot escape death. I often take comfort in the knowledge that others have been able to die before it comes to me, and then I think "If they can, surely I can, too. Perhaps they took it like an adventure or they experienced it as a surprise." Alas, one cannot ask them how they did it, and what they felt during the process of dying. Watching someone die can be a very difficult experience, as there is the painful struggle towards the end when the body gives up its live functions in agony and confusion. In previous times Christians saw this struggle as the mental suffering of the sinful, and much sacred music has been written about this coming to terms with one's sinfulness and the hoped-for salvation through the grace of God. In J. S. Bach's cantata "Ich habe genug", there is this sense of a giving up, of resigning oneself to the inevitable, as in Hamlet's "shuffling off this mortal coil". This mood of resignation rather than of fear and defiance at the point of death, this acceptance of "my time has come", is enshrined in the expressive and highly ornamental funeral music and particularly in the passions and requiem masses by Bach and his contemporaries, which celebrated the release of the body from the painful sufferings of earthly existence and represented a moving towards the spiritual (Yeardsley, 2002).

The *ars moriendi* of the Baroque period was a "project of purification" rather than stoicism, which Luther had disparaged as an "artificial virtue and a fabricated strength". It represented a conscious preparation and an "unsparing contemplation of death", in order to be able to die with dignity. This attitude, which reflects the stern spirit of Lutheran Protestantism, in which I was brought up, has also been criticized as a defensive fascination with death, a moral fatigue that contravenes the imperative towards life that should be lived to the full right until the end. However, it also reflects accurately what happens to people of biblical age in their "declining years", when the body grows weak and is assailed by numerous incapacitating age-related illnesses. There can be a longing for release mixed into the fear of extinction, an attitude of waiting and resignation that can turn into a saintly "so be it".

I remember being moved when reading some excerpts from the diary of Joseph Haydn, written in old age in a shaky hand-writing, where he described himself as weak and unable to go on composing. The occasion was an exhibition at Schloss Esterhazy in Hungary, where Haydn had spent most of his summers creating and making music, and the text spoke of a melancholic acceptance of the inevitable. Haydn was, of course, supported by his simple Christian belief. One of his last works was the beautiful chamber music piece "The Seven Last Words on the Cross", a fitting contribution to the *ars moriendi*, and his final statement before he fell silent after fifty years of vigorous composing.

Haydn's dignity in the face of death reminds me of the dignity that both C. G. Jung and Sigmund Freud attained in old age, when their bodies were failing and death was approaching. Jung, unlike Freud, believed in God, as his "Answer to Job" demonstrates, in his own, inimitable way of certitude. That made him say in his *Face to Face* interview, when asked by John Freeman whether he believed in God, "I do not take his existence on belief—I know that He exists" (Brome, 1978, p. 255). It was a statement seemingly rooted in personal experience, but perhaps also in his thinking on archetypes, with Jesus Christ being considered the archetype of the self. In his eighty-fifth year, Jung wrote in his reminiscences,

> while the man who dies in the belief that he will not survive after death marches towards nothingness, the one who placed his faith in the archetype follows the tracks of life and lives right on to his death. Both, to be sure, remain in uncertainty, but the one lives against his instincts, the other with them.

He also wrote: "The older I become, the less I have understood or had insight into or known about myself. And so I am disappointed and not disappointed. I cannot form any final judgment." Quoting Laotse, he said, "All are clear, I alone am clouded. And that's exactly as I feel. Once I was alienated from the world, now it is transferred to my inner world. I have a very surprising unfamiliarity with myself" (Hugo Charteris, interview, 1963).

This way of veering between certainty and uncertainty is characteristic of the mystic and it led Jung to further elaborate the answer he gave to Freeman, as he knew that it was "controversial, puzzling or even ambiguous", by saying "I do know that I am obviously confronted with a factor unknown to itself which I call God". Which is a shrewd way of leaving the matter open. When he died he was confused, as many old people are at the point of death, which makes the custom of giving deep meanings to the "last words" of famous people so dubious. Goethe ostensibly called for "more light", which lends itself to symbolic interpretation, when it might simply have been the request for more candles. And Jung, according to his carer Ruth Bailey, said "Let's have a really good red wine tonight". The interpretation might be that the wine is for the Last Supper or it could have been just what it said.

What we know of Freud's last words is connected with the instruction he had given to his personal doctor Max Schur at their first meeting: "Promise me, when the time comes, you won't let them torment me unnecessarily". He had survived another operation in 1938, was talking about "being overdue, with nothing to do but wait, wait", and wrote to a friend that "an illness that would cut off the cruel process would be very desirable", as "at my age every postponement has a painful connotation". People who visited him during his last weeks described him as "already far away", and when the time had indeed come, on 21 September 1939, he took Dr Schur's hand and reminded him of their contract: "Now it is nothing but torture and makes no sense". "Schur indicated that he had understood and, after consultation with Anna Freud, gave him a small dose of morphine, after which Freud lapsed into a coma from which he did not awake" (Gay, 1988, p. 651). Forty years earlier he had written to his friend Oscar Pfister, wondering what one would do one day "when thoughts fail or words do not come", and admitted that he could not suppress a tremor before this possibility. That is why with all the resignation before destiny that suits an honest man I have one wholly secret entreaty: only no invalidism, no paralysis of one's powers through bodily misery. Let us die in harness, as Macbeth says.

Schur helped Freud die with dignity by giving him morphine, when he indicated that he could no longer bear the pain.

The words "weakness", "struggle", and "peace" appear in all three cases describing the decline of the physical functions which lead to the "natural death" in old age, but also the anxieties, pain, and suffering experienced by the dying. What seems to have been a common mitigating factor in these three cases was the presence of carers, close friends and relatives, like Jung's companion Ruth Bailey, who was living with him after his wife's death, and Freud's daughter Anna, of whom he said, "Fate has been good to me that it has granted me the relationship to such a woman . . ." (Gay, 1988, p. 640). And there was also the sense of a benign regression, a resigned psychic withdrawal that ushered in the eventual letting go, the indescribable moment of death to which Shakespeare refers when Claudio talks of going "we know not where" in *Measure for Measure* (III: 116). Vincentio, the Duke of Venice, admonishes him sternly:

> Be absolute for death. Either death or life
> Will thereby be the sweeter. . . . Though hast nor youth nor life,
> But, as it were, an after-dinner sleep, dreaming on both.

This poetic metaphor has often been quoted, for instance by T. S. Eliot. But what of the harrowing fear of death that plagues young Claudio as he is condemned to an untimely death, and so afraid that he exclaims:

> 'tis too horrible!
> The weariest and most loathed worldly life,
> That age, penury and imprisonment
> Can lay on nature is a paradise
> To what we fear of death.

Many people say, it is not death they are afraid of, but the thought of "how to get there", i.e., the process of dying. A patient of mine, whose husband, a policeman, had been murdered, was very empathic about that because she had not been with him as he was bleeding to death. She was traumatized and, as she said, she "died with him". Not knowing how he died was troubling her for a long time and making her feel guilty, while the thought of death had no fears for her any more. So it was not the uncertainty of where we go or will be, but the certainty of how awful dying can be that made it difficult for her. To know that, as in his case one would be murdered, or that one would die of a long-drawn out degenerative or incurable illness, would surely be very difficult. How would we be able to bear the knowing? *Mors certa, hora incerta*! How much the Ancients knew about the fear of death! The crime of Aeschylus' Prometheus is that he asks Zeus to give the promise that human beings be allowed not to know the time of their death.

We all have a preferred mode of how we would like to die, perhaps in our sleep, or suddenly and painlessly of a heart attack. Once again, it is the not-knowing that is troubling, and it is in particular a depressive fear about the loss of the known self, of consciousness, and of what, if anything, would take its place. This fear is only absent in the person who is mortally afraid of life, like the suicidal depressive who has lost all hope, who imagines that death would be preferable to life, and that an action to stop living would be better than no action. But the suicidal person is not genuinely "absolute unto death", and when he "acts out", as suicide is described in analytic language, he often deceives himself with fantasies of release or of merging with the universe. "Humankind cannot take much reality", T. S. Eliot famously said. In other words, the human mind is by definition incapable of conceiving of its own extinction.

Even very old people are afraid of death, and the example of people with near-death experiences, who tell afterwards that they had seen a light, is instructive as a form of denial, as they are still alive then. I am reminded of the "jumpers", who leapt from the collapsing and burning buildings on 9/11, as if there was any hope of surviving when, in fact, much like suicide cases, they were "acting out" in mad desperation to do something rather than waiting passively to be engulfed by the flames. Any action must have seemed better to them than no action, but then it all turned into death.

Analysts come closest to describing this mortal fear, when they talk of the unconscious anxieties of annihilation and disintegration, from which Freud's controversial death instinct can be considered a regression, a wishful fantasy of peaceful non-being rather than self-destructiveness. This was also was my infantile solution to the fear of death. It amounts to a practice of denial: "I know I will die, but I do not believe it nor can I imagine it".

I cannot resist another quote from John Donne, this time in his pamphlet with the title "Biothanatos", where he writes about "the reasons, the purpose, the way and the end of the author":

> Whether it be that I had my first breeding and conversation with men of suppressed and afflicted religion, accustomed to the despite of death, and hungry of an imagined martyrdom . . . or that a faint cowardliness beget it, whensoever any affliction assails me, me thinks that I have the keys to my prison in mine own hand, and no remedy presents itself so soon to mine own heart as mine own sword. [1929, p. 420]

Donne here explains the suicidal mind in his inimitable way, and he prophetically anticipates the complex aetiology of the suicide bomber that baffles the contemporary politician. Nothing, apparently, concentrates the mind so much as the desire for an "imagined martyrdom" that promises paradise.

This brings me back to the beginning, to death as unthinkable unless there is an illusion that it is "a way out of the prison of the body or of the mind". The poetry of Philip Larkin was haunted all through by the fear of death and in one of his last poems "Aubade" (1977) he waxes eloquent like Shakespeare when he writes:

> the total emptiness for ever
> The sure extinction that we travel to
> And shall be lost in always. Not to be here
> Not to be anywhere,
> And soon; nothing more terrible, nothing more true.
>
> [in: *Collected Poems*, 1989]

It seems there are no consolations, there is only the waiting for one's time to come and for the traumatic, the inevitable catastrophe to happen. Philosophers have come up with enigmatic answers to the conundrum. Seneca said, "we learn how to die all throughout our life", and Epicurus, in a more oracular mode: "when we are present death is not and when death is present we are not . . ." These paradoxes are true, but not truly comforting, as they imply the extinction of the mind and of consciousness, which is the really frightening and mind-boggling fact for the individual human being. The French philosopher Montaigne thought constantly about death, about his own death, in terms of melancholia, with its manic-depressive bipolarity, which accounts for the melancholic's creativity but also puts it close to madness.

What did Freud and his followers have to say about the matter? In a recent book *Making Death Thinkable* (2004) the Italian analyst Franco de Masi declares that "it is possible to accept our own death as individuals by coming to terms with and integrating the legacy from the past and opening ourselves up to the possibility of investing and projecting onto other people's future lives" (from the book's blurb). This is another way of saying that we perpetuate ourselves in our children and grandchildren, or become immortal as writers, composers, and scientists by creating works of lasting value. It does not directly address the mortal fear, of which Shakespeare and Larkin speak so eloquently, but offers instead the Darwinian and the Socratic solutions, which replace the Christian definition of an afterlife by a biological definition of individual survival through "transgenerational transmission". In Kleinian terms, this might be seen as a form of "collective reparation". Klein did not share Freud's views on the absence of death in the unconscious, and stated that

> my analytic observations show that there is in the unconscious the fear of annihilation of life . . . since the struggle between the life and the death instincts persists throughout life, this source of anxiety is never eliminated and enters as a perpetual factor in all anxiety. Anxiety has its origins in the fear of death. [1948]

Thus, the capacity to face death is closely linked to the state of an individual's internal world:

> The inescapable fragmentation, loneliness and abandonment, which characterise the beginnings of our psychic functioning re-emerge cyclically in the course of our life. For this reason, the fear of death can be likened to the state of agony and chaos in the internal world. The more an individual's internal world is peopled by good objects, the more the thoughts of one's own death can arouse regret and sadness, but not fear of chaos, agony and nameless dread. [de Masi, 2004, p. 148]

The advice is ultimately to sharpen the ability to mourn, to prepare, and thus to consider death not as an unthinkable catastrophic event but as the natural conclusion of one's existence. There is thus "an alternative way of redemption, a consolation based on feeling part of humanity which goes on living".

Then the "internalization" of good objects, which is the result of the successful mourning envisaged first in Freud's "Mourning and Melancholia" (1917e), becomes the secure base of an integrated self. In other words, the achievement of a whole person, which is the goal of psychoanalysis and psychotherapy, will make it possible to look at death serenely (Searles, 1961): "The fear of one's death is in itself an immanent element of non-integration" or "Just as one can be a truly whole person only through facing the inevitability of death so too can one become able to live fully only if one lives in the light of this recognition" (*ibid.*, p. 361). In essence, this amounts to toler-ating the thought of the passage of time and the transience of human life. In another, more paradoxical vein, this is enshrined in the words of the existentialist philosopher Heidegger, from *Being and Time*, that "death is the most likely possibility of all our impos-sibilities".

Erik Erikson (1950) considered old age the life stage of "integrity versus despair", and later elaborated on this (1989), saying that

> integrity equals the gathering of life into a meaningful pattern. The major involvement is relationships with children and grandchil-dren. The life cycle curves back on the life of the individual, allowing a re-experiencing of earlier stages. It can be called a growth towards death. And individual life is the accidental coincidence of but one life cycle of one segment of history. The style of integrity by one culture thus becomes the "patrimony of the soul". Ego integrity implies an emotional integration which permits participation by followership as well as acceptance of leadership. The one and only life cycle will need to be accepted as the ultimate of life. Adaptation is vital at any stage. [p. 260].

And further: "Old age is a time of relinquishing, of interdependence rather than of independence. Growing old is an interesting adven-ture, full of surprises".

Thus, for Erikson, the fear of death is not a problem for the aged individual who has achieved ego integrity. While Kleinians would consider the fear to be a pathological psychotic fear, not compatible with integration and the depressive position, it was different for Freud, who stated that "the unconscious seems to contain nothing that could give any content to our concept of the annihilation of life", and "nothing resembling death can ever have been experienced. I am therefore inclined to the view that the fear of death, like the fear of conscience, should be regarded as analogous to the fear of castration", and that it probably covers other unconscious ideas (1926d). These explanations are analytic attempts at thinking about death similar to the rational statements of the Stoic philosophy, which confirmed that we can only think of death calmly as long as we are not unreasonably attached to living: "Seneca took the view that death is no evil and that therefore suicide is a rational act. Ultimately, the question for him was whether in living 'one is lengthening one's life or one's death'". The Buddha conceived of Nirvana, of nothingness, as the best solution to human suffering, and to the unbearable and often psychotic anxieties that human beings are likely to feel when they are facing the certainty of their extinction. Neither Freud's death instinct nor Klein's concept of the depressive position can offer the same consoling wisdom, as they operate within the consciousness of the living individual.

A comforting and convincing picture of death, akin to the Buddhist view, emerges from the reports of carers and priests who are present with the dying until their end and unanimously report that after the agonizing physical struggle there always is a moment of letting go, when all the bodily functions have ceased and the dying person, no longer able to speak or to breathe, becomes unreachable. This is the moment when the phrase "he/she has passed away peacefully" feels most appropriate as a metaphor. In the past, people stayed with their relatives in order to assist them through this transition, whether it was the priest taking confession, the wife wiping her husband's brow, or the lover holding the hand of his beloved. The dying need this help, in order to let go of the fear of death, and of the fear of loneliness. In essence, human beings are object-seeking. Apparently, people cannot die unless they are helped to settle any "unfinished business", any unresolved conflict they still have with someone, involving feelings of anger, guilt, and shame, and also any remaining secrets that need to be put into words, before they are finally able to let go of life.

I have come to the conclusion that what we fear most when we think of dying is unbearable pain and abandonment. The near-death experiences people have reported may be similar moments of feeling released from suffering either physically or psychically.

Too many old people nowadays die alone in hospital, attached to intravenous drips and oxygen masks (Aries, 1975). My prayer, therefore, is to not be left to die alone in a medical ward. Many of us now make a "living will", in which we ask to be allowed to die rather than have to continue suffering incurable illnesses of the aged mind or body. When we make this will, we face our death squarely, it is an act we make consciously, asking to be allowed to die with dignity. Like Freud and many other very old people, we do not want to be a burden or to go on living, having lost our mobility, our mind, our independence, all of which would feel undignified. Animals, after all, decide to die when they feel very sick.

Two examples here come to mind of people seeking an end to their own lives at this stage. They are the analysts Nina Coltart and Bruno Bettelheim in recent years, both of whom took their own lives in old age, when they had reached the point of no return. And there is, of course, the classical example of Socrates who believed as a philosopher that philosophy is the contemplation of the mystery of death and calmly took the cup of hemlock, surrounded by his friends and disciples, when he had been condemned to death for impiety and for having corrupted the young.

In our time and age there was the poet Sylvia Plath, who committed suicide in 1966 in a state of despair, having written that "Dying is an art, like everything else, I do it exceptionally well". This indicates that the thought of death must have been ever-present for her and perhaps a consolation, like John Keats's "Too much in love with easeful death". There are, of course, many ways of looking at this, and of facing or not facing death. For instance there can be angry resistance, as expressed in a poem by Dylan Thomas, another poet who burnt his candle at both ends, drowned his sorrows in drink, and died young. He admonished his aging father "Do not go gentle into that good night . . . / Rage, rage against the dying of the light". A little later, in 1978, R. D. Laing wrote a cycle of poems with the title *Life before Death*, which ends with a grand ironic flourish:

> To live our life's a great adventure: fit
> For any hero. Nothing else can be

> The meaning of our absurd mystery
> We'd like to think that there's some benefit
> Somewhere, to something, someone, to the All
> That we're such sacks of comic lust: or good
> For us that we are thus.
>   At least we are food
> Good for worms. However spirit fail, the call
> Of death's a reconciliation
> For our flesh, its contribution to the feast
> Which we partake of. Eater eaten, beast
> For beast. From dust to dust. No less, no more.
>
> We can be sure of death's utility
> Whatever we've accomplished of futility

In a secular age like ours, this may be small comfort, but it is a dark poetic prescription of how to face reality. It resembles Andrew Marvell's stark words to his coy mistress:

> Thy beauty shall no more be found
> Nor, in thy marble vault, shall sound
> My echoing song: then worms shall try
> That long preserv'd virginity:
> And your quaint honour will turn to dust;
> And into ashes all my lust.
> The grave's a fine and private place,
> But none I think do there embrace.

Finally, there are always the measured words of Ecclesiastes:

> To everything there is a season, and a time to every purpose under the heaven;
> A time to be born and a time to die; a time to plant and a time to pluck up that which is planted;
> All go unto one place; all are of the dust and all turn to dust again . . .
> Wherefore I perceive that there is nothing better, than that man should rejoice in his own works; for that is his portion; for who shall bring him to see what shall be after him?

REFERENCES

Alexander, F., & French, T. M. (1946). *Psychoanalytic Principles and Application.* New York: Ronald Press.

Ardagh, J. (1995). *Germany and the Germans. New Edition: The United Germany in the mid-1990s.* Harmondsworth: Penguin.

Aries, P. (1975). *The Hour of Our Death.* Oxford: Oxford University Press.

Baker Miller, J. (1976). *Toward a New Psychology of Women.* Harmondsworth: Penguin.

Balint, M. (1968). *The Basic Fault, Therapeutic Aspects of Regression.* London: Tavistock/Routledge.

Balint, M. (1972). *Focal Psychotherapy. An Example of Applied Psychoanalysis.* P. H. Ornstein & E. Balint (Eds.), London: Tavistock.

Barker, P. (1991). *Regeneration.* Harmondsworth: Penguin.

Barnett, R. (1992). Two or three sessions? *British Journal of Psychotherapy*, 8(4): 430–431.

Bateson, G. (1978). *Steps to an Ecology of the Mind.* London: Granada.

Benjamin, J. (1990). *The Bonds of Love: Psychoanalysis, Feminism, and the Problem of Domination.* London: Virago.

Bennett, A. (1998). *Talking Heads 2.* BBC.

Bennett, A. (2001). *The Laying on of Hands.* London: Profile Books.

Bettelheim, B. (1975). *The Uses of Enchantment.* London: Peregrine.

Bion, W. R. (1961). *Experiences in Groups.* London: Tavistock.

Bion, W. (1967). A theory of thinking. In: *Second Thoughts: Selected Papers on Psycho-Analysis*. London: Maresfield Library.

Bion, W. (1982). *The Long Week-End*. London: Karnac.

Birkett, D. (1992). Psychoanalysis and war. *British Journal of Psychotherapy, 8*(3): 300–306.

Bleger, J. (1967). Psychoanalysis of the *psychoanalytic* frame. *International Journal of Psycho-analysis, 48*: 511–519.

Bollas, C. (1986). The transformational object. In: G. Kohon (Ed.), *The British School of Psychoanalysis. The Independent Tradition*. London: Free Association.

Bollas, C. (1999). *The Mystery of Things*. London: Routledge.

Bollas, C. (2004). The structure of evil. In: *Cracking Up: The Work of Unconscious Experience* (pp. 121–130). New York: Hill & Wang.

Bonhoeffer, D. (1971). *Letters and Papers from Prison*. London: SCM Press.

Bowlby, J. (1965). *Child Care and the Growth of Love*. Harmondsworth: Penguin.

Bowlby, J. (1988). *A Secure Base. Clinical Applications of Attachment Theory*. London: Routledge.

Britton, R. (1992). The missing link: parental sexuality. In: R. Britton, M. Feldman, & E. O'Shaughnessy (Eds.), *The Oedipus Complex Today: Clinical Implications* (pp. 83–102). London: Karnac.

Britton, R. (2004). *Sex, Death and the Super-Ego*. London: Karnac.

Brome, V. (1978). *Jung, Man and Myth*. London: Macmillan.

Budd, S., & Sharma, U. (1994). *The Healing Bond, The Patient–Practitioner Relationship and Their Therapeutic Responsibility*. London: Routledge.

Casement, P. (1985). *On Learning from the Patient*. London: Tavistock.

Chasseguet-Smirgel, J. (Ed.) (1970). *Female Sexuality*. London: Virago.

Coleman, D. A. (1998). Reproduction and survival in an unknown world: what drives today's industrial populations and to what future? Nidi Hofstee Lecture Series 5, Amsterdam: Social Science Council.

Coles, P. (2002). *The Importance of Sibling Relationships*. London: Karnac.

Coltart, N. (1987). Suitability for psychoanalytic psychotherapy. *British Journal of Psychotherapy, 4*(2): 127–133.

Coltart, N. (1996). Endings. In: *The Baby and the Bathwater* (pp. 141–154). London: Karnac.

Corney, R. (1993). Studies in the effectiveness of counselling in general practice. In: R. Corney & R. Jenkins (Eds.), *Clinical Counselling in General Practice*. London: Routledge.

Corney, R. (1999). Evaluating clinical counselling in primary care and the future. In: J. Lees (Ed.), *Clinical Counselling in Primary Care*. London: Routledge.

Craig, G. (1983). *The Germans*. New York: Meridian.

Crashaw, S. (2004). *Easier Fatherland, Germany and the Twenty-first Century.* London: Continuum.

Cummings, N. A., & Samaya, M. (1995). *Focused Psychotherapy: A Casebook of Brief Intermittent Psychotherapy throughout the Life Cycle.* New York: Brunner/Mazel.

Davanloo, H. (1980). *Short-term Psychodynamic Psychotherapy.* New York: Jason Aronson.

de Masi, F. (2004). *Making Death Thinkable.* London: Free Association.

de Mause, L. (Ed.) (1974). *The History of Childhood.* London: Bellew.

de Mause, L. (1991). The universality of incest. *The Journal of Psychohistory, 19*(2): 1–17.

de Mause, L. (1998). The history of child abuse. *The Journal of Psychohistory, 25*(3): 1–12.

Donne, J. (1839). Meditation XVII. In: Henry Alford (Ed.), *The Works of John Donne,* vol. III. London: John W. Parker.

Donne, J. (1929). *Complete Poetry and Selected Prose.* London: Nonsuch.

Draucker, C. B. (1992). *Counselling Survivors of Childhood Sexual Abuse.* London: Sage.

Eigen, M. (1993). *The Psychotic Core.* London: Karnac.

Eisold, K. (1994). The intolerance of diversity in psychoanalytic institutes. *International Journal of Psycho-analysis, 75*(4): 785–800.

Erikson, E. (1950). *Childhood and Society.* Harmondsworth: Penguin.

Erikson, E. H., Erikson, J. M., & Kivnick, H. Q. (1987). *Vital Involvement in Old Age.* New York: W. W. Norton.

Faulks, S. (1994). *Birdsong.* London: Vintage.

Fonagy, P., & Roth, A. (1996). *What Works for Whom?* New York: Guilford.

Fordham, M. (1985). Ending phase as an indicator of the success or failure in analysis. *Journal of Analytical Psychology.*

Forrest, T. (1963). The paternal roots of male character development. *American Journal of Psychiatry, 54*(2): 61–99.

Frame, J. (1984). *An Angel at My Table. Autobiography 2.* London: Paladin.

Freud, A. (1937). *The Ego and the Mechanisms of Defence.* London: Hogarth.

Freud, S. (1895d). *Studies on Hysteria. S.E., 2.* London: Hogarth.

Freud, S. (1900a). *The Interpretation of Dreams. S.E., 4–5.* London: Hogarth.

Freud, S. (1909d). *Notes upon a Case of Obsessional Neurosis. S.E., 10:* p. 151. London: Hogarth.

Freud, S. (1913c). On beginning the treatment. *S.E., 12:* p.121 London: Hogarth.

Freud, S. (1914g). Remembering, repeating and working through. *S.E., 12:* p. 145. London: Hogarth.

Freud, S. (1915). Thoughts for the times on war and death. *S.E., 14:* p.237. London: Hogarth.

Freud, S. (1917e). Mourning and melancholia. *S.E.*, *14*: p.237. London: Hogarth.

Freud, S. (1919a). Lines of advance in psycho-analytic therapy. *S.E.*, *17*: p.157. London: Hogarth.

Freud, S. (1921c). Group psychology and the analysis of the ego. *S.E.*, *18*: p.65. London: Hogarth.

Freud, S. (1923a) Two encyclopaedia articles. *S.E.*, *18*: p.233. London: Hogarth.

Freud, S. (1924f). A short account of psychoanalysis. *S.E.*, *19*: p.189. London: Hogarth.

Freud, S. (1925h) Negation. *S.E.*, *11*: p.233. London: Hogarth.

Freud, S. (1926d). Inhibitions, symptoms and anxiety. *S.E.*, *19*: p.271. London: Hogarth.

Freud, S. (1937c). Analysis terminable and interminable. *S.E.*, *23*: p.209. London: Hogarth.

Freud, S. (1940e). Splitting of the ego in the process of defence. *S.E.*, 30: p.271. London: Hogarth.

Friedrich, J. (2006). *The Fire: The Burning of Germany, 1940-1945*. New York: Columbia University Press.

Fromm, E. (1956). *The Art of Loving*. World Perspectives, Vol. 9. New York: Harper.

Frosh, S. (2005). Hate and the "Jewish Science", Anti-Semitism, Nazism and Psychoanalysis.

Garfield, S. L. (1994). Research on client variables in psychotherapy. In: S. L. Garfield & A. E. Bergin (Eds.), *Handbook of Psychotherapy and Behaviour Change; An Empirical Analysis*. New York: Wiley.

Garland, C. (1998). *Understanding Trauma. A Psychoanalytic Approach*. London: Tavistock.

Gay, P. (1988). *Freud. A Life for Our Time*. New York: W. W. Norton.

Gilligan, C. (1982). *In a Different Voice: Psychological Theory and Women's Development*. Cambridge, MA: Harvard University Press.

Glasser, M. (1992). Problems in the psychoanalysis of certain narcissistic disorders. *International Journal of Psycho-Analysis*, *73*(3): 493–505.

Glover, E. (1946). *War, Sadism and Pacifism*. London: Allen & Unwin.

Glover, E. (1955). *The Technique of Psychoanalysis*. New York: International Universties Press.

Goldman, D. (2003). The outrageous prince: Winnicott's uncure of Masud Khan. *British Journal of Psychotherapy*, *19*(4): 483–502.

Green, A. (1960). The dead mother complex. In: *On Private Madness*. London: Karnac, 2003

Green, A. (1983). *"The Dead Mother", On Private Madness*. London: Karnac.

Greenson, R. (1967). *The Technique and Practice of Psychoanalysis*. London: Hogarth.

Guggenbuhl-Craig, A. (1982). *Power in the Helping Profession*. Dallas: Spring.

Halmos, P. (1965). *The Faith of the Counsellors*. London: Constable

Heimann, P. (1975). Sacrificial parapraxis—failure or achievement. In: *About Children and Children No Longer, Collected Papers 1942–80* (pp. 276–294). London: Routledge.

Heimann, P. (1989). The evaluation of applicants for psycho-analytic training. In: *About Children and Children-No-Longer; Collected Papers, 1942–80*. London: Tavistock/Routledge.

Hemmings, A. (1997). Counselling in primary care: a randomised controlled trial evaluation. *Patient Education and Counselling, 32*: 219–230.

Herman, J. L. (1992). *Trauma and Recovery. From Domestic Abuse to Political Terror*. London: HarperCollins.

Hinshelwood, R. D. (1991). Psychodynamic formulation in assessment for psychotherapy. *British Journal of Psychotherapy, 8*(2): 166–174.

Holmes, J. (1997). Too early, too late: endings in psychotherapy—an attachment perspective. *British Journal of Psychotherapy, 14*(2): 159–171.

Hopper, E. (1991). Encapsulation as a defence against anxieties of annihilation. *International Journal of Psycho-Analysis, 72*: 607–624.

Howard, K., Kopta, M. S. I., Orlinsky, D. E., & Brown, D. E. (1986). The dose-effect relationship in psychotherapy. *American Journal of Psychiatry, 146*: 775–778.

Khan, M. M. (1963). The concept of cumulative trauma. *The Privacy of the Self*. London: Hogarth Press.

King, F. T. (1918). *The Natural Feeding of Infants*. Auckland: Whitcombe & Tombs.

King, F. T. (1923). *Feeding and Care of Baby*. London: Macmillan.

King, M. T. (1937). *Mothercraft*. London: Simpkin.

King, M. T. (1948) *Truby King, the Man. A Biography*. London: Allen & Unwin.

Kipling, R. (1888). Baa Baa Black Sheep. In: *Wee Willie Winkie*. Allahabad: The Indian Railway Library.

Klauber, J. (1986). *Difficulties in the Analytic Encounter*. London: Free Association.

Klein, J. (1999). Assessment—what for? Who for? *British Journal of Psychotherapy, 15*(3): 333–345.

Klein, J. (2003). *Jacob's Ladder, Essays on Experiences of the Ineffable in the Context of Contemporary Psychotherapy*. London: Karnac.

Klein, M. (1940). Mourning and its relationship to manic-depressive states. *International Journal of Psycho-analysis, 21*.

Klein, M. (1948). On the theory of anxiety and guilt. In: *Envy and Gratitude and Other Works, 1946–1963* (pp. 25–42). London: Hogarth Press.

Lacan, J. (1988). *The Seminars of Jacques Lacan.* New York: W. W. Norton.

Laing, R. D. (1978). *Life before Death.* London: Charisma.

Lambert, K. (1981). *Analysis, Repair and Individuation.* New York: Academic Press.

Langs, R. (1994). *Doing Supervision and Being Supervised.* London: Karnac.

Larkin, P. (1977). In: *Collected Poems, 1989.* New York: Farrar, Straus & Giroux.

Liddiard, M. (1938). *The Mothercraft Manual* or *The Expectant and Nursing Mother and Baby's First Two Years.* London: Churchill.

Lifton, R. J. (1973). *Home from the War. Vietnam Veteran: Neither Victims nor Executioners.* New York: Simon and Schuster.

Luborsky, L., & Crits-Christoph, P. (1990). *Understanding Transference. The CCRT Method.* New York: Basic Books.

Mace, C. (1995). *The Art and Science of Assessment.* London: Routledge.

Maddox, B. (1975). *Step-Parenting: How to Live with Other People's Children.* London: Unwin.

Mahler, M. (1975). *The Psychological Birth of the Human Infant: Symbiosis and Individuation.* London: Hutchinson.

Malan, D. (1963). *A Study of Brief Psychotherapy.* London: Tavistock.

Malan, D. (1979) *Individual Therapy and the Science of Psychodynamics.* London: Butterworth.

Malan, D. (2003). *Anorexia, Murder and Suicide. What Can Be Learned from The Stories of Three Remarkable People.* London: Butterworth-Heinemann.

Mander, G. (1996). The stifled cry, or Truby King, the forgotten prophet. *British Journal of Psychotherapy, 13*(1), pp. 3–13.

Mander, G. (1997). Towards the millennium: the counselling boom. *Counselling,* Feb. 1997, pp. 51–56.

Mander, G. (1999). Echoes of war, the absent father and his return. *British Journal of Psychotherapy, 16*(1): pp. 16–26.

Mander, G. (2000). *A Psychodynamic Approach to Brief Therapy* London: Sage.

Mann, J. (1973). *Time-Limited Psychotherapy,* Cambridge, MA: Harvard University Press.

Maslow, A. (1962). *Toward a Psychology of Being.* New York: Van Nostrand.

Mead, M. (1971). Anomalies in American post-divorce relationships. In: P. Bohannan (Ed.), *Divorce and After.* New York: Anchor.

Melville, H. (1856). *Bartleby and Benito Cereno.* New York: Dover Publications.

Menninger, K. (1958). The psychiatric diagnosis. In: K. Menninger, P. W. Pruyser, & M. Mayman (Eds.), *Manual for Psychiatric Case Study*. London: Tavistock.

Mitchell, J. (1974). *Psychoanalysis and Feminism: A Radical Reassment of Freudian Psychoanalysis*. Harmondsworth: Penguin.

Mitchell, J. (2000). *Mad Men and Medusas. Reclaiming Hysteria and the Effect of Sibling Relations on the Human Condition*. London: Penguin.

Mitscherlich, A., & Mitscherlich, M. (1975). *The Inability to Mourn: Principles of Collective Behaviour*. New York: Grove.

Mollon, P. (1993). *The Fragile Self, The Structure of Narcissistic Disturbance*. London: Whurr.

Momigliano, L. N. (1992). *Continuity and Change in Psychoanalysis,* London: Karnac.

Murdin, L. (2000). *How much is Enough? Endings in Psychotherapy and Counselling*. London: Routledge.

Parker, R. (1995) *Torn in Two, The Experience of Maternal Ambivalence*. London: Virago.

Paulsen, L. (1967). The unimaginable touch of time. In: M. Fordham, R. Gordon, J. Hibbard, K. Williams, & M. Williams (Eds.), *Analytical Psychology. A Modern Science*. The Library of Analytical Psychology, Volume 1. London: Heinemann.

Pearson, M. (1995). Problems with transference interpretations in short-term dynamic therapy. *British Journal of Psychotherapy, 12*(1): 37–48.

Phillips, A. (1993). *On Kissing, Tickling, and Being Bored*. London: Faber and Faber.

Pietroni, M., & Vaspe, A. (2000). *Understanding Counselling in Primary Care. Voices from the Inner City*. London: Churchill Livingstone.

Pincus, L., & Dare, C. (1978). *Secrets in the Family*. London: Faber.

Pines, D. (1993). *A Woman's Unconscious Use of Her Body*. London: Virago.

Plath, S. (1965). "Lady Lazarus". In: *Ariel*. London: Faber & Faber.

Remarque, E. (1954). *All Quiet on the Western Front*. A. W.Wheen (Trans.). London: Putnam.

Roth, A., & Fonagy, P. (1996). *What Works for Whom? A Critical Review of Psychotherapy Research*. New York: Guilford.

Sagan, E. (1979). *The Lust to Annihilate. A Psychoanalytic Study of Violence in Ancient Greek Culture*. New York: Psychohistory Press.

Samuels, A. (1989). *The Plural Psyche: Personality, Morality and the Father*. London: Routledge.

Samuels, A., Shorter, B. & Plant, F. (1986). *A Critical Dictionary of Jungian Analysis*. London: Routledge & Kegan Paul.

Sandler, J. (1988). Psychoanalysis and psychoanalytic psychotherapy: problems of differentiation. *British Journal of Psychotherapy, 5*(2): 172–177.

Schwartz, E. (1990). Supervision in psychotherapy and psychoanalysis. In: R. C. Lane (Ed.), *Psychoanalytic Approaches to Supervision* (pp. 84–94). New York: Brunner-Mazel.

Searles, H. F. (1958). Positive feelings in the relationship between the schizophrenic and his mother. In: *Collected Papers on Schizophrenia and Related Subjects* (pp. 216–253). London: Maresfield Library.

Searles, H. F. (1961). Schizophrenia and the inevitability of death. *Psychiatric Quarterly, 35*: 178–182.

Sebald, W. G. (2003). *The Natural History of Destruction.*

Sereny, G. (2000). *The German Trauma.* London.

Shakespeare, W. (1987). *Twelfth Night.* In: S. Wells & G. Taylor (Eds.), *The Complete Oxford Shakespeare, vol. II: Comedies.* London: Guild.

Sifneos P. E. (1973). *Short-term Dynamic Psychotherapy, Evaluation and Technique.* New York: Plenum.

Spurling, L. (1997). Using the case study in the assessment of trainees. In: I. Ward (Ed.), *The Presentation of Case Material in Clinical Discourse* (pp. 64–76). London: Freud Museum Publications.

Steiner, J. (1995). Psychic Retreats. London: Routledge.

Stern, D. (1985). *The Interpersonal World of the Infant. A View from Psychoanalysis and Developmental Psychology.* New York: Basic Books.

Stern, D. (1995). *The Motherhood Constellation. A Unified View of Parent–Infant Psychotherapy.* London: Karnac.

Stern, D. (2004). *The Present Moment in Psychotherapy and Everyday Life.* New York: W. W. Norton.

Stone, M., & Duckworth, M. (2003). Frequency of sessions and the analytic frame. In: R. Withers (Ed.), *Confrontation in Analytical Pyschology.* pp. 307–333.

Sullivan, A. S. (1953). *The Interpersonal Theory of Psychiatry.* New York: Norton.

Symington, N. (1993). *Narcissism, A New Theory.* London: Karnac.

Welldon, E. (1992). *Mother, Madonna, Whore. The Idealization and Denigration of Motherhood.* New York: Guilford.

Winnicott, D. W. (1958). Primary maternal preoccupation. In: *Through Paediatrics to Psychoanalysis.* London: Hogarth.

Winnicott, D. W. (1958). The capacity to be alone. In: *The Maturational Processes and the Facilitating Environment.* London: Hogarth.

Winnicott, D. W. (1965). Dependence in infant care, in child-care and in the psycho-analytic setting. In: *The Maturational Processes and the Facilitating Environment.* London: Hogarth.

Winnicott, D. W. (1971). Fear of breakdown. In: G. Kohon (Ed.), *The British School of Pyschoanalysts: The Indpendent Tradition.* Lonodn: Free Association.

Wolff, H. (1988). The relationship between psychonanalytic psychotherapy and psychoanalysis attitudes and aims. In: G. Kohon (Ed.) *British School of Psychoanalysts: The Independent Tradition. London:* Free Association.

Woolf, V. (1977). *The Diary of Virginia Woolf 1920–1944.* London: Hogarth.

Wordsworth, W. (1850). *The Prelude, XII.* Oxford: Oxford University Press.

Yeardsley, D. (2002). *Bach and the Meanings of Counterpoint.* Cambridge: Cambridge University Press.

BIBLIOGRAPHY

Abram, J. (1992). *Individual Psychotherapy Trainings: A Guide.* London: Free Association.

Adamson, J. (1997). *Melville, Shame and the Evil Eye, A Psychoanalytic Reading.* New York: State University of New York Press.

Coren, A. (2001). *Short-Term Psychotherapy, A Psychodynamic Approach.* London: Palgrave.

Coughlin Della Selva, P. (1996). *Intensive Short-Term Dynamic Psycho-therapy.* London: Karnac.

Feltham, C. (1997). *Time-limited Counselling.* London: Sage.

Graves, R. (1929). *Goodbye to All That.* London: Cape.

Greer, G. (1988). *Daddy We Hardly Knew You.* London: Hamish Hamilton.

Kuebler-Ross, E. (1974). *Questions and Answers on Death and Dying.* New York: Collier.

Levine, R. S. (1998). *The Cambridge Companion to Herman Melville.* Cambridge: Cambridge University Press.

Messer, S. B., & Warren, S. (1995). *Models of Brief Psychoynamic Therapy. A Comparative Approach.* New York: Guilford.

Murray Parks, C. (1972). *Bereavement, Studies of Grief in Adult Life.* London: Tavistock.

Rank, O. (1929). *The Trauma of Birth.* New York: Harcourt Brace.

Sassoon, S. (1930) *Memoirs of an Infantry Man,* London: Faber.

Smith, D. (1990). *Stepmothering.* London: Harvester Wheatsheaf.

Wiener, J., & Sher, M. (1998). *Counselling and Psychotherapy in Primary Health Care.* London: Palgrave Macmillan.

Winnicott, D. W. (1945). From dependence towards independence in the development of the individual. In: *The Maturational Processes and the Facilitating Environment, Studies in the Theory of Emotional Development.* London: Hogarth.

Woolf, V. (1925). *Mrs. Dalloway.* London: Hogarth.

Zinkin, L. (1998). All's well that ends well. In: H. Zinkin, R. Gordon, & J. Haynes. *Dialogue in the Analytic Setting* (pp. 240–248). London: Jessica Kingsley.